# The Elite Connection

## PROBLEMS AND POTENTIAL OF WESTERN DEMOCRACY

## Eva Etzioni-Halevy

D1232887

Polity Press

Copyright © Eva Etzioni-Halevy 1993

The right of Eva Etzioni-Halevy to be identified as author of this work has been asserted in accordance with the Copyright, Designs and Patents Act 1988.

First published in 1993 by Polity Press in association with Blackwell Publishers

Editorial office:
Polity Press
65 Bridge Street
Cambridge CB2 1UR, UK

Marketing and production:
Blackwell Publishers
108 Cowley Road
Oxford OX4 1JF, UK

238 Main Street
Suite 501
Cambridge, MA 02142, USA

ISBN 0 7456 0891–4
ISBN 0 7456 1068–4 (pbk)

A CIP catalogue record for this book is available from the British Library and The Library of Congress.

Typeset in 10½ on 12 pt Bembo
by Times Graphics, Singapore
Printed in Great Britain by
T.J. Press (Padstow) Ltd, Cornwall

This book is printed on acid-free paper

# Contents

# Acknowledgements

The intellectual debt I owe practically every scholar whose work is cited in this book should be evident from the book itself. In addition, I owe a debt of gratitude to Professor Dafna Izraeli, Professor Bernie Laserwitch and Professor Zvi Bachrach of Bar-Ilan University, and to Professor Peter Self, Dr Thelma Hunter and Dr Jenina Frentzel-Zagorska of the Australian National University for their most helpful comments on parts of the material. Finally, I am deeply grateful to my husband Zvi Halevy for his expert assistance in the research for the chapter on Eastern Europe, and for his invaluable comments.

# Introduction: the elite connection and Western-style democracy

Following the collapse of Communism in Eastern Europe, it seemed for a short while that Western democracy had enjoyed a resounding victory, and its future seemed well assured. This, however, was but an optical illusion. This is so not because Islamic fundamentalism may now replace Communism as a formidable world rival to Western democracy. Rather, it is so because the main threat to the principles of democracy springs primarily not from external enemies, but rather from inside itself. The recently celebrated (but already eclipsed) idea of Francis Fukuyama that the collapse of Communism heralds the triumph of Western democracy makes even less sense if we consider that democracy was created more by domestic struggles than by external ones. And its future seems to be less assured if we consider that its problems have always sprung first and foremost from domestic subversions of its own principles, the very principles that are the result of previous struggles.

In this context, this book's basic assumption is that elites,[1] their connections and struggles, are of prime importance in shaping, threatening or changing democracy. Hence, the aim of the book is, first, to explore the pivotal role of elite relations and conflicts in Western democracy in order to reach a better understanding of how this political system emerged and how it functions in the contemporary world. Second, its aim is to identify the threats to democracy that emanate from certain elite relations which subvert democratic principles, and the manner in which these threats may be countered. Third, it intends to show how these struggles may also lead to a more equitable and democratic democracy.

The book is designed as a combination of a text, or supplementary reading (for courses in political theory, political sociology, comparative politics and the like), a theoretical statement supported by empirical-historical illustrations, and a warning. As a text, the book presents a brief, critical, overview of relevant theories, in the context of which its own contribution is to be understood. As a theoretical statement, it is written from the perspective of democratic elite theory. But it differs from several other writings in this tradition in that it espouses an egalitarian bent. The illustrations it brings are from recent history and current events. And the warning it contains is that unless a better understanding of the threats that face democracy leads to a deliberate attempt to counter them, and unless we work to reform democracy, even what has been achieved is anything but assured.

Democratic elite theory has its basis in liberal thought and in the thought of some classical social scientists at the turn and the beginning of the twentieth century. As such, of course, it is by no means new. But this book refocuses attention on it for several reasons. First, for some time now this theory has been unduly neglected. It is my intent to show that, although not currently trendy, it has much to contribute to our understanding of Western democracy – that is, of the system in which we live our daily lives.

Second, although some of the greatest thinkers in the social sciences have adhered to democratic elite theory, they have also concentrated much of their effort in other areas. Hence they have merely presented this theory's bare essentials. For this reason, the theory has been frequently misunderstood. For instance, it has sometimes been seen as tantamount to elite theory on the one hand, and to pluralist and pluralist elite theory on the other hand. I intend to show that although it is a certain variant of elite theory, and although it shares elements with pluralist theory as well, it nonetheless differs from both. And it is only through an understanding of these differences that the special contribution of democratic elite theory to our understanding of democracy can be appreciated.

Third, because only the essentials of democratic elite theory have been presented, it warrants further development. In the framework of what I refer to as a demo-elite perspective, I intend to pinpoint some of the new directions in which the theory may be taken. Finally, my aim is to show how democratic elite theory can be developed in an egalitarian fashion. It is a widespread belief that Marxism, the class theory derived from it and similar conceptions are egalitarian, while liberalism and the theories derived from it espouse liberty at the expense of equality. It is my intent to demonstrate that Marxism and its related ideas do not have a monopoly over egalitarianism, and that liberalism-derived democratic elite theory – even if it was not egalitarian at the outset – can be elaborated in this direction. The intent is to show how it can be used to help in the analysis of struggles for a more democratic and egalitarian democracy.

Part I of the book begins with the observation (chapter 1) that, in the social sciences so far, the analysis of elites has been overshadowed by the attention lavished on classes. It presents a brief overview of the main themes of both class theory and elite theory. It thus sets the theoretical context in which the overshadowing of one by the other has taken place. It then makes the argument that the factors which have led to elite theory being partly squeezed out by class theory are largely coincidental. Despite the image elite theory has gained in the intellectual community, and despite some actual examples which justify this image, elite theory is not *inherently* simplistic, elitist, undemocratic and disparaging of the public.

Indeed, democratic elite theory – which (as noted) is one variant of elite theory – illustrates that the theory does not necessarily suffer from these deficiencies For instance, elite theory does not necessarily work with a simplistic division of society into elites as power holders and masses as powerless: sub-elites as lesser power holders and the power of the public may be taken into account as well. Also, elite theory is not necessarily undemocratic and elitist. For example, in the framework of democratic elite theory, the present analysis puts major emphasis on identifying the conditions under which elites and sub-elites may contribute to democracy and equality. This analysis defines elites as including not only bastions of the establishment, but also those who endeavour to change it. Thus the analysis shows how elites may play a role in making democratic regimes more democratic and egalitarian than they are at present.

Next (chapter 2) the book makes a plea for paying greater attention to elites and sub-elites because their role in society (for good or for bad) is much greater than class theory has been willing to admit. This plea is first set in its theoretical context. It is then argued that contrary to the message that emanates from Marxist and other class theories, classes as entities are not historical actors, and cannot act. Elites and sub-elites are and do. Hence, many of the deeds – both exploitative and egalitarian – that have been widely attributed to classes, have in fact been carried out by elites and sub-elites (whether established or non-established ones). And what have frequently been dubbed as class struggles have in fact frequently been elite struggles. Thus, the role of elites and sub-elites both in creating and sustaining despotism and in generating and defending the liberties of democracy is much more central than class theory has acknowledged. This is so even though elites themselves are constrained in their actions by their relations with the public.

As elites and sub-elites have both despotic and liberating potential, the next question is: what turns them into either oppressors or champions of democracy? Part II of the book presents a brief, critical overview of various political theories that have some relevance to this question. First, the analysis (chapter 3) turns to liberal thought and to democratic elite theory, recapitulating some of its main themes. These include most centrally the tenet that concerted power is despotic power. And only the separation of powerholders, and the mutually countervailing power of elites, limits the power of the ruler, increases the liberty of the ruled and forms one of the hallmarks of democracy.

Next the book presents a brief review of other pertinent theories (chapter 4). I then argue that it is the above simple but crucial tenet that each of them has neglected. Because of this disregard, Western Marxist theorists have inadvertently lent legitimation to the Communist regime, which has suppressed elite autonomy, and thereby has crushed democracy. In this manner, they have also helped legitimize a rigid regime which – by suffocating the autonomy of the elites of social movements – was rendered incapable of sustaining reforms initiated from below that might have preserved its essence. Thereby they have – however marginally – helped prevent gradual changes that might have led to the development of a communist democratic regime, the very regime they claim to propound.

Marxist thought has had an important impact also on the West. In its pervasive critique of capitalist democracy it has made a great contribution by focusing attention on the inequality and exploitation embedded in this regime. Yet it has had a less than felicitous effect as well: it has helped divert attention from both the existence and importance of the autonomy of elites in Western democracy. Thereby it has helped delegitimize not only the inequalities of capitalism, and not only the distortions to democracy caused by capitalism, but also democracy itself.

Marxist theory, however, is not alone in disregarding both the existence and the importance of the autonomy of elites in a democracy. Some elite theorists, for instance, regard elites – even in a democracy – as highly concerted, and hence have little to say on the difference between democratic and non-democratic regimes. Pluralists, and even pluralist elite theorists, in their own way, have also neglected this tenet. For they have seen the dispersion of power among a large number of interest groups – rather than the autonomy of even a limited number of power holders – as a distinguishing feature of democracy (though some of them have later reneged on this view). State-centred theorists emphasize the autonomy of the state from other forces of society and corporatists focus on the coalition between state and certain peak organizations. Thus neither has much to say on the autonomy of elites within and from the state in democratic regimes.

Part III of the book presents my own view, the demo-elite perspective (chapters 5 and 6). One aim of this perspective is to refocus attention on the achievements of Western democracy in this respect. Defined by the principles of free competitive elections, universal suffrage and civil liberties, this political regime is far from being 'government of the people by the people for the people' as solemnly proclaimed by Abraham Lincoln. Yet it is unique in that the relative autonomy of elites and sub-elites (from the state and within the state, and particularly from the government) has developed in it more than anywhere else. And this relative autonomy (though it varies among different democratic countries) is of crucial importance in underpinning the principles of democracy.

In emphasizing this point, the demo-elite perspective (as part of democratic elite theory) differs from the other theories reviewed. Unlike elite theories it does not view elites in a democracy as forming a concerted power structure. Unlike pluralist and similar theories it looks not primarily at interest groups or 'civil society' (no matter how fashionable the concept may currently be) but at elites and sub-elites – whether or not they have interest groups or parts of the public to back them up. The aim is to demonstrate that, beyond a certain minimum, what counts for the preservation and further democratization of democracy is not the plurality of elites but their *independence* from the government *in terms of the control of resources*, a topic that has been explicated neither by pluralist theory nor by several proponents of the concept of civil society.

Democratic elite theory has been virtually unique in promoting the idea of the importance of the autonomy of elites for democracy, and it has been successful in turning it into a central theme of Western thought. Yet even this theory has not fully explored and amplified the idea. Another aim of the present analysis is to elaborate this idea further, and bring out the contribution it can make in the contemporary world. Thus, while previous democratic elite theories have discussed the relative autonomy of elites in general terms, the present analysis spells it out in more concrete terms. It explicates the relative autonomy of elites and sub-elites in terms of control over several types of resources, including coercive, material, administrative, symbolic and psycho-personal resources. It is its relative (though never complete) immunity in the control of these resources which lends an elite or sub-elite relative autonomy, and it is through the use of these resources that it can manifest such autonomy.

Also, while previous democratic elite theories have discussed the relationship between elite autonomy and democracy in general terms, the present demo-elite analysis spells out the actual relationship between the autonomy of elites and the principles of democracy, including the principle of free elections and various civil liberties. It highlights the paradox that the relative autonomy of elites is not an explicit principle of democracy and not formally enshrined in democratic constitutions, laws or rules. Indeed, if elite autonomy were to be referred to explicitly in these rules, they would be considered undemocratic. And yet it forms part of their semi-hidden agenda, without which the explicit principles of democracy could not be sustained.

The analysis spells out how each democratic principle protects and legitimizes what may be referred to as the meta-principle of relative elite autonomy and for its part is promoted, legitimized and protected by it. It spells out the relative autonomy of elites as an information-providing mechanism. This mechanism is seen as crucial because without it the adversary public discourse – necessary for the electoral principle and for civil liberties could not be implemented.

Established elites generally have a common interest in the maintenance of the system from which their elite positions derive. This common interest is likely to foster a degree of voluntary cooperation among them, without which no political system can function smoothly. This analysis makes a contribution over previous ones also in an initial exploration of the relationship between elite cooperation as a requirement of any political system, and elite autonomy as a requirement of democracy.

The relative autonomy of elites is not presented as a miracle cure that relieves democracy of all ills of inequality and injustice. But it is argued that it protects the ability of the disadvantaged to stand up for their rights and struggle for justice and thus for change. This is precisely the right that despotic regimes, in which elite autonomy is lacking, have denied. And this denial, though not the only factor, is one of the most important features that has turned them into oppressive and exceedingly inegalitarian regimes. It follows that relative elite autonomy – producing clashes of elites and sub-elites of the disadvantaged with established elites – may have a liberating and equalizing potential, which we would disregard only at our peril.

How do we know, however, that the principle of elite autonomy is really so important for democracy? This becomes clear from an exploration of the historical relationship between the two. Here the contribution of the present book lies in the specific thesis it puts forward. The thesis is that the relative autonomy of elites and sub-elites constitutes an important condition for the *subsequent* development and stabilization of democracy. This is not to say that such autonomy is democracy's ultimate or sole cause. Previous and other factors, dealt with by other theories, are important as well. Moreover, these factors themselves may well be interrelated with the autonomy of elites and sub-elites. My thesis, however, is that such relative autonomy is not an automatic reflection of these other factors, but an important condition in its own right for the successful evolution and stabilization of democracy.

Part IV of the book presents historical-empirical analyses that provide illustrative support for this thesis. Such support comes, first, from a brief delve into European history (chapter 7). It shows that in Britain, where key elites and sub-elites have successfully struggled and obtained relative autonomy, democracy has subsequently taken root. Conversely, in Germany the elites' struggles for autonomy have been much less successful. Here, too, democracy – even though in some respects it preceded the advent of democracy in Britain – was not successfully stabilized. It subsequently suffered a breakdown, which came even *before* the ascent of Nazism to power. It is only because of this previous breakdown that Germany was so vulnerable to the onslaught of Nazism, the price of which has been paid in atrocities suffered by millions of human beings.

The lesson to be learned from this is clear, and I submit (chapter 8) that recent events in Eastern Europe may be looked at in the light of this lesson. The crumbling of the old regime in these countries does not necessarily herald the advent of stable democracy. Even where multi-party elections have been occurring already, democracy cannot be expected to stabilize as long as the self-sustaining power of elites and sub-elites *vis-à-vis* and within the state has not been assured. In several Communist countries some stirrings in this direction have been perceptible already. Still, calling attention to this factor necessarily leads to a more cautious view of occurrences in the Eastern bloc than does the focusing on multi-party elections as such.

This is so because the autonomous power of elites depends on the flow and control of resources and hence – unlike competitive elections – cannot simply be legislated into existence. In a system in which the resources have long been concentrated in the hands of one super-elite, where they have flowed chiefly from the top downwards and from the centre outwards, the reversal of their flow necessarily is an arduous process. Contrary to initial appearances, then, instant democracy is not necessarily stable democracy.

The importance of elite autonomy for democracy also becomes clear from a comparison of different East European countries. For although at the time of writing (Spring, 1992) in all of Eastern Europe stable democracy was still somewhere in between wishful thinking and well-founded hopes, there were differences among the countries. By 1991 Poland, for instance, was far more advanced on the path to democracy than was the Soviet Union (as an entity). There, some steps towards democracy were later disrupted by a failed coup (a coup being a major hallmark of a non-democratic regime), and the erstwhile centralized government was replaced by a looser federation before democratic governance of the whole had been given a chance. A brief look into these countries' history, both under Communism and before, shows that this difference may be explained in part by *previous* differences in the autonomy of elites and sub-elites in them: this autonomy was clearly more highly developed and sturdier in Poland than it was in the Soviet Union.

As the demo-elite perspective puts so much stress on the autonomy of elites, and also claims that this phenomenon has developed in Western democracy more than anywhere else in the world, this approach may seem to be overly self-satisfied. The impression that one might gain is that it conjures up an excessively favourable image of our own regime. And in a sense this is correct: unfashionable as this may sound, I admit that when the conception is used to compare Western democracy to any other hitherto existing regime, democracy in the West comes up with flying colours.

Nonetheless, in the final part of the book I show that the demo-elite perspective is far from complacent. Chapter 9 makes the point that looked at in the light of this theory, even Western democracy gives no grounds for great joy. On the contrary: my argument is that even in the West there have always been cracks in the walls separating elites from each other, elites have always shown a tendency to subjugate other elites, the relative autonomy of elites has never been assured, and it is anything but safe today.

Accordingly, the chapter highlights the fact that absence of elite autonomy as an explicit principle of democracy, as well as the haziness, inconsistency and controversiality of democratic principles, facilitates infractions of this meta-principle, and thereby also of democratic principles themselves. It brings examples of some recent subversions of democratic principles which, although they seem to be unrelated to each other, have a common denominator. They all involve incursions of elites into the autonomy of other elites and sub-elites. This occurs through non-legitimate, excessively close, dependency or interdependency relations of elites, either in subjugation of other elites or in collusion with them.

Such incursions result in threats to civil liberties and human rights. Or else they result in non-legitimate, or less than legitimate, appropriations of public resources, that is, in impropriety and corruption at the expense of the public. And this impropriety and corruption, no less than the threats to civil liberties, jeopardize democracy. So far these occurrences have still been relatively mild and the danger they pose to democracy has therefore been limited. But it is important to highlight them so as to put us on guard, lest such threats become more formidable in the near future.

Notwithstanding all this, the fact that some elites have been transgressing democratic principles does not signify that this is their preordained and invariable pattern of behaviour. The final contribution of the book over previous democratic elite theories is its argument (chapter 10) that although democracy is a political system with many deficiencies, beset by inequalities and many subversions of its own principles, it is a system that also has the built-in potential to counter its own subversions. The counter-elites and sub-elites of social movements are still relatively independent and are still powerful enough to struggle for change, as they have in the past. They may help us thread the path towards greater freedom, participation, equity and equality, that is, towards a more democratic democracy in the future.

## Note

1  Defined as wielders of power and influence on the basis of their control of resources, the term is explained in detail below. Elites include the political elite (of the government and opposition), the business elite, the elite of trade unions and of the media, as well as some others, as also explained below.

# PART I

# ELITES AND CLASSES: BRINGING ELITES BACK IN

# 1

# *Why class theory has overshadowed elite theory: a matter of coincidence*

In all known societies, as George Orwell put it 'some are more equal than others,' meaning that some are better off than others. And as Ralph Miliband added, 'some are more plural than others.' This means that while a plurality of groups may have an impact on the political processes, some are more powerful or influential than others.

In view of these two dimensions of inequality, two strategies have been devised in the social sciences for mapping social structure. One strategy involves the analysis of classes, differentiated from each other by the extent to which they own and control various resources and most prominently material resources. The other strategy involves the analysis of elites, differentiated from non-elites by the extent of their power and influence. The first strategy is known as class theory, the second – as elite theory.

To understand a sociopolitical structure, we need to understand the role of elites versus the public, no less than the role of classes in it. Yet, in the social sciences, elite theory has been overshadowed by class theory: when the theory of classes – fathered by Karl Marx – and the theory of elites – sponsored by Vilfredo Pareto – have confronted each other in the almost Darwininan struggle for survival and dominance in the social sciences, the former has easily gained the upper hand. While neither theory has enjoyed a resounding victory and neither has suffered a crushing defeat, the analysis of classes has clearly fared better than that of elites.

This partial eclipse of elite theory by class theory has been evident particularly since the Second World War. Since the mid-1970s, there has been a modest revival of the popularity of elite theory (Moyser and

Wagstaffe, 1987, p. 5) But even so, there has not been a reversal of the two theories' fortunes, and class theory has continued to outshine elite theory.

In this chapter, I first present a brief overview of some of the major contours of class theory and of elite theory. I then analyse the shortcomings of elite theory that have led to its overshadowing by class theory. Next I argue that these drawbacks are largely coincidental, in that they are not inherent in elite theory's logic. They have in fact beset much of what is generally considered as *the* elite theory. Yet there is another type of elite theory – democratic elite theory – which overcomes some of these drawbacks. And this theory must be used to bring elites back into the centre of sociopolitical analysis.

## Class theory: some major themes

Class theory was fathered by Karl Marx, and to this day Marx's and Marxist class theory occupies a special position in the social sciences. This is so because, more than any other theory, it has successfully called attention to the inequalities and exploitation inherent in capitalist societies. But Max Weber has left his mark on class theory as well. Thus class theory is commonly divided into a Marxist and a 'main-stream' – chiefly Weberian – strand. Marxist theory sees classes as based on the relationship to the means of production. It also sees them as social actors and as conflict groups. Mainstream theory views classes as based on various resources, with material resources as a major but not the only basis of class division. And only in some mainstream conceptions – not in others – do classes emerge as actors and conflict groups.

For Marx,[1] every society is divided at least into two categories sharing common relationships to the means of production: those who own and control them (the ruling class), and those who do not (the exploited class). The class that controls the means of material production also controls the means of mental production; thus it rules not only econom-ically, but also by disseminating its ideology. Yet at some stage the exploited class organizes and becomes conscious of its common interests; it thus turns from 'a class in itself' into 'a class for itself'. That is, it turns from what is merely a category of people into a militant entity.

In feudal society, which featured an agrarian economy, the most important means of production was the land. Hence those who held and controlled the land – the feudal nobility – formed the ruling class. In capitalist society the main means of production are machinery and financial resources. And those who control those means – the capitalists or the bourgoisie – are the ruling class. In feudal society the main exploited class was the serfs, who were tied to the land. In capitalist society the main exploited class is the proletariat, which has no ties and is formally 'free' – yet actually compelled – to sell its labour.

In capitalist society there are other classes as well: the small bourgoisie, whose members control minor means of production and are self-employed; the lumpenproletariat, made up of the marginal and parasitic elements of society; the landlords; and the peasantry. But as capitalist society advances, most of the small bourgeoisie is absorbed into the proletariat, while a minority manages to work its way up into the bourgeoisie. In this manner society is gradually polarized into two mutually opposing camps. Marx was aware of the growth of a new petty bourgeoisie. But as Abercrombie and Urry (1983, p. 50) point out, he paid insufficient attention to the consequences of this develop-ment for what he nonetheless perceived as the polarization of society into two adversarial camps.

In all societies the subjected classes are exploited through the expropriation of surplus value, whereby part of the value of their work product is appropriated by the exploiting class. In capitalist society this derives from the difference between the value of labour which the capitalist buys in the marketplace and the value of the product of labour which the capitalist sells in the marketplace. Put simply, it takes the form of the capitalist paying the worker for only part of the work s/he does, with the rest (when all expenses are deducted) pocketed by the capitalist as net profit.

Consequently, the polarization of society also entails a polarization in standard of living, as that of capitalists goes up and that of workers goes down in either absolute or relative terms. As a result, workers produce but cannot serve as consumers for large parts of the multitude of products which their work – in conjunction with modern machinery – throws on to the market. The worsening situation of workers is thus exacerbated by the contradictions of capitalism, manifested in crises of overproduction. The combination of these factors leads to a heighten-ing of the consciousness of the prolertariat, until it is ready for the final showdown, the revolutionary class struggle, which is to bring about the demise of capitalism.

Some present-day Marxists have reservations with respect to various elements of this theory, but they accept its basic tenets. They also believe that these hold for the end of the twentieth century no less than they held for Marx's time. The bourgeoisie is still the ruling and exploiting class. While the living standards of workers have risen, and while there is some movement from manual to non-manual occupations, there is little mobility into the capitalist class. And workers are still in a subordinate and exploited position in the production process, which has become more alienating and dehumanized than it ever was before.

Marxist class theorists recognize that the revolutionary class consciousness which Marx had expected the proletariat to develop did not materialize. Some also note that class conflict has been institutionalized and reduced to the bargaining over wages and working conditions. This they attribute, among other things, to the perfection of hegemony, that is, the ideological domination of the working class by its exploiters.

However, several Marxists believe that the potential for concerted class action and struggle is still there. The fact that class conflict has recently been regulated does not indicate that it has become less salient. Rather, it demonstrates that the contradictions of capitalism have deepened, that the opposing interests of classes have remained as contradictory as ever, and that the struggle between them is still as potentially disruptive (see Braverman, 1975; Connell, 1977; Korpi, 1983; Mandel, 1975; Miliband, 1973, 1977, 1989a; Poulantzas, 1978; Therborn, 1978; Wright, 1980).

A certain problem for Marxist class theory is posed by the growth of what has been termed 'the new middle class', composed of people engaged in tertiary occupations: certain service, white-collar, managerial, administrative and knowlege-related occupations. These groups do not fit neatly into the Marxist scheme as they neither own the means of production as do capitalists, nor simply sell their labour power as do proletarians. According to some Marxists, it is possible to perceive a process of proletarianization of several of these groups, as evident in their deskilling and general degradation (Braverman, 1975; Carchedi, 1977). Other Marxists conceptualize these groups as a separate class, engaged in unproductive labour, whose main action is to ensure continued extraction of surplus value and the perpetuation of the class structure on behalf of capital (Poulantzas, 1975, 1977; Ehrenreich and Ehrenreich, 1979).[2]

There are still others, occasionally referred to as 'analytical' Marxists, who have a particular concern with these groups. As McLennan (1989, p. 97) notes, analytical Marxists depart considerably from the Marxist tradition in that they extend the idea of relationship to the means of production to include not only ownership, but also organizational position, or control. These theorists regard the previously mentioned categories as torn between classes, by virtue of occupying contradictory class locations: they do not own the means of production, but they participate in their control, or at least enjoy a considerable degree of self-control within the work process (Roemer, 1986, as cited by McLennan, 1989; Wright, 1985).

While Marxist class theory is descended directly from Marx, mainstream class theory is of mixed theoretical ancestry, with Weber its most prominent progenitor. Weber (Gerth and Mills, 1958) posited three separate though interrelated dimensions of social stratification: (1) class, based on property and position in the market, or life chances; (2) status, based on consumption and lifestyle; and (3) party, based on a struggle of different groups for political power. On the basis of property and market position he distinguished mainly three classes: the holders of property, those who hold no property but whose market position is enhanced by their skill and knowledge; and those who can only sell their labour.

Although many mainstream class theorists use Weber as their point of departure, different scholars have developed different strands of his thought. Thus some mainstream sociologists follow Weber in using a multidimensional scheme with respect to the bases of inequality. In their analysis the concept of classes has been practically abandoned in favour of the concepts of status, occupational position, socioeconomic background and the like (Lenski, 1954), or else classes are defined as resting on various bases such as market and work situation, occupation, prestige, income and education (Lockwood, 1958; Landecker, 1981). Or else, again, occupation itself is held to incorporate the dimensions of income and prestige, and classes are defined on the basis of occupations (Stewart et al., 1980).

Other sociologists use Weber's emphasis on power as a dimension of inequality to argue that a new dominant class has now come into being. Thus, Dahrendorf (1959) accepts Marx's view of society as divided into classes that stand in conflict with each other. But he maintains that Marx conceived of these too narrowly: class conflict is based not on relationship to the means of production, but rather on the resource of authority and power or lack thereof. In Marx's time, classes were in fact differentiated by ownership of the means of production, since ownership also implied control, and hence – power. In present-day society, however, there has been a differentiation of ownership and control.

Ownership is dispersed among large numbers of shareholders, while control is concentrated in the hands of a few managers. The managerial class has thus become the dominant class of industrial society. This class, however, is confronted by another class. The latter is made up of those who are devoid of power, but who struggle to increase their share of this central resource.

For his part, Bell (1973) follows up the Weberian emphasis on skills and knowledge as a basis of class differentiation: he argues that a newly constituted 'knowledge class' has gained ascendancy in what he terms postindustrial society. In industrial society, in which capital was the central resource, the capitalist class was dominant. In postindustrial society, in which knowledge forms the central resource, those who possess such knowlege (including scientists, professionals, academics, engineers and other experts) approach dominance. Ultimately it is still the capitalists and the politicians who hold the power to make vital decisions. But neither capitalists nor politicians can get along without the expertise provided by the knowledge class.

Giddens (1973), too, regards skills or lack thereof as a major factor in influencing market and thus class position. Yet he sees the educational and technical qualifications of knowlege holders as endow-ing them with no more than middle-class position. The capitalist class thus remains dominant, though Giddens (1982a) also highlights the power of the working class to act against exploitation.

The Weberian idea of multidimensional inequality has also been used to place top bureaucrats, independent businesspeople, and profes-sionals (who all base their positions on different resources) at the top, or close to the top, of the class hierarchy. In one case, this class has been designated as a service class (Goldthorpe, 1982). In another case, it has been designated as a dominant class, by virtue of its ability to use property, credentials or legal monopoly over professional services to exclude others from top positions (Parkin, 1979).

In an attempt to overcome the antinomy between Marxist and mainstream class theory, Abercrombie and Urry (1983) suggest that social classes should be conceptualized in terms of both market and work situation. On this basis they argue that what is traditionally viewed as the middle class is actually composed of two classes. The one is a small service class, which is performing certain tasks delegated to it by capital – particularly control and reproduction; the other comprises a large group of deskilled white-collar workers, which increasingly shares the market and work situation of the working class.

Also using a combination of Marxist and Weberian lines of thought, Bourdieu (for instance, 1988–9) sees the dominant class as rooted in 'economic capital', but also in 'cultural capital'. Members of this class can thus use their cultural capital to perpetuate and reproduce their dominant class position: they appear distinguished (that is, of dominant class affiliation) simply by being themselves (that is, by giving outward indications of their cultural capital). And they produce their position in large part by transmitting this cultural capital to their children, through education.

It can be seen, then, that class theory assumes different forms. It includes two schools of thought, with variations within each school. It includes attempts to bridge the gap between the two schools, but thereby still more variations are created. Beyond all variations, however, there is the common conception of inequalities based mainly on economic resources and to a lesser extent on resources of skill, knowledge and power. There is also the common conception that such inequalities yield at least two, and in most conceptions at least three (though not always clearly distinct), categories of people. In Marxist theories they (or at least the capitalist class and the working class) are seen as turning into actors and confronting each other in an inevitable class struggle. In mainstream theory the emphasis is on gradations more than on confrontation, but in some cases class action and conflict is visualized as part of the constellation as well.

## Elite theory: some major themes

Elite theory is distinguished from class theory in that it focuses almost exclusively on inequalities based on power or lack thereof. Power, in turn, is based on other resources, (such as economic assets and organizational bases) and for its part may give rise to control over other resources as well. But elite theory is concerned primarily with power and only secondarily (if at all) with the other resources that are related to it. Accordingly, the central tenet of elite theory is that societies are divided into the few who hold power or rule, and the many who are ruled. The ruling group, or elite, effectively monopolizes power; it almost inevitably gets its way whenever important decisions are made. The second group – the non-elites, the masses, the rank and file, or the public – has no choice but to acquiesce in this arrangement. The presence of – largely concerted – power holders is universal in complex societies, and democracy is not exempt from their rule any more than are other regimes.

This model of society was introduced into the social sciences by what came to be known as the classical elite theorists: Vilfredo Pareto, Gaetano Mosca and Roberto Michels, with Pareto considered as its chief founding father. Pareto (1935) begins with the observation that people are unequal in their personal endowments. Those who are the most capable (though not necessarily the most honest) in any particular area of activity may be called an elite. The rest of the population forms the non-elite. Pareto then distinguishes two types of elites: the governing elite, comprising those who directly or indirectly take part in government, and a non-governing elite, comprising all others endowed with excellence in their areas.

Although, in principle, elites are made up of those who excel, this is not always so in practice. Because of factors such as wealth and family connections, elite positions may come to be occupied by people who are not so endowed. It is here that Pareto's ideas on the circulation of elites come in: as long as elites are open and absorb into their ranks the most talented people from the non-elite, talent and elite positions largely coincide. But at times elites close themselves to the influx of capable elements from the population at large. When that occurs, talent and elite position increasingly diverge; people in the governing elite lose the qualities that are needed to keep them in power. At the same time people of superior quality are coming to the fore among the non-elite.

This, in turn, has a crucial impact on society at large. As long as elites are open, there is a free circulation of elites (the talented enter the elites and the non-talented leave it), society is in a state of equilibrium, and it changes but moderately and gradually. But when the circulation of elites is impeded, social equilibrium is upset, and social order decays. It is then that society becomes prone to violent upheavals and revolutions. Such upheavals, however, are not capable of eliminating the rule of elites. When the governed overthrow their rulers, this merely means that new elites will arise and institute more effective elite rule.[3]

In some ways the ideas of Mosca resemble those of Pareto, but instead of referring to those who hold power and rule as an elite, he referred to them as the ruling class. In all societies, writes Mosca (1939), from the simplest to the most advanced, two classes of people appear: a class that rules, and a class that is ruled. The first enjoys power and its advantages, while the second is controlled by the first. The ruling class may be a group of warriors, a group of religious functionaries, a landholding aristocracy, a wealth-holding or a know-ledge-holding class, or some combination of these. In any case it is its political power that sets it apart from the rest of society.

The ruling class is always less numerous than the class which it rules. According to democratic theory, majorities rule minorities. In fact, minorities rule majorities even in a democracy. Because they are minorities, they have the ability to organize, while the masses remain unorganized. The political domination of an organized minority over an unorganized majority is inevitable. When a ruling class is deposed, there will be another to take its place. Indeed, the whole history of civilization comes down to the struggle between existing ruling classes and their contenders.

Ruling classes never rule merely by brute force; they justify their rule by political formulae (such as 'divine right' or 'the sovereignty of the people'), which frequently are accepted by those they rule. When ruling classes are vigorous in their capacity to impose their political formulae, to manage society and render a service to it, when they are open to the more talented and ambitious people among the ruled, gradual change and progress in society will take place.

When, however, ruling classes lose their vigour, when they can no longer render their previously rendered services, or when they become closed to talented outsiders, violent upheavals are likely to take place. These frequently result in the total replacement of the ruling classes. There usually follows a period of rapid innovation in which people from the bottom of the social ladder can easily force their way up. This, in turn, is followed by a period of crystallization of the new ruling class, which also spells a period of social stability. Thus the character and structure of the ruling class is of major importance in determining the structure, and rate of change, of society.[4]

While Pareto and Mosca were concerned with power in society at large, the topic with which Michels (1915) was most prominently concerned was that of power in political parties and trade unions. Drawing his material from European socialist-democratic parties and unions around the turn of the century, he showed that even organizations whose principles were democratic came to be organized in an oligarchic manner.

As Michels sees it, the democratic principles call for guaranteeing to all equal participation and influence in regulating the affairs of the organization; for free elections in which all members are eligible for election; and for control of the electors over those they elect. In fact, however, each organization becomes divided into a minority of leaders and a majority of led. At first, the leaders are merely the executive organs of the collective. But eventually they come to exert almost unlimited power over the rank and file. The external forms of democracy are preserved, but underneath them oligarchy becomes more and more pronounced.

Why do inequality and oligarchy develop in organizations that were aimed precisely at struggling against inequality and oligarchy? Michels explains these trends on the basis of several interrelated factors. These include the size of the organization, which makes common decision-making practically impossible. Hand in hand with size of the organization goes the complexity of its tasks. These become less and less comprehensible to the rank and file, hence the need for delegation. Also, for the organization to run efficiently, decisions have to be made quickly. Democratic procedures invariably cause delays, hence the temptation for leaders to forgo such procedures.

Because of the growing complexity of tasks, the organization's decision-making processes require expertise. The leaders gain such expertise through training and long experience. Inside information on what is going on in the organization is also monopolized by leaders, as are means of communication. To this must be added the leadership skills which leaders gain through experience, the need for continuity, as well as the general apathy of members, all of which make the leaders' positions practically impregnable.

In view of all this, Michels formulated his famous law of oligarchy: 'who says organization says oligarchy' (1915, p. 418) and the more developed the organization, the stronger the oligarchy. Such oligarchy is undemocratic also because, once in office, the leaders develop their own interests and no longer represent those of the rank and file. Their own interest, now, no longer is to promote the socialist aims of the organization, but rather to maintain the organization on which their elite positions depend. Organization thus creates oligarchy, which in turn creates conservatism.

After the Second World War, elite theory was further elaborated, and applied to the United States, by C. Wright Mills (1959). Mills sees modern (and especially American) society as dominated by the upper political, military, and corporate economic personnel, whose power is derived from their key positions in their respective institutional structures. These three groups are in a perpetual though uneasy coalition with each other. Together they form a conglomeration of power or a 'power elite', which manipulates the masses into accepting its rule. Members of Congress and trade union leaders make up the middle levels of power. And at the bottom there are the masses that, in America no less than in other contemporary societies, are mostly passive and have little influence of their own. 'In many countries,' writes Mills, 'they lose their will for rationally considered decision and action; they lose their sense of political belonging because they do not belong; they lose their political will because they see no way to realize it' (1959, p. 324).

Several contemporary elite theorists, too, have posited a concerted power elite or something closely akin to it, sharing a commonality of interests, an ability to impose political unity, interlocking positions, cohesiveness, or other close interrelations (see for instance Domhoff, 1983; Dye, 1985; Dye and Zeigler, 1987; Stone, 1987; Useem, 1984). Some contemporary elite theorists have also posited a procedural consensus among elites in stable (including stable democratic) regimes. 'Elites', write Dye and Zeigler, 'share a consensus about fundamental norms underlying the social system. They agree on the "rules of the game"' (1987, p. 4).

In connection with this, some elite theorists are laudatory of elite rule. Field and Higley (1980), for instance, adopt this stance, which is clearly though subtly evident throughout their book. Thus they characterize their paradigm not merely as an elite theory, but explicitly as one of elitism in the normative sense. They further characterize elitism as antithetical to extreme egalitarianism, and regard egalitarian values as crippling liberalism. For their part, Dye and Zeigler (1987) characterize elites as a major repository of political knowledge, in contrast to the public which is characterized by pervasive ignorance and lack of interest in all matters political. In their view, it is the irony of democracy – which is ostensibly the rule of the people – that even democracy itself is safeguarded by elites rather than by the people themselves.

In line with this, argue Dye and Zeigler, as well as some others (such as Poggi, 1978), the most prominent feature of Western democracy, competitive elections, forms only a very imperfect instrument of holding government elites accountable to the public. For competing elites or parties – among whom the public may choose – do not usually offer distinct policy alternatives. Candidates for election avoid as far as possible taking a stance on issues, and even if they do, are not usually bound by their election pledges once they are elected.

Even if elites wished to give the public what it wanted, they would not be able to do so. For they cannot clearly interpret the policy mandates emanating from elections. This is so because most voters base their electoral choices on personalities rather than on issues, and in any case they frequently misinterpret the candidates' policy preferences. As candidates take positions on many issues, they cannot know which policy position resulted in their election. Hence elites do not usually have reliable knowledge on public preferences, and cannot shape policies to suit those preferences.

In short, according to this view, voters can but rarely affect policy by selecting a particular candidate for office, and elites influence the opinions of the masses more than the masses influence elites. In fact, elections serve as little more than a symbolic exercise designed periodically to reaffirm a common belief in democracy and to lend the masses a feeling that they do play a role in the system. In other words, elections are merely a ritual, the function of which is to legitimize the power of the elite.

Overall, the elite theory here reviewed has found various forms and expressions, but it is somewhat less variegated than class theory. Its common focus is on the division in society created by power. Mostly it sees this division as generating two groups: the rulers and the ruled, the elites and the masses (though Mills conceives of three echelons of power). Mostly it views the elites as a concerted conglomeration of power and the masses as largely unorganized, passive and powerless. And, generally, it applies this conception to all complex societies, and it devotes little analytical effort to the identification of differences in these respects between democratic and non-democratic regimes. Thus it has little to say on what makes democracy distinctive, and on how this distinctiveness may be enhanced.

## Why class theory has overshadowed elite theory

The chapter set out with the observation that in the social sciences today, class theory has been fairly successful in squeezing out elite theory from the centre of intellectual attention. The foregoing brief overview of class and elite theories should provide some indications as to why this has occurred.

### The halo effect of the founding fathers

First, as the theories are of different descent, there has been a halo effect: each has been affected by the status of its founding father. And in this respect Marx has fared much better than Pareto. Although widely maligned and for some time partly ignored in the social sciences in the West, Marx has eventually made a massive comeback. He did more than generate a multitude of influential disciples, and a highly prominent school of thought. Marx's influence radiated far beyond that: he became one of the most influential thinkers which the social sciences have claimed as their own.

By contrast, Pareto has been considered but one of the minor classical theorists of the turn and the beginning of the twentieth century. And while lip service is still paid to Pareto, he is generally viewed condescendingly. Moreover the two other classical elite theorists, Mosca and Michels, have not fared much better. Although they are not overlooked, only perfunctory attention is paid to them in contemporary academic life.

## The halo effect of ideology

This disadvantage is compounded by another factor: Marx developed his conception of classes in conjunction with a socialist ideology. His theory therefore came to be associated with the vision of socialism which, in turn, came to be equated with egalitarianism, humanism and progress. Pareto, on the other hand, developed his conception of elites in early twentieth-century Italy. This was the time and place in which Fascism made its ascent – and he seemed to be initially sympathetic to that development. Thus his theory, justifiably or not, came to be associated with a fascist ideology and with reaction. Although he distanced himself from Fascism later on when its true character became evident, the damage had been done already; the association between Fascism and elite theory had already impressed itself on people's minds.

The two other classical elite theorists, Mosca and Michels, were active in the same era and country in which Pareto also made his mark. On top of this, Mosca in his early years expressed disdain for democracy, and Michels became an apologist for Fascism in the 1920s. Classical elite theories were also adopted by European fascist ideologues. On the face of it, what better proof could there be for the link between elite theory and the ideology of fascism?

Eventually Marxist theory came to be associated not only with beautiful, utopian albeit non-existent socialism. It also came to be linked with less beautiful though actually existing Communism. However, Marx had a great number of protagonists who were quick to point out that this regime was far from what Marx had had in mind. By contrast, there were few protagonists of Pareto, Mosca and Michels who were motivated to point out anything at all in their defence.

## Problems of terminology

Further, elite theory has been plagued by some problems of terminology. There have also been some problems with the term 'class' for, as we saw, there is little agreement concerning either class bases or class boundaries. But the term 'elite' is much more problematic. A term for those who wield power and influence was direly needed for sociopolitical analysis. Yet the introduction of the term 'elite' into the theory that bears its name was from the beginning beset by misfortune. Pareto's choice of the term was itself unfortunate, for in everyday language, the word denotes a select group of people: the 'cream' of society. This choice of terms, moreover, was not by chance. For the concept was intended by its sire in the social sciences (somewhat indecisively) to denote both those who excel in various areas of social life and those who have power and rule.

As seen before, it was evident even to Pareto himself that the most capable are not always the best from a moral standpoint. By his own testimony, it was also clear to him that those who hold power are not necessarily the most capable, and that power holders do not necessarily excel in anything except in power. Yet he did not coin separate terms for each of the various categories of people, as his realization of the distinction among them would have necessitated. Instead he retained the rather confusing meaning of the term elite, which implied an unjustifiably favourable evaluation of elites as rulers.

Thus, even though Pareto qualified his positive evaluation of elites, in this respect too the damage had already been done. In the mind of many critics the use of the term elite came to be associated with elitism, or the adulation of elites and endorsement of their rule. Thus the favourable connotation which Pareto had lent the term had a boomerang effect: it made people wary of the term elite, and by implication of the theory of elites.

The terminology of elite theory seemed to fall short in another respect as well. The term 'classes' embraces people at the top, the middle and the bottom of the social hierarchy. As such, it opens the possibility for any number of categories to be included in the structural map of society. As noted, Marx's own theory, as well as most other class theories, have in fact been working with three or more such categories. The term 'elites', on the other hand, refers to one category of people – the power holders – only. Seemingly, it thus generates merely one other category of people – those who are subject to the elite's power. Apart from its other misfortunes, elite theory thus has suffered because it seems to call for an overly simplistic, dichotomous map of the sociopolitical structure.

To this must be added the fact that Marxist class theory has spawned the apt term 'working class' or 'proletariat' to designate the major echelon at the bottom of the class structure. But elite theory has not come up with an equally feliticious counter term to designate the lowest in its power structure, that is, the majority of society.

As seen before, the terms variously used by elite theorists to refer to those who are not elites have been: non-elites, the masses, the public, or the rank and file. Contrary to the term working class or proletariat in Marxist class theory, none of these terms has become a powerful analytical tool in elite theory. For while in class theory both the ruling class and the working class have been defined by some criteria which are at least apparently clear, in elite theory only elites have been clearly defined. By contrast, the term non-elites and its equivalents have been used as a residual category of people, characterized not on their own, but simply by their exclusion from the category of elites.

## The neglect of the public

These terminological difficulties have been related to another problem. As noted before, in Marxist class theory the category that is low on the hierarchy, the working class, has been characterized as potentially active in shaping its own fate, as having the potential of struggling for the implementation of its own interests. As will be argued in the next chapter, there is a fallacy in this conception. But it certainly looks good: it is seemingly democratic and egalitarian and therefore has been greatly attractive to intellectuals.

By contrast, in elite theory, those low in the hierarchy have been characterized as being not only a residual category, as implied by the term 'non-elites', but also as largely apathetic and passive, as implied by the term 'masses'. In either case this has conjured up an image of a non-entity, whose main mission in life is to serve as the object of elite rule. In contrast to class theory, which has emphasized conflict between classes, elite theory has thus been unable to conceptualize conflict between elites and the masses. And although elite theory has much to say on the periodic overthrow of elites, it has never held out the (attractive, but false) hope of non-elites being able to abolish elites altogether, or of the public at large taking over.

## Elitism and concerted power

Another problem which may have detracted from the popularity of elite theory is the fact that, even after Pareto, some elite theorists have been manifestly or latently approving of elites. As shown above, some recent theorists have espoused an elitist line of thought which (rightly or wrongly) has seemed to be inegalitarian. This has been in contravention of the ideology popular among intellectuals – including social scientists – many of whom have therefore distanced themselves from this theory.

In conjunction with this, the elite theory, as here reviewed, despite its invaluable contribution to our understanding of political systems, has conjured up an image of concerted elites, closely allied with each other through structures, interests and opinions. Several elite theorists have applied this image to democratic no less than to authoritarian regimes. Thereby these scholars have viewed Western power structures as more concerted than they actually are, belittling the differences between democratic and non-democratic regimes. Thereby, too, several elite theorists have failed to present a convincing theory of democracy, and they have not been notable for their appreciation of this regime. This, too, may well have antagonized intellectuals – and social scientists as intellectuals – particularly those who have greater faith in Western democracy than have those elite theorists.

For all these reasons, class theory came to be regarded as progressive, egalitarian and democratic, while elite theory has come to be regarded as conservative, elitist, inegalitarian and undemocratic. For many intellectuals elite theory, no less than elitism, has come to be a pejorative term. Through all this, the less than brilliant careers of the term elite and of elite theory have been perpetuated into the present, and both have been partly delegitimized and marginalized in the social sciences today.

# A matter of coincidence

These reasons for the partial eclipse of elite theory, however, are coincidental in that they are extrinsic rather than intrinsic: they have little to do with the logic and validity of elite theory as such. Thus, as will be argued, elite theory is not *inherently*, by its very essence, what in some of its major manifestations it has turned out to be in actual practice. This can be exemplified *inter alia* by presenting some features of another version of elite theory, democratic elite theory, and within its broader framework the present analysis. As will be clarified below, democratic elite theory is not in the confines of *the* elite theory proper in the tradition of Pareto, Michels or Mills. Rather it follows the liberal tradition of thought, introduced into the social sciences by, for instance, Max Weber, Joseph Schumpeter and Raymond Aron. But it is still *an* elite theory. Hence if, as will be shown, it does not share some of the features that have led to elite theory's misfortunes, this indicates that these features are not an immutable part of elite theory.

## Elite theory is not inherently simplistic

To begin with, there is no eternal obligation for elite theory to work with a simple division between elites and the rest of society. While it has most commonly worked with this division, the latter is not indigenous, so to speak, to elite theory. This theory can equally well work with a more complex conceptualization of the hierarchy of power. For this, as mentioned before, the theory of Mills provides the best – though not the only – proof.

The present version of democratic elite theory does not accept the Millsian conception of a concerted power elite and a powerless public. But the present analysis has a similarity to Mills's in suggesting a trichotomous hierarchy of power structures. The rationale for this lies in the conception of elites, power and influence used in the present analysis. By this conception, the term elites refers to those who wield power and influence on the basis of their active control of a disproportionate share of society's resources.

From this it should be clear that – as here conceived – elite position, or power and influence, are not an either–or proposition. Rather, since they are based on the distribution of resources of which one may have more or less, they generally are a matter of degree. For in no society are resources divided equally, but neither are they divided so that some have everything while others have nothing. It follows that in elite or power structures, in principle, gradations are more feasible than dichotomies. And gradations are better characterized by a trichotomous division than by a dichotomous one. Hence the present analysis works with a division of social power and influence structures into three echelons: elites, sub-elites, and the public.

This division, too, is oversimplified; but not more so than the division of society into three classes, with which several prominent class theorists work as a matter of course. And a certain oversimplification of the complexities of society is, of course, necessary in order to facilitate analysis. As is the case with the division of classes, subdivisions within each category in the elite structure are possible as well. But the advantages of greater precision have to be weighed against the disadvantages in loss of clarity and incisiveness of the analysis. Hence it is a trichotomous division of power that is being suggested here. The more such a trichotomous gradation proves itself, the more it will go to show that elite theory is not inseparably wedded to a dichotomous one.

## Elite theory is not inherently elitist

It is frequently thought that because elite theory is concerned with elites, it must be elitist, and we have seen that occasionally it is. But the elitism of elite theory is not inevitable. Just as elite theory is not irreversibly locked into a dichotomous view of power structures, so too is it not irrevocably committed to an elitist view of those structures. Elite theory must, by definition, focus on the indisputable fact that in all societies there are especially powerful and influential minorities. But in itself elite theory is ideologically neutral, and it is only the ideological preferences of elite theorists which may imbue it with one or another ideological bent.

Hence there is nothing in elite theory which makes it inherently elitist, or approving of elite rule, any more than the Marxist theory of the ruling class makes it 'classist' or approving of class rule. Elitism is one legitimate ideological stance of elite theory, but there are others, and they are no less legitimate. There is manifest proof of this. It lies in the fact that while some elite theorists have expressed elitist views, others have promoted antithetical views. The most prominent example of this, of course, is once again Mills, who thoroughly vilified what he conceived as the power elite. Another example is Domhoff (see 1983), whose analysis may also be read as a comprehensive condemnation of elite rule.

By the same token, an elite theory may neither praise nor condemn elites *in toto*, but rather examine elite actions in their context and by their (either positive or negative) ramifications for democracy. This is the stance adopted in most of democratic elite theory, including the present version of this theory.

In addition, although a term for those who hold power and influence is central for elite theory, it need not be used in a laudatory sense. True, we are now stuck with the term elite and its originally praiseful connotations, since no alternative, neutral term is available to designate power holders. Nonetheless, several elite theorists have stripped the term of its complimentary connotations by deliberately imbuing it with neutral ones. For instance, Lasswell and Kaplan have defined elites simply as 'those with most power in a group' (1950, p. 201), and most contemporary elite theorists have worked with similar definitions. And the same is true of democratic elite theory, and also of its present incarnation. All this goes to show that elite theory is not necessarily elitist, and that elites need not be seen as the 'cream' of society, as people who are better (or, for that matter, worse) than anybody else.

## Even elites are not inherently elitist

It is of interest to note that not only elite theory but even elites are not necessarily elitist. The term elites (as previously defined) refers first and foremost to the overprivileged, well-entrenched bastions of established power structures. But as defined in the present analysis it covers more than those, for resources also include psycho-personal resources of motivation, energy and the like. These latter resources (which I unjustifiably neglected to pinpoint in my previous analyses, 1989a and 1989b) are actually of prime importance. For their inclusion as bases of elite position enables one to focus on – among others – people who are *not* socially advantaged and whose disproportionate power and influence emanate from their own personalities alone. Thus, as here conceived, elites are not only the establishment, but also *those who stand up to* the establishment, or are out to demolish or change it.

## Elite theory is not inherently undemocratic

Once elites are conceptualized in this manner, moreover, it becomes clear that they must not be seen as an invariably concerted conglomeration of power, as some elite theorists have been wont to see them.

While the elites of the establishment have some interests in common, some elites are clearly opposed to other elites in their interests.

In connection with this it should also become clear that elite theory is not inherently undemocratic. It has been and can be successfully wedded to democratic theory, to form a democratic elite theory. This theory, to which the present analysis adheres, concentrates in particular on the cleavages between elites, which it sees as one of the most distinctive features of Western democracy. Once the existence of such cleavages is accepted, this also opens the way for another type of analysis. This is an analysis of the strategies by which some elites try to overcome these cleavages and gain ascendancy over other elites, and the manner in which other elites may use the same cleavages in distinctly democratic struggles, to make democracy more democratic. All this will be argued, explained and shown at length in the following parts of this book.

### Elite theory is not inherently neglectful of the public

Similarly, although those who are not part of the elites have been direly neglected by elite theorists, this 'view from the top' is not intrinsic to elite theory any more than is the belittling of democracy. In democratic elite theory, at any rate, the public is not *necessarily* disregarded or disparaged (though it sometimes has been). And neither is it necessarily seen as less crucial than elites in shaping society.

This may be once again exemplified by the present discussion. In it, it should become clear that while elites and sub-elites exert disproportionate power and influence, their power is not exclusive or impregnable. They themselves are greatly constrained by their interface with the public and public opinion. The actions and sociopolitical structures that emerge are thus the combined result of relations among elites and of relations between elites and the public.

## Conclusion

This chapter has started out with the observation that in the social sciences today, elite theory has been partly eclipsed by class theory. This has been followed by a brief review of class theory and of what is usually considered as *the* elite theory. This review of the two theories has then been used as an explanation for the eclipse of one theory by the other; it has shown how this eclipse was the result of a series of shortcomings that have beset elite theory in comparison to class theory. Next it has been argued that these shortcomings stem from particular circumstances, misfortunes and idiosyncratic patterns which elite theorists have adopted, and which have little to do with the essence and logic of elite theory as such. Some versions of elite theory proper along with democratic elite theory, including its present manifestation, have been used to illustrate that elite theory is not inherently simplistic, elitist, inegalitarian, conservative, undemocratic and contemptuous of the public. Rather, it is capable of working in favour of democracy and of adopting an egalitarian ideological bent.

This has not been widely admitted, however. And it is for this reason that elite theory – including democratic elite theory – has been partly delegitimized in the social sciences. This is unfortunate because, among other things, it has led to the hegemony of an analytical framework in which classes alone have been deemed to be important, and the complex but intriguing relations between elites and classes have been neglected.

## Notes

1  Marx's theory of classes stands as the centrepiece of his entire work and of all his writings; see in particular Marx and Engels, 1969a, 1969b, and Marx, 1976. On Marx's class theory in relation to his theory of the state, see for instance Marx, 1969a, 1969b.
2  Carchedi, Ehrenreich and Ehrenreich and, later, Parkin are cited on the basis of their analysis in Abercrombie and Urry, 1983.
3  There are other parts of Pareto's theory of elites, such as his distinction between 'lions' and 'foxes'. These, however, seem so dated today that they do not warrant more extended comment.
4  While Mosca was one of the founding fathers of elite theory, and a large part of what he wrote obviously fits this model, some of his ideas also made a major contribution to democratic elite theory. These elements of his ideas are reviewed in chapter 3.

# 2

# *Why class theory should not have overshadowed elite theory: a matter of democracy*

The fact that class theory has partly overshadowed elite theory (including democratic elite theory) is unfortunate from an additional viewpoint as well. In this chapter I argue that it has produced a misleading image of social reality, one which has hampered our understanding of democracy.

## A misleading image of social reality

It was seen in chapter 1 that a large part of class theory, particularly but not only of the Marxist variant, has seen classes as important social actors. Interests have been attributed to classes, and they have been deemed to act in line with (and occasionally against) those interests. At the same time elites and their interests and actions have not played a role in this theory: class action and class conflict alone have been regarded as central to the constellation of society.

Therefore, when class theory has moved towards the centre of the stage, pushing elite theory out to the margins, this has produced a biased view of social reality. It has led to the hegemony of an analytical framework in which classes have had attributed to them both demonic and heroic deeds which they could not possibly have perpetrated or accomplished. These are actions which, for good or for bad, usually have been carried out by elites and sub-elites.

This is not to say that only elites are capable of effective action. All people are actors and do act. They can and do act in their own lives, as private individuals, or as members of classes or of other social entities. Thus, people – all people – can act, but classes – all classes, as entities – cannot. And actions which class theorists have attributed to classes have generally been carried out by small minorities of people within them, which – by the definition proposed in the previous chapter – are elites and sub-elites.

## The myth of class action

As noted, Marx distinguished between a class in itself, a category of people with a common relationship to the means of production, and a class for itself, which is also conscious of its common interests and acts to promote them. Some modern class theorists, too, speak of classes as actors or of class action (see Przeworski, 1977; Bechhofer et al., 1978). Others speak of classes as 'doing' things, as when Therborn (1978) asks 'What does the ruling class do when it rules?' Some non-Marxists, too, have adopted the conception of class action. For instance, Goldthorpe regards the working class as the 'social vehicle through whose action' there is a good probability for egalitarian social change to be realized (1980, p. 28). He further highlights 'the shared beliefs, attitudes and sentiments that are required for concerted class action' (p. 265).[1]

Yet, both in principle and in practice, there is no possibility for classes as units to be actors, to do things, to act. There are several intertwined reasons for this. As Hindess (1989) has noted, for action to occur a decision has to be reached and, at the very least, an attempt has to be made to implement it. Yet classes as entities have no mechanisms for making common decisions and acting on them. In fact, classes do not have formal membership, and so it is not clear who would be entitled to participate in such (hypothetical) decision-making processes anyway. And formal membership is precluded at the very least by the fact that the boundaries of classes are unclear and controversial. It is also precluded by the fact that objective and subjective boundaries do not necessarily coincide.

Then, too, in contemporary societies classes generally are large, if not huge, categories of people. And what Michels turned into common knowledge almost a century ago still holds: sheer size makes collective decision-making processes, as well as united action, practically impossible. Even the capitalist class, small as it is in comparison to other classes, is generally too large to become a common decision-making body. And this holds even more for other, much larger classes. Indeed, class theorists would be hard put to come up with historical instances in which all (or even most) members of any one class, in any one society, have got together, reached a decision and acted on it in unison. Thus attributing action to classes is really the creation of a myth.

When class theorists refer to class action presumably what they really mean is that some members of certain classes have taken common action. They mean that, in addition, this common action has been regarded by the participants, or by themselves as class theorists, or by both, as being in line with the class's interests and as carried out in its name.

However, regarding this as class action is highly misleading. For not only has such action not been carried out by an entire class, but it has not necessarily been *supported* by the entire, or even by the majority of the class. Most members of the relevant class may not have regarded those purporting to act in their name as entitled to represent their interests. Some, or most, members of the relevant class may even have been totally unaware of the fact that the action has taken place in their name. Indeed in most cases of what has been dubbed as class action, it has never been clear whether, and to what extent, such action has been endorsed by the members of the class it was meant to benefit.

Classes are important components of the structure of society. They are categories of socioeconomic inequality in it. They may become focuses of identification. Their members may have interests in common, and some people may act in their name to promote what they consider those interests to be. Others may act to the detriment of those interests. But these actions cannot involve all, or even most people in each class, and so cannot involve the classes as entities. Hence this may be action for or against classes, but it is not action *by* classes, or class action.

## The myth of class struggle

'The history of all hitherto existing society', wrote Marx and Engels in the *Communist Manifesto*, 'is the history of class struggles' (Marx and Engels, 1969b). These forceful words have inspired not only multitudes of revolutionaries but also large numbers of scholars. Marxist class theorists have imbued particularly the working class with the potential of engaging in a class struggle to overthrow the capitalist system. Some may have become sceptical with regard to the prospects for the immediate realization of this potential, but most (as noted in chapter 1) have not abandoned the hope that revolutionary class struggle will ultimately materialize. As Miliband has aptly summarized this position: 'For many Marxists, past and present . . . the important thing was to concentrate on class struggle . . . and at some point, the class struggle would reach a moment of extreme crisis, out of the deepening and irresoluble contradictions of capitalism . . .' (1989b, p. 34).

Pending such an outcome several class theorists focus their attention on what they regard as the class struggle within the capitalist system. For instance, Dahrendorf (1959) regards classes as conflict groups. Also, some Marxist class theorists stress the primacy of class warfare as a key for understanding extant capitalist societies (see Wright, 1980). And Korpi maps out the topic of his analysis as follows: 'In this book the conflicts of interest manifested in the political arenas of Western nations are conceived of as a democratic class struggle' (1983, p. 4). In a similar vein Wetherly (1988) views the Western welfare state as an arena of class struggle. Others, such as Arrighi, Hopkins and Wallerstein (1987) analyse class struggles in the perspective of world politics.[2]

In fact, however, the alleged potential for revolutionary class struggle can never be realized, and neither can the allegedly more limited class struggle within extant societies. The simple reason for this is (as should be clear by now) that if classes as entities cannot act, and if struggle is a type of action, then classes cannot struggle either. In other words, classes as entities cannot struggle any more than they can act. And the working class as an entity is no more capable than any other class of struggling either in support or in negation of the capitalist system, or indeed in any way at all.

To be sure, the term class struggle may be used in different ways. Some Marxists, and others influenced by them, favour a wide-ranging designation. They refer to any struggle in which individuals of different classes are involved as a class struggle. For Tilly and Tilly, for instance, class struggles include a variety of struggles, even when the people participating in them do not cast their actions in terms of class and are not aware of their class interests (1981, p. 17). Miliband similarly believes that class struggles include clashes between workers and employers even when those 'do not define [the] struggles in which they are engaged in class terms at all . . .' (1989a, p. 6).

Indeed, it can hardly be denied that people of different classes may clash, and frequently have clashed, with each other. But to refer to this as a 'class struggle' is again the imposition on reality of a misleading terminology. How can a clash between individuals of different classes be a class struggle when most of the people belonging to the relevant classes may not be involved, may not be aware of its taking place, or may even be opposed to it?

Other Marxists and likeminded thinkers define class struggles even more broadly as any struggle that has something to do with classes. Korpi, for one, characterizes class struggle as 'a struggle in which class, socio-economic cleavages and the distribution of power resources play a central role' (1983, p. 21). With respect to this overarching characterization of class conflict, there is very little to argue against. But by the same token it also means very little. Most social struggles, past and present, fall into this category. Any struggle between people, even if they are not of different classes but merely, say, of different ethnic groups or opposite genders, clashing over issues related to class or power would be included. Indeed, one would be hard put to come up with a social conflict in which class, socioeconomic cleavages and power resources do *not* play a central role. Surely, to make sense, the term class struggle must mean something more clearly delimited than this.

By contrast, Poulantzas defines class struggle narrowly as the 'mutual opposition' of classes (1978, p. 14). Abercrombie and Urry also propose a narrow designation when they claim that for a certain conflict to qualify as a class struggle it be, *inter alia*, 'in some sense generated by the underlying struggle between the classes' (1983, p. 131). But it is precisely this that begs the question: what, if anything, is the 'mutual opposition' or the 'underlying struggle' between the classes when classes – as such – cannot oppose each other and struggle.

So when the term class struggle is conceived of merely as the struggle between individuals or groups of different classes, or as in some vague way related to classes, it is misleading and has little meaning. On the other hand, when class struggle is understood in a straightforward manner, as a clash between classes as entities, it does not and cannot exist. Like class action, then, the struggle between classes, or class struggle, is nothing but a myth.

## Can organizations act as proxies for classes?

As against this, class theorists may, and have, argued that there are organizations that represent social classes and that it is they who engage in class action and class struggle. Thus capitalist enterprises, employers' associations, chambers of commerce and the like may be said to represent the capitalist class and engage in capitalist class action. Trade unions may be said to do the same for the working class.

In line with this, Goldthorpe maintains that for the working class 'trade unionism . . . is the normal mode of action' (1978, p. 207).[3] Similarly, Korpi regards the class struggle as one in which 'class organizations in the sphere of production, i.e. unions and employers' (or business) organizations, emerge in the central roles' (1983, p. 24). Applying a similar line of thought Wardell and Johnston (1987) describe what they regard as a historical case study of class struggle as represented by a clash between mine owners and a labour union. By the same logic, political parties may be said to engage in class action and struggle on behalf of whatever classes they may claim to represent. But even leaving aside the question of whether such bodies can represent entire classes – including non-members of those bodies – the more interesting question is whether as such, as organizations, they are even capable of acting (or struggling).

Hindess (1989) has argued that while classes are not actors, organizations are. For, unlike classes, they have mechanisms for reaching decisions and implementing at least some of them. And, unlike classes, they can be held legally responsible for their actions. Coleman (1990), too, speaks of organizations – purposively entered by individuals – as (corporate) actors. I argue, however, that in reality the overwhelming majority of organizations, as entities, cannot be actors either.

Legally, to be sure, organizations may be deemed to be actors. In empirical reality, however, organizations, like classes, in most cases have no means of formulating common decisions and turning them into common action. However, the reasons in each case are different. Classes cannot reach common decisions and act on them because they are not organized, and organizations cannot reach common decisions and act on them because they *are* organized. And because they are organized they are, in most cases, oligarchies, or multilayered and hierarchical (today this is so obvious that it is no longer necessary to invoke Michels's name in saying it). Hence their mechanisms for reaching decisions, which Hindess attributes to the organizations as wholes, are mechanisms in which only small numbers of people actively take part. More often than not these are the persons situated at the peak, or immediately below the peak, of the pyramid: top and middle management, or leaders and officials.

Coleman, who shows great awareness of the oligarchical tendencies of organizations, still refers to organizations as corporate actors, apparently because he sees their formal agents as acting in their name. Here, however, it is argued that formal agents cannot act in the name of an organization as an entity, because mostly it is not only a multilayered, but also a multi-interest social conglomeration. Thus, as an extensive literature on the topic has shown, organizational layers frequently consist of people from different classes. And even if all layers are recruited from the same class, frequently they have diametrically opposed interests. Thus decisions and actions supposedly taken by organizations and proclaimed by their agents to be in their name may, but frequently do not, reflect the interests or the wishes of the lower layers or rank-and-file members of those organizations.

To say then that an organization acts when in reality only its top layers are involved, and when the action may well be against the interests of rank-and-file members, is to disregard the latter's very presence as a component of the organization. Given that industrial – or workplace – democracy has had but limited success (Lansbury, 1980; Ogden, 1982; Clarke, 1987), this certainly holds for capitalist enterprises.

For instance, when we read in the press that Mitsusuba Motorcars Company (a fictitious name) has decided to make 20 per cent of its workers compulsorily redundant, this merely means that Mitsusuba management has decided to do so. It means that the decision is against the interests of, at the very least, those 20 per cent of Mitsusuba workers who are about to be made redundant, who may strenuously oppose the decision, and who certainly outnumber the management. For social scientists to accept at face value the statement that it is indeed the Mitsusuba organization that has taken the decision to retrench, and that it acts on it, would be to identify the organization with the management, and disregard those 20 per cent of workers altogether.

This argument, moreover, holds not only for capitalist corporations. Many trade unions, too, are oligarchies today no less than they were in Michels's time. In such trade unions, just as in capitalist corporations, the interests of the leadership may diverge from those of the membership. And so-called union action may well be action by, and in the interests of, those at the top. Researchers have also identified unions or associations in which democratic processes have been quite vigorous. For this the International Typographical Union in North America, studied by Seymour Martin Lipset and his associates (1956), has been the most famous, though not the only example.[4]

Yet usually this merely means that in these unions there have been proper procedures of representative democracy: fair, competitive and regular elections, following vigorous electoral campaigns, and strong oppositions. It may also mean that relatively larger percentages of members than is the case in other organizations have been politically active. Even in organizations such as those, however, because of size and other factors, it is usually the elected leaders and officials who have become the organization's major decision makers. And even in these types of organizations the interests of leaders and members may diverge. For instance, certain strategies of bargaining and industrial action may well favour the interests of one but not of the other. The decision taken by leaders either in favour or against such strategies thus may be in their own rather than in their members' interests.

To be sure, in hierarchical organizations those at the top do not always have things their own way. Sometimes rank-and-file members engage in action of their own. For instance, where the organization is a capitalist enterprise this may include industrial action by workers aimed against the interests of the management, which supposedly *is* the organization. In trade unions it may include wildcat strikes and other action against the wishes of the leadership, or even challenges to the leadership itself. Occasionally, too, participants lower down in organizations (for instance inmates in prisons) revolt. In these cases, however, it becomes even clearer that decisions and actions are not taken by the organization, but only by part of it.

While most organizations are expressly hierarchical, some proclaim themselves, or are proclaimed to be, participatory types of organizations. In these, all members supposedly have an equal share in the decision-making process. But, even in participatory organizations, decisions and actions are effected mostly by minorities, though with varying degrees of input from the rest of the members.

This has been the case, for instance, for many, if not most, workers' cooperatives. Enduring cases of such cooperatives of substantial size are conspicuously rare, and they have played only a peripheral role in Western industrial societies. And even in those relatively few cases where sizable workers' cooperatives have endured, participatory democracy has frequently had to be tempered by representative democracy: general meetings of all members have been intermittent only and major decisions have had to be delegated to managers or boards of directors.[5]

A similar situation prevails, for instance, with respect to the kibbutzim in Israel. In these collectives, seemingly effective (and widely celebrated) mechanisms for common decision making were put into place: weekly general assemblies were to be the decision-making bodies. But, as a large volume of research has conclusively shown, things have not worked out quite like that in practice. As time went on, members' attendance at assemblies has generally dropped off. Even among attenders, the majority have become relatively passive. In all but matters of exceptionally critical importance, the actual managing of assemblies, as well as that of kibbutz matters generally, has been left to a small (albeit elected) minority.[6]

Occasionally, organizations have been located which are participatory not only in ideology but in practice as well. For instance, Rothschild-Whitt (1979) and Rothschild and Whitt (1986) have studied five such 'alternative' workplaces in California. However, not only were those organizations small as well as unusual, but even in them the bases of power and influence that individuals 'carry in their person' (1979, p. 524) could not be eliminated. In other words, even in these organizations there were still persons who had a greater input than others into the decision-making processes.

Moreover, Rothschild-Whitt (1979) lists a variety of constraints which hampered the implementation of full participation by all members in these decision-making processes. Interestingly they sound very much like the lists of factors hampering democracy in trade unions and socialist parties in Europe at the turn of the century, on which Michels based his 'iron law of oligarchy'. Finally, the organizations in question were studied in the early 1970s for limited timespans (from six months to two years) only. It would be of interest to find out whether these workplaces (if they still exist) continue (even in their limited way) to be as participatory today as they were almost two decades ago.

In short, the overwhelming majority of organizations have identifiable individuals who are the locus of decisions and the centre of action. It must be concluded then that, like classes, the great majority of organizations – as entities cannot act. And even organizations which supposedly represent social classes, such as employers' associations and trade unions, generally cannot act as units any more than classes themselves can. Thus there is no greater advantage in focusing on organizational actions than on class actions: both are phenomena of a different order, which class theory has disregarded.

## What class theory has disregarded

What class theory has disregarded is that it is neither classes nor organizations, but rather elites and sub-elites, who conduct the actions usually attributed to classes or organizations. Both so-called class actions and so-called organizational actions are, in effect, elite actions. The elites concerned may be those of organizations, of classes, or of parts thereof, but in any case they are still elites.

This statement would obviously be false if we subsumed under the term elites and sub-elites only those people who stand at the head of organizations and their seconds in command. The statement would also be false if (as is customary in some of the literature) we were to equate elites and sub-elites with the upper classes, or the top and second-rank position holders of the state. But, as clarified in chapter 1, the present definition of elites and sub-elites is different. It is based on the active control and deployment of disproportionate resources. These include psycho-personal resources of charisma, time, motivation and energy. As such, it may include people at the top, at the bottom or outside organizations. As such it may also include people in the capitalist, middle, working, or other disadvantaged classes. And it is my argument that it is elites and sub-elites (by this definition) who do what supposedly has been done by classes.

With respect to organizations, this is obvious when we consider actions initiated at the top of their pyramid. But it holds equally for action taken at the *bottom* of an organizational pyramid. For, as the extensive literature on this topic has shown,[7] action of this type is not generally initiated and engaged in by the organization's lower participants collectively. Enterprises, unions and prisons are usually large-scale organizations, most of whose members belong to its lower echelons. Hence, in cases such as these, decisions are usually made and actions are spearheaded and controlled by the lower participants' – formal or informal – leaders and their immediate collaborators, that is, by their elites and sub-elites. The same, moreover, holds for social classes.

## Elites within classes

The fact that class theory has overshadowed elite theory has led to bias in another respect as well. It has led to a neglect of the fact that even within classes not all are equal. By most definitions, members of the same class are roughly equal in their access to economic goods. But access to such goods does not necessarily entail their active control.

And in this respect members of the same class may differ widely. In addition, even within each class, people differ from each other in the control of other, non-economic resources.

Even within classes, therefore, there are elites and sub-elites. They may be those, who – even within their own classes – have a greater share of active control over organizational/administrative resources of power. Or they may be those who have a greater share of resources of knowledge, ambition, charisma, time, motivation and energy. In any case, they are the men and women within each social class who, on the basis of these resources, have the ability and the willingness to engage in certain actions which are of wider significance and have an impact on society. They are simply the most powerful, influential and active elements of social classes, and those who are next in line in these respects.

Now this goes for all social classes: in modern Western society it goes for the capitalist class no less than for the middle class or the working class. Obviously the capitalist class includes not only the people who actively control the corporations and enterprises which lend them economic power, but also passive owners who never use their ownership to exercise control over those enterprises in practice. It also includes the members of the owners/controllers' families who may be but are not necessarily involved in the enterprises' control.

However, because the capitalist class is small in numbers compared to other classes, because all members of the business elite belong to this class while relatively large numbers within this class belong to the business elite, the proportion of the elite component within it is relatively large. This renders the non-elite component within it less visible, and blurs the distinction between the capitalist class as a whole and the business elite as part of that class.

Not so with other classes which, numerically, are so much larger. Since elites and sub-elites are usually small groups of people, the larger the class, the smaller the proportion of the elite component in it. And the smaller proportion of the elite component within a class, the more clearly it stands out from the rest of the class.

Thus, there are several elites and sub-elites that belong over-whelmingly to the middle class, especially the new middle class. For instance, most members of the media elite and the academic/intel-lectual elite and their sub-elites belong to this class, by virtue of the occupations in which they are engaged. In addition, research has shown (see for instance Offe, 1985) that the leaders and activists of the new social movements in the West are recruited disproportionately from this class. But although the elites and sub-elites that belong to the middle class may (or may not) exceed the elite of the capitalist class in numbers, they still constitute relatively small minorities within their own class. And as such they are clearly identifiable as distinct from the rest of that class.

In principle, however, there is no difference between the various classes in their relationship to elites. Whether we look at the capitalist class or at the middle class (or at any other class), each of those classes includes especially powerful, influential and active components, and these constitute elites, with sub-elites as next in line.

## Class actions and struggles are really elite actions and struggles

What class theory has also failed to highlight is that some of these elites and sub-elites within classes engage in actions that have implications for those classes as wholes. Also, some elite members cross class lines and act in the name of classes to which they do not belong. And when certain deeds are attributed to classes, it is invariably those active elements who are to blame – or to be praised – for them. In short, it is elites and sub-elites who engage in what commonly has been referred to as class action.

This includes, in the first instance, the exploitation attributed by Marxist theory to the capitalist class. This in fact has been (and can be) carried out only by the part of this class which *actively* controls economic resources, or by its elite and sub-elite.[8] It encompasses, in the second place, the political rule attributed by Marxist theory to what is referred to as the ruling class, which in contemporary Western society is also the capitalist class. This rule, in fact, is also carried out by an elite and sub-elite, even though its members may (or may not) all belong to the same class. It has been carried out by an elite and sub-elite even though its members may (or may not) represent a certain class's interests, and may (or may not) act with the tacit acquiescence of the other members of that class.

The deeds attributed by class theory to classes include, thirdly, the attempts to better the lot of lower or exploited classes, particularly the working class. Some of these attempts may be engaged in by people who actually belong to those classes, others by those who identify with them. Yet what is true but not so clearly evident at the top, is eminently clear closer to the bottom of the social hierarchy: the endeavours to better the lot of the less privileged in society have not been carried out by entire classes.

Whether engaged in to better their own lot, to better the lot of other groups of people, or to better the lot of entire classes, whether engaged in in organized fashion or spontaneously, through reformist action or violent upheavals, these attempts have generally been engaged in by small minorities. While facing varying degrees of support or non-support from the members of the relevant classes, they have been carried out by those who are especially powerful, influential and active: by leaders, agitators, functionaries, activists. Hence, although these are actions for (or against) classes, they are actions by elites and sub-elites.

The endeavours to better the lot of the less privileged have frequently (though not always) met with the active opposition of ruling elites and sub-elites, and frequently the latter have acted in the interests of the more privileged classes. This being the case, it must be concluded that frequently elites and sub-elites of, or for, different classes have confronted each other, and those actions dubbed by Marxists and others as class struggles have also been perpetrated by elites, and are in fact elite struggles.

In illustration of this, we may look back into the recent history of Western countries. When we do so, we see quite clearly that even those large-scale collisions which are seen by class theorists as the epitome of class struggles have been perpetrated by minorities within their classes. This goes, for instance, for events such as the storming of the Bastille which signalled the beginning of the French revolution, the uprisings of 1848, or the shortlived mushrooming of the Paris Commune.

Each of these uprisings was conducted by (albeit spontaneously created) elites and sub-elites – of or for lower classes – and was opposed by the elites of the most privileged classes. And even the so-called masses that participated in the street events connected with them were merely small minorities within their own classes. And if this is true for apparently spontaneous mass events, it is certainly true for more organized struggles such as those of the Chartists or Suffragettes in Britain, or of trade unionists or labour activists up to the present (see for instance Etzioni-Halevy, 1989a, ch. 3).

Thus even struggles for greater equality and for democracy have been carried out by elites. And if we look forward into the future, and towards the prospects of greater equity and equality, and for a more democratic democracy, these too can be realized not by class struggles but exclusively by struggles of the most active elements within classes.

## The public within elite struggles

Because class theory has neglected the fact that class struggles are really elite struggles, it has also neglected what I would call the less active, but distinctive and crucially important, role of the public in these struggles. Clearly it is easier to analyse this distinctive role in the framework of democratic elite theory than it is to analyse it in the framework of class theory.

For in this framework it becomes clear, in the first place, that when we say that so-called class struggles are really elite struggles, this does not imply that members of the public are precluded from participating in them. But to participate actively they need to muster unusual resources of time, motivation and energy, if not some more tangible resources. When those engaging in the struggles are organized, members of the public wishing to participate must find the means of penetrating into the relevant organizations, movements or associations, which may be more or less open to outsiders.

Even if these members of the public do join, or are already rank-and-file members of those organizations, moreover, there is no certainty that the leaders and officials of those organizations will carry out their wishes. To gain certainty on this count, they must struggle to figure among those associations' leaders, or their close associates, themselves. In some cases this may be easier, in other cases it may be more difficult. But, in any case, members of the public wishing to engage in class struggles *actively* must themselves become members of elites or sub-elites.

In the framework of democratic elite theory it also becomes clear, in the second place, that even if members of the public do not become elites they still *are* important in elite struggles. Their importance lies in the climate of opinion and in the support they either lend or do not lend to those who conduct the struggles. Elites and sub-elites acting in the name of certain classes are strengthened in their struggles against the elites of other classes when they can mobilize rank-and-file support. And they are weakened (and occasionally made impotent and defeated) when they cannot. For the threat which elites of disadvantaged classes pose to elites of the establishment is directly proportional to the numbers of demonstrators they can bring out into the streets, the numbers of rioters they can lead on to the barricades, the numbers of strikers and picketers they can muster in enterprises, or the numbers of votes they can channel into the ballot boxes.

Even when rank-and-file support for struggles is forthcoming, however, such support (although it may include occasional participation in mass events such as demonstrations) is different from, and must be clearly distinguished from, active, sustained engagement in struggles. These struggles are sustained, not by the public, that is the rank-and-file members in each class, any more than by the classes in their entirety, but by elites and sub-elites – of and in classes.

## Discussion: a matter of democracy

It may be argued that the contention that classes as entities cannot act, and that elites and sub-elites engage in the actions commonly attributed to classes, is either false or unfalsifiable. And, indeed, as noted, the contention would certainly be false if elites and sub-elites were defined as those standing at the apex of the upper classes, or those standing at the helm of the state or of other organizations. But as explained in detail, what is here meant by elites is different: it overlaps with those categories of people, but it also includes the most active people in the middle and at the bottom of organizational and class structures. If so, however, is not the statement a tautology and therefore unfalsifiable? Does it not merely contend that the people who do not act – do not act; while those who act – do act?

This, I say, is not the case. By contending that elites and sub-elites are the ones who do what is commonly attributed to classes as wholes, I make a statement that *is* falsifiable. It could be falsified if the boundaries of classes could be clearly set, and if it were to be shown that entire classes do in fact reach common decisions in which all members actively participate, and that they act on them in unison. Common decision-making and action-taking by classes is after all not logically precluded, but rather (as I have argued) empirically non-existent, or virtually non-existent.

Moreover, if the idea that classes as entities cannot act and elites do what is commonly attributed to classes were, in fact, a tautology and unfalsifiable, then it would be all the more astounding that so many class theorists have disregarded it and do attribute common action to classes. Pointing out a curiosity such as this would thus be doubly interesting.

Weightier, however, than the accusation that the above contention is a tautology would be the accusation that it is a truism. In other words, that it is so self-evident as to be unworthy of attention. To put it differently, it could be argued that the distinction between what Marxists and other class theorists refer to as class struggles and what are here referred to as struggles of elites within classes is merely nitpicking. When class theorists speak of class action and class struggle, they know of course (and some explicitly admit) that not all or most members, or the classes as concerted units, are involved. They still speak of class action or conflict, but they do so in a figurative, or metaphorical sense, *as if* the classes as entities were included.

All this would be all right except for the fact that class theorists subsequently tend to forget this truism. Perhaps they disregard it *because* it is a truism. But even so, I maintain that it is still important to call or re-call attention to this truism, for disregarding it leads such theorists to take their own metaphor literally. And it is through this literalization of a metaphor that the myth of class struggle is created.

What is particularly unfortunate is that out of this disregard of a truism, and out of this literalization of a metaphor, springs an entire theoretical conception which belittles one of society's most important aspects: the despotic but also democratic potential which invariably springs not from classes but from elites and their aides. It is therefore a conception which also belittles the role of elites in a democracy and hence detracts from our understanding of this regime.

There is another possibility to consider: perhaps class theorists prefer to disregard elites-within-classes, to attribute to classes what has actually been done by elites, for ideological reasons. As noted before, emphasizing elite action sounds elitist and conservative; talking of class struggles seems more egalitarian and progressive. If however (as is the case here) elites are conceived as including not merely some of those who stand at the top of the social hierarchy in wealth, prestige and the like but also some who stand at the bottom of the hierarchy in these respects, then neither the elites themselves, nor an analysis which puts major emphasis on such elites, is necessarily elitist. The case for disregarding elite action within classes is thus much weakened.

Bringing elites and sub-elites back into class theory, not as supporting actors for classes but as star actors in their own right, positioning them at centre-stage, not instead of but in conjunction with classes, and exploring the relationships between the two, is thus a legitimate and a much needed endeavour. And so is the exploration of the effect which elites and elite structures have for democracy. It is with this latter endeavour that the present analysis is concerned.

Analysis of elites, however, is not synonymous with their admiration. If elites have both despotic and democratic potential, it follows that, as such, elites are not necessarily either the one or the other. The point, therefore, is not to condemn elites or to praise them. Rather the task is to use democratic elite theory in order to explore the conditions under which they may become despotic, as against the conditions under which they may contribute to democracy. This, as will be shown below, leads to a better understanding of democracy which is not merely of academic value, but has tangible implications for democracy's future.

## Notes

1  Also cited in Hindess, 1989, pp. 103, 110. On alleged working-class action see also Wardell and Johnston, 1987.
2  See also Kesselman, 1983.
3  Cited in Abercrombie and Urry, 1983, p. 145.
4  There is an extensive literature on this. On oligarchical unions see for instance Gulowsen, 1985; Fairbrother, 1986; Wippler, 1986; Seifert, 1988. On democratic unions see among others Willey, 1971; Hemingway, 1978; Edelstein and Warner, 1979.
5  On the short lives and the obstacles to the survival of worker cooperatives, see Gamson and Levin, 1984. On delegation of decision making in cooperatives, see for instance French and French, 1975; Bernstein, 1976; Roy, 1976; Greenberg, 1984 and 1986; and Stirling et al., 1987.
6  The literature on the problems of democracy in the kibbutz is legion. For an example see Rosner and Cohen, 1983.
7  See for instance Etzioni, 1961, ch. 5, who reviews an extensive literature on the topic.
8  Although other members of the capitalist class, such as passive owners of economic resources, may have exploitation carried out in their name and thus participate in it by default, and all members of the capitalist class, including the members of the capitalists' families, may benefit from exploitation.

# PART II

# THE AUTONOMY OF ELITES AND WESTERN THOUGHT

# 3

# *Democratic elite theory*

As elites may be both despotic and democratic, what turns them into the one or the other? The attempt to answer this question has been the main focus of democratic elite theory. Hence one way to work out the answer is to trace some developments in this theory. Its roots are to be found, first, in Western liberal thought, from the seventeenth century onwards, and second, in some of the classical social science theories of the turn and the beginning of the twentieth century. Let us turn, in the first instance, to liberal thought.

## The separation of powers in liberal thought

This thought has had as its centrepiece the claim that state power must be limited in the interest of individual rights and liberties. Such restriction of power must occur through its dispersion among different agents and through their institutionalized separation. This conception, pioneered by John Locke, David Hume, and James Madison, was most clearly formulated in the eighteenth century by Charles Montesquieu in his doctrine of the separation of powers.

Concentrated power, taught Montesquieu, was dangerous and led to despotism and abuses. 'Constant experience', he wrote in his book *De l'Esprit de lois*, 'shows us that every man invested with power is apt to abuse it ... until he is confronted with limits.'[1] But how are such limits to be imposed? Montesquieu's answer was that there was to be a separation of powers within government, so that one power might check another power, for 'power halts power.' Where the legislative, executive and judicial powers are united in the same person or governmental body, there can be no liberty. If the same body that enacted laws were to execute them and judge those who transgressed them, rule would be tyrannical, arbitrary and oppressive. Only the separation of these powers from each other can ensure the freedom of the citizen.

The value of the doctrine of the separation of powers was further enhanced in the liberal thought of the nineteenth century when (after initial misgivings) it became wedded to the idea of electoral, representative democracy. For James Mill and Jeremy Bentham, liberal democracy had to be based on the division of powers within the state, on freedom of the press, of speech and association, and on accountability of the governors to the governed through periodic elections. Although the logic of their arguments pointed in the direction of universal suffrage, they at one time excluded women and large parts of the labouring classes from this right. But Bentham later abandoned his reservation about universal male suffrage.[2]

Subsequently, John Stuart Mill advocated the separation between parliament and administration, and he also advocated universal suffrage – including voting by women. He still favoured a system of plural voting for those with knowlege and skills, so that the political order would not be subjected to 'ignorance'. But this arrangement was to be only for a transitional period, until the masses attained a higher intellectual standard. At that time it was to be replaced by a system of one-person-one-vote.[3] Gradually, then, the idea of the separation of powers became a core element of Western liberal democratic theory.

Even so, at the time, this notion was still rudimentary. It referred to power mainly within the state. And it obviously made no explicit reference to elites, as power holders, as we now understand this term. This means that there was no explicit awareness that holders of power and influence were not confined to the state and that they existed in other spheres as well. And although there was some awareness of pressure groups, there was no stress on the importance of the autonomy of non-state elites for the limitation of state power and the promotion of civil liberties. Therefore what these philosophers advocated, though of overwhelming importance, did not go far enough.

# The countervailing power of elites in classical theories

The theme was brought to the fore again at the turn and first part of this century by some of the great thinkers we now call classical social scientists. These included most notably Max Weber, a Western liberal in his affinities.

## The Weberian framework

Weber's political theory is best known for its contribution to the analysis of authority and bureaucracy. These elements of his theory, however, are intimately connected to another area of his analysis: that of both bureaucratic and political elites in a democracy.

*Weber on authority and bureaucracy* Weber's conception of authority is based on his definition of power as 'the probability that one actor within a social relationship will be in a position to carry out his will despite resistance'. Power in a hierarchy creates domination, which is 'the probability that a command . . . will be obeyed by a given group of persons' (1947, p. 152). When obedience is based on the belief in the command's legitimacy, we may speak of authority. Three types of authority may be distinguished by virtue of their claim to legitimacy. Traditional authority is legitimated by time, that is, by its existence in the past; charismatic authority is legitimated by the outstanding personal leadership characteristics of its bearer, and legal-rational authority is legitimated by being in accordance with formally correct rules and by the right of those in authority, under such rules, to issue commands.

This typology of authority provided Weber with the basis of a further classification: traditional authority forms the basis of tradition-alist organizations (such as patriarchal kinship units); charismatic authority forms the basis of charismatic movements (such as early Christianity under the charismatic leadership of Jesus); and legal-rational authority forms the basis of bureaucracy. Bureaucracy is distinguished from other types of organizations by its clear demarcation of duties among offices, by its ordered hierarchical structure, and by its operation by general, abstract and impersonal rules.

Because of these, claims Weber, bureaucracy is, from a purely technical viewpoint, capable of attaining the highest degree of rationality and effectiveness. Bureaucracy has developed, and is becoming pervasive in the modern world, because its rationality and technical superiority make it the most appropriate tool for dealing with the complex tasks and problems of modern society. Because of this superiority, bureaucracy is bound to become even more pervasive in the future (Weber, 1947; Gerth and Mills, 1958).

Weber refers to his model of bureaucracy as an 'ideal type' (not to be confused with an ideal), which is a theoretical construct, combining several features of a phenomenon in their purest and most extreme form. An ideal type as such is never found in actual reality. Thus Weber never claimed that all modern organizations, or even all state administrations, displayed the aforementioned features. He merely claims that in modern society there is a general tendency in this direction.

Because Weber regards bureaucracy as rational and effective, he is frequently – though mistakenly – considered as an advocate of bureaucracy. In fact, Weber is quite ambivalent about this phenomenon: he sees it as efficient, yet he is deeply concerned about its effects both on the individual and on society. He sees the impact of bureaucracy on the individuals within it, the bureaucrats, as the crippling of their personality. Bureaucracy creates persons who are nothing but little cogs in a big machine, desperately clinging to their positions and hoping to become bigger cogs. Bureaucracy creates technical experts: 'specialists without spirit, sensualists without heart' (Weber, 1958, p. 182) who replace the previously prevalent cultured persons.

According to Weber, bureaucracy holds equally grave dangers for society. In the past, bureaucratization (as part of a growing rationality) had a liberating effect on society in that it destroyed oppressive traditions. But he fears that further bureaucratization will lead to the permeation of a bureaucratic mentality, a compulsive quest for order and nothing but order, throughout the population. He fears that it is apt to lead to over-organization, a prospect he did not find heartening.

Most of all, however, Weber fears that bureaucracy may come to be the master of society. On the one hand, Weber stresses that bureaucracy is an instrument of power held by others, bound by obedience to its political master. He adds, however, that in practice the bureaucratic official, because of his technical expertise, knowledge and information, may easily become insubordinate to his political master if he so chooses.

Bureaucracy could thus become the unfettered, oppressive ruler of the state (Weber, 1947, 1958, 1968).

*Weber on the countervailing power of political elites*   It is here that Weber's analysis of political elites in a democracy comes in. Weber has few illusions about this political system. He recognizes the inevitability of elites even in democratic regimes. He does not believe in the feasibility of the sovereignty of the people, and he has little faith in the ability of the people themselves to judge the merits of political issues. He further believes that representative democratic institutions provide for little control of the elected by their electors. But he is nevertheless a champion for democracy. He argues that democratic institutions (including political parties, parliamentary assemblies and their leaders) are still of the utmost importance in that they serve to keep the increasingly powerful bureaucracy in check.

It is here, too, that Weber's analysis of charismatic authority and charismatic leaders becomes highly relevant. He emphasizes the importance of the democratic process as a competitive struggle of leaders for public support. For this struggle brings to the fore the most qualified leaders, that is to say, those who have genuine charisma. For Weber such autonomous charismatic leaders – committed to democratic values – have a special role to play. For it is up to them to give new directions to political regimes, to countervail bureaucratic inertia and to keep society at least partly exempt from bureaucratic oppression.

Like the power of bureaucracy, the power of these leaders is to be held in check in turn by parliamentary assemblies. Such assemblies form a counterweight to elected leaders by acting as a safeguard against the routinization of their charisma. Once leaders lose their charisma, or their grip over the masses, they might be tempted to turn to oppression to prop up their power. It is up to parliamentary assemblies to avert this danger. Weber also points out that such countervailing forces have, in fact, emerged in modern democratic societies (Gerth and Mills, 1958).[4]

## Mosca: on the countervailing power of the bureaucratic elite

It is customary in the social sciences to view the classical theorists Vilfredo Pareto, Gaetano Mosca and Roberto Michels as a trio whose theories belong to the same school of thought and generally complement each other. As we saw in chapter 1, in some respects, this is the case: all three focus their analyses on the rule of elites (which Mosca terms 'the ruling class' and Michels equates with oligarchy).

At least in one respect, however, there are substantial differences among Pareto, Mosca and Michels: of the three, only Mosca devotes a substantial part of his analysis to the importance of the countervailing power of separate elites. Mosca vied with Pareto over the paternity of elite theory. While he lost out in this paternity suit, he nonetheless has an advantage over Pareto (and Michels). This advantage lies in the fact that it is he who introduced the ideas of the separation of powers into what we now think of as elite theory, and only his theory may thus be regarded not merely as an elite theory, but also as a democratic elite theory in its own right.

In Mosca's conception (1939), the character and structure of the ruling class is important in determining a society's political structure. There are a few major types of such regimes, most important among them the feudal and the bureaucratic. The feudal system is one in which the same members of the ruling class exercise all governmental functions: the economic, the judicial, the administrative and the military. The bureaucratic regime is one where there is a greater specialization within the ruling class. Here this class is divided into separate sections, including a governmental-bureaucratic and a military one. The absolute bureaucratic state may be regarded as fully established in Europe in the seventeenth century. In less than a century and a half, however, it was transformed into the modern bureaucratic-parliamentary, representative state.

In Mosca's view, as in that of Weber, representative democracy does not spell the sovereignty of the people, as democratic theory would have it. A ruling class is unavoidable even in this type of regime, as it is in any other. But, as he believed particularly in his later years, the emergence of the democratic state is still significant. This is so because in it political forces – which in an absolute state would remain inert – become organized in a representative system, and so exert an influence on government. In addition, there are advantages in a system in which all government acts are subject to public discussion. Parliamentary, individual and press liberties serve to call attention to abuses of power. This forces the ruling class to take account of mass sentiments and public discontent.

The democratic state, moreover, is important also because it divides the ruling class even further into separate branches: the one derived from bureaucratic and judicial appointment, the other from popular suffrage. Like Weber, Mosca sees the unmitigated power of the bureaucracy as holding grave dangers: unless checked, it would result in an absolutist and highly repressive regime. The importance of elections lies in that they create elected assemblies. These, then, curb the power of the bureaucracy and prevent it from becoming omnipotent. Importantly, however, Mosca also points to the danger inherent in the uncurbed power of elected politicians, because of its tendency to bring about abuses through party-related political corruption.

Elected representatives tend to concentrate excessive power in their own hands. Moreover, in an electoral democracy government control goes astray under personal and partisan electoral ambitions. The ability of elected representatives to govern well is distorted by their tendency to pursue their own interests, especially those of getting themselves elected, and by their tendency to pursue the interests of the party which backs their election. This calls forth improper partisan interference of elected representatives in court procedures, in public administration and in the distribution of funds that accrue to the state through taxes and levies. In its more extreme form it leads to the transformation of administrative departments into electioneering agencies, and thus to the improper interference of bureaucracies in elections. This results ultimately in the negation of the democratic principle itself.

Mosca therefore emphasizes the role of an autonomous bureaucratic elite for the restriction of the corrupting power of politicians. He also stresses the role of a judiciary independent from the political elite, so as to prevent politicians penalizing their rivals in order to further their own careers. According to Mosca, in democratic regimes, since different parts of the ruling class are aligned with different and separate political institutions, they exercise reciprocal control. In this manner, power limits power, thereby restraining the arbitrariness of the rulers and increasing the liberty of the ruled.

## More recent theories: Schumpeter and Aron

Like the liberal philosophers then, the classical theorists Weber and Mosca are still concerned mainly with the separation of power holders within the state. However, the topic of the autonomy of elites is taken up once more towards the middle of this century when, at last, the autonomy of non-state elites comes to be emphasized as well. This is evident in the theory of the liberal Austrian scholar Joseph Schumpeter.

## Schumpeter: on competitive democracy and the countervailing power of elites

Schumpeter (1962) rejects the prevalent notion that democracy is capable of realizing certain ideals, or that it is able to lead to widespread public participation in the political decision-making process. Like Weber and Mosca he sees such ideas as unrealistic. Like his two predecessors he emphasizes that democracy is not rule by the people, but by elected elites. For Schumpeter the essence of democracy lies in its being a certain arrangement for reaching political, legislative and administrative decisions. The arrangement is the leaders' attainment of power – and thus the ability to make such decisions – through competition for the people's votes. He does not believe that this makes it posssible for the electors to control those they have elected, except through their ability to refuse to reelect them.

Consequently, argues Schumpeter, since the power of elected politicians may be only minimally controlled by their electors, it has to be limited through independent agencies, or elites. Like Weber and Mosca, he thus emphasizes the crucial importance of the countervailing power of autonomous elites. Unlike Weber and Mosca, however, Schumpeter sees the issue in a broader perspective, in which not only state elites but non-state elites are included as well.

For Schumpeter, a most important requirement of democracy is that the effective range of political decisions be limited. This implies that several types of organizations, and their top position holders, have a large measure of independent power as against that of the elected political leadership. These include – besides the state elites such as the judiciary, the top of the state bureaucracy and the central bank – also universities, or academic elites. He further expresses his belief that in most democracies such autonomy does in fact accrue to these elites. In this manner he draws together the liberal idea of the separation of powers within the state with the notion of the independence of elites outside the state as well, in what has come to be known as democratic elite theory.

## Aron: on the distinctiveness of democracy and the countervailing power of elites

Thereafter, the thinker who most clearly recognized the importance of – both state and non-state – elite autonomy for democracy was the

French sociologist and liberal thinker Raymond Aron. Aron's focus on elite autonomy results from his conception that elites are universal, and that their power is formidable (1968, 1978). He adds that in modern society the power of elites over the life and death of millions is expanded beyond measure by thermonuclear armaments. His interest in elites also results from his conception that elite structure is more than a mere reflection of the structure of society, and, indeed, has a major impact on it.

Hence the importance Aron sees in mapping out the type of elite structure that limits elite power and ensures a free society. For him, this is also the combination of particular elite features that distinguishes Western-democratic from autocratic regimes. And, in similarity to Weber, Mosca and Schumpeter, Aron believed that these distinctive features are to be found not in the absence of elites, but in the unique limitations with which Western societies have shackled their rulers. In spite of growing centralization, Western societies have remained democracies because they have been suspicious of rulers and hence have been stingy in granting them the authority to rule. Hence the checks and balances they have put on their power have survived well into the twentieth century.

For Aron the unique structure of elites in a democracy is *not* the result of their proliferation or multiplicity. For he makes it clear that, although there are many power groups, in all modern societies there are but five major elites: political leaders, government administrators, economic directors, labour leaders and military chiefs. And neither are the checks on elite power the result of total disunity among them. For while a totally unified elite means the end of freedom, a totally disunited elite means the end of the state. Freedom prevails in the intermediate region, and Western democracies have been more successful than, say, Communist regimes in maintaining this balance. For although there is a basic consensus among democratic elites on the most basic issues, elites are internally divided on a whole variety of less fundamental issues.

In Aron's view, the essence of the restraint on power in democratic regimes also lies in the fact that it is attached to well-defined spheres of action, and is fought over by many claimants. Also, those who exert power all form separate organizations and defend their separate interests. They therefore are in constant, free and legitimate rivalry with each other. Thus the other elites have a relative independence from political rulers, who lack the force to overpower them. Because of all this, reasons Aron, in a democracy there is a clear differentiation between state and society, and the authority of rulers is controlled and limited.

## Elitist versions of democratic elite theory

Apart from these thinkers, there have been some American scholars whose work has also been classified as falling in the tradition of democratic elite theory. These include, for instance, Berelson and his associates (1954). Analysing the role of voting in democratic politics, they make the point that non-voters and marginal voters, who are the most inconsistent in their political views and have the least interest in politics, provide the system with the flexibility it requires to function properly.

Writing at about the same time, Kornhauser (1959) expresses the view that American democracy is promoted by countervailing and mutually limiting focuses of power. Relatively autonomous power groups, which mediate and act as a buffer between the elites and the masses, fulfil a twofold function for democracy: they countervail and thus limit the power of elites, but they also restrain the undemocratic tendencies of the masses, thus bolstering democracy.

These scholars thus have something in common: possibly in the shadow of the rise of Nazism, Fascism and Communism in Europe, they developed a fear of the alleged totalitarian tendencies of the 'masses', whose impact on the political system has to be moderated and buffered if democracy is to survive. In one way or another, they and some other scholars (see Milbrath and Goel, 1965) therefore promote the idea that successful democracy depends on widespread public apathy, and that if the 'masses' were to participate in politics in large numbers, peaceful competition among elites – and thus democracy – would be apt to break down.

## Other versions of democratic elite theory: Lipset and Eisenstadt

### Lipset: on the conditions for democracy

Also working broadly within the democratic elite Schumpeterian tradition is Seymour Martin Lipset. Much of his work, spanning several decades, focuses on the conditions for, and the transition to democracy. In the classical study of the political processes in a trade union, Lipset and his colleagues (1956) demonstrate the role of relatively independent centres of power – whose members still maintain their loyalty to the whole – for the promotion of democracy within the organization. The authors further emphasize that democracy in an organization is not so dissimilar from democracy in the state that understanding the one cannot also help us in understanding the other.

Subsequently, Lipset (1981) seeks to provide an explanation for the development and maintenance of liberal democracy in the state proper. Lipset now argues that stable democracy is related to levels of economic development, and also to levels of education among the population. Comparing stable democracies to unstable ones and to dictatorships, Lipset demonstrates that the former have higher levels of economic development and higher levels of average education than the latter.

The interpretation which Lipset suggests for these differences is that widespread affluence and education moderates radicalism and authoritarianism among the working classes. These factors also increase the middle class which acts as a buffer between the upper class and the working class, reducing conflict between them. Importantly, his further interpretation of the above findings is that a large middle class is likely to generate autonomous associations, or centres of power, acting as intermediaries between government and the public.

In his other work, Lipset analysed the role of intellectuals in society, as well as student protest and a variety of other topics. Recently, however, Lipset working with some associates (see Diamond et al., 1989–90) has returned to the topic of the conditions for democracy. Analysing the transition from non-democratic to democratic regimes, they posit *inter alia* the role of autonomous power centres in such transitions (see in further detail below). The idea of autonomous power centres as a condition for, and as guardians of democracy may thus be seen as a major, core idea of Lipset's contribution to political sociology.

## Eisenstadt: a new synthesis of antagonistic theories

Also relevant in this context is the work of the Israeli sociologist Shmuel Eisenstadt, which, like that of Lipset, has spanned over several decades. Eisenstadt's work cannot be neatly compartmentalized within any one area of sociology or within any one school of thought. In his comparative studies of empires, civilizations and modernization, he has managed to reconcile seemingly incompatible paradigms, including a structural-functional consensus model and a Weberian-Schumpeterian one.

Within the distinctive approach that has emerged from this reconciliation, Eisenstadt (see for instance 1966) proposes the idea that the success of a modern, democratic political system may be measured by its ability to absorb change without major breakdowns and crises. In Eisenstadt's view, there are two seemingly incompatible conditions for this success: a differentiation of elites, leading to a competition among various power centres, and a solidarity of elites, as well as a consensus among them on basic values and on the rules of the political game. Only a balance of such elite cleavages on the one hand, and elite solidarity and consensus on the other hand, can ensure democratic elite conflict. For only such a balance makes it possible for elites to bridge conflict and reach the sort of compromises that prevent the breakdown of the system. Once again, then, the separation of elites, elite cleavages, are put forward as one of the central conditions for democracy.

## Critique and evaluation

Liberal philosophers, as well as the social scientists working within the democratic elite tradition, have been widely criticized. Generally the critique levelled at them has little to do with their factual analysis, most aspects of which have not been put into question. Rather, the critique has to do with the focus of their analysis: with their emphasis on elites at the expense of the public. It also has to do with their ideological bent: their concern with liberty, civil rights and political democracy at the expense of economic equality. In addition, some of them have been taken to task for being not only democratic elite theorists, but democratic elitist theorists, for praising elites while denigrating the public in Western democracy (see, for instance, Pateman, 1970).

With respect to this latter accusation I would argue that while it has a kernel of truth in it, it is not valid for all democratic elite theory: it is more justified for theorists such as Berelson and Kornhauser than it is for other theorists in the same school of thought. With respect to these two theorists I join this critique. But I submit that there are some separate elements in their work: their analysis of the countervailing role of relatively autonomous power groups, and their analysis of what they see as the negative function of massive public participation – or conversely the positive function of public apathy – for democracy. These are not logically inseparable. It is quite possible to accept the one yet reject the other. And while doing so, it is possible to assign a much more substantial and positive role to the public in a democracy, as I will endeavour to do in my analysis.

## Conclusion

The core idea of democratic elite theory, then, is – to put it in simplistic terms – that what turns elites into democratic ones is the separation among them. It lies in stressing the importance of countervailing and relatively autonomous elites for the limitation of despotic rule and for the promotion of democracy. Whatever problems may have beset some of their work, the social philosophers and social scientists who have developed this idea have certainly succeeded in bringing it to the forefront of attention in the West, and there is no doubt that these ideas have become central to Western thought. In addition, it can hardly be disputed that these scholars were influenced by, but some of them were also influential, in the shaping of Western reality. For in some albeit limited ways, this reality has come to mirror their ideas, as I will argue further below.

Recently, however, democratic elite theory has not been faring well. Thus not only has elite theory in general been overshadowed by class theory, but even within elite theory, democratic elite theory has been overshadowed by what is considered as the elite theory proper, thereby emerging as unjustifiably low on the theoretical totem pole. Perhaps this is so because even the giants of social thought who have worked in this field have supplied only its basic contours; they have not developed their pertinent ideas as fully as could have been wished. Perhaps for that reason, these ideas were not suitably elaborated by other modern social scientists.

The latter point is not immediately evident, because quite a few social scientists have been labelled as working within the democratic elite tradition, while they actually do not. These include chiefly pluralist, neo-pluralist and pluralist elite theorists, most prominent among them Robert Dahl and John Kenneth Galbraith. In fact, the work of all these scholars is highly relevant for democratic elite theory and has some basic affinities with it. Yet it differs in some important respects from democratic elite theory, as should become evident in the next chapter.

## Notes

1 Montesquieu, 1952, book XI, ch. 4.
2 These ideas are to be found in various parts of their work. See for instance Bentham, 1960; Mill, 1937.
3 Mill, 1982. For an informative review of these ideas, see Held, 1987.
4 For a more detailed anlaysis of Weber's ideas on bureaucracy in relation to democracy see Etzioni-Halevy, 1985. Good analyses of Weber's theory on the countervailing power of elites in a democracy are provided by Mommsen, 1974, and by Held, 1987.

# 4

# *Other theories: a comparison*

To understand the contribution of democratic elite theory, it is necessary to place it in its theoretical context. Its place in relation to what is usually considered as elite theory proper has been clarified in chapter 1. It is now necessary to look briefly at how some additional theories have dealt with similar issues, so that the democratic elite theory can then be seen in comparison to those as well. In this respect, the contrast is clearest with respect to the theories of Marx and Marxism.[1]

## Marx and Marxist theories

### *On the state and democracy*

The unique contribution of Marx and Marxism to unmasking the inequalities and exploitation inherent in capitalism has been noted before, it has been widely acclaimed, and is not in question. But it must also be said that unlike liberalism Marx and Marxists have not emphasized the dangers inherent in the indigenous and potentially oppressive power of the state. And neither have they stressed the importance of the separation of powers – or the autonomy of elites and sub-elites – for limiting that power and for democracy. Hence, also, their neglect of the dangers that stem from crushing such autonomy.

Perhaps Marx's unique understanding of the exploitation inherent in capitalism and his disregard of the repressive potential of the state are not unrelated to each other. For Marx regarded the modern state as nothing more than an organization of the bourgeoisie for the management of its common affairs and for the mutual protection of its interests. This view, which Marx and Engels expressed in *The German Ideology* (Marx and Engels, 1969a) and in the *Manifesto of the Communist Party* (Marx and Engels, 1969b), was the basis of Marx's whole conception of the state, which he occasionally qualified, but never rejected.

Thus, in his more empirical writings, Marx recognized that under certain circumstances the state may gain some independence from the capitalist class. This, wrote Marx (1969a), had occurred for instance in France, under the dictatorship of Napoleon III. It happened because the bourgeoisie's economic interests had to be secured by a strong state, and subsequently the bourgeoisie was too weak to control the state it had strengthened. This state thus became oppressive of its own account. But once the bourgeoisie was freed from political care it attained unprecedented economic prosperity. This led eventually to the recapture of its political power as well. Thus the state was not a passive instrument of the capitalist ruling class. But even when it gained a degree of autonomy from the bourgeoisie, it still served its interests.

In light of this conception, it is not surprising that Marx was greatly ambivalent with respect to what he termed bourgeois democracy. He denounced such democracy as nothing but a purely developed form of bourgeois rule. Nevertheless, he thought it had some advantages, because it deprived the bourgeoisie of absolute power and of the absolute assurance of its power. However, the bourgoisie could not afford to let democracy prevail in the long run, as it would eventually destroy its rule. Whenever this rule was really threatened, the bourgeoisie would not hesitate to repudiate democracy (1969b).

Marx envisioned that this system would be overthrown by a revolution, followed by a transitionary period of the dictatorship of the proletariat. This, however, would give way to a communist society, in which for the first time a true democracy would come into being. For only in that society would there be individual freedom and the abolition of classes. This would include the abolition of the ruling class, which prevents the realization of democracy in capitalist society. Also, in this post-revolutionary society, the state, which had previously represented the interests of the ruling class, would wither away (although Marx never clarified what this withering away would entail).

Using Marx's ideas as a point of departure, contemporary Marxists have added to it the distinction between governing and ruling. Governing entails the execution of the day-to-day routine tasks of administration and decision making which make the political process run smoothly. Ruling, on the other hand, implies the holding of decisive power which constrains the political process to serve the rulers' interests. It makes little difference who governs in capitalist society for, in any event, it is the capitalist class that rules. Indeed, the state apparatus best serves the interests of the ruling class when the latter is not a governing class. Through this separation between governing and ruling, the state has a relative autonomy from the ruling class. But this itself works in favour of that class, since the state can promote its common purpose only in so far as it is not exclusively committed to any of its frequently warring fractions.

There are various reasons for the state serving the interests of the ruling class. These include the common background and mentality of capitalists and those in command of the state apparatus, as well as their social interconnections. They also include the fact that capitalists act as an extremely powerful interest group which can pressure the state by threatening to withdraw its investments and transfer them overseas. Finally, it includes the fact that the state acts in a capitalist system of production, and is thus structurally constrained to serve the interests of capitalism. And by serving the capitalist economy, the state necessarily serves the class in charge of that economy. Failing that, it would undermine the economy and thereby the basis of its own power (Miliband, 1973, 1977, 1989a; Mandel, 1975; Poulantzas, 1975).

Marx's ambivalence towards democracy is reflected in the writings of modern Marxists as well. According to the Marxist view, democracy is not a serious hindrance to the state serving the interests of the ruling class. For the capitalist state manages to promote the interests of the ruling class while appearing to be class neutral. The electoral system gives people the illusion that insurmountable cleavages exist among political parties. But in reality there is a basic consensus among them on the preservation of the existing economic system. It follows that bourgeois democracy is but the rule of the bourgeoisie through the instrument of free elections. It is a system whereby the acquiescence of the ruled classes is assured through their political participation.

Despite all this, democracy is not to be dismissed lightly. In the bourgeois democratic state the powers of repression are circumscribed in various ways. Hence there are important qualitative differences between it and dictatorship. All in all, bourgeois democracy is still preferable to all past and present alternatives (Jessop, 1978; Miliband, 1973, 1977, 1989a; Poulantzas, 1978; Therborn, 1977, 1978).

There are certain divergencies among different strands of contemporary Marxism. Some Marxists, such as Miliband, put more emphasis on the close connections between capitalists and those staffing the state apparatus as a major factor in making the state serve capitalism. Others, such as Poulantzas, put more stress on structural factors, or the constraint of the capitalist system, in creating the same effect.

Marxists also differ with respect to their belief in the power of the capitalist state to integrate the working class into the system. It will be remembered (chapter 1) that Marx imputed to the dominant class not only economic rule, but mental or ideological rule as well. In the wake of this idea, Antonio Gramsci coined the term hegemony, which several contemporary Marxists have adopted as well. The concept encapsulates the idea that in capitalist democracies the dominant ideology – promulgated by the ruling class – mystifies the working class into identifying with its exploiters. It entices it into accepting the status quo, even though it works against its interests (see Althusser, 1971; Connell, 1977; Miliband, 1989a). Other Marxists, or writers inspired by Marxism, believe that the capitalist state suffers from crises, expressed in the breakdown of the legitimation it had previously enjoyed (see Habermas, 1989; O'Connor, 1987; Offe, 1984).

There is nevertheless sufficient common ground between Marx and modern Marxists, and among modern Marxists themselves, for them to suffer from a common problem. Unlike liberalism and democratic elite theory, they have (albeit inadvertently and by default) contributed to the shaping and legitimation of Communism in Eastern Europe. Thereby, dialectically, they have also carried within their theories the seeds of its downfall.


## The legitimatory effect on Communism

The idea that Marx has helped shape and legitimize the Communist regime has been stated – and disputed – many times. Lovell, for one, states (what has also been said before) that it is not Marx's theory, but rather the modification introduced into it by Lenin which is to blame for pressing its imprint on Communism (1984). To this Miliband (1989b) adds that one would be hard put to it to find an endorsement of Communist-style dictatorship in Marx's writings. True as all this may be, it misses the point.

The point is that, despite all this, it is clearly not by a mere freak that Marx's theory (rather than, say, John Stuart Mill's) was chosen by Lenin for adaptation. Marx's theory could not have been adapted to serve as the official doctrine of the despotic Communist regime had there not been something in it which made this conversion feasible. This something is certainly not an endorsement of Communist dictatorship. Rather, it has to do with Marx's analysis of state and society under *capitalism*.

With respect to this, and in contrast to liberalism, his theory lacked an important insight. Because he saw the state mainly as the lackey of the capitalist class, most of his theoretical writings lacked the understanding that the state necessarily had an indigenous interest: that of exercising power and of accumulating more of it. Hence he was not truly concerned about the danger of oppressive state rule. He failed to visualize that the state would necessarily encroach on liberty unless the mechanism for restraining its might were incorporated into its own structure. Despite Lovell's and Miliband's argument, it is the fact that Marx practically disregarded the separation of powers and elites as a mechanism for limiting state dominance that has made his theory suitable as justification for a regime which has purposely prevented such checks and balances.

Like Marx, modern Marxists have never endorsed Communist dictatorship. Instead, they have envisioned a future socialist or communist democracy. Like Marx, they focus their analyses on society more than on the state. It is also true (as will be seen below) that Gramsci, Habermas and some of their followers have been concerned with civil society as standing apart from the state. Some Marxists have also recognized and advocated a plurality of social forces. But perusal of the work of the most prominent Western Marxists such as that by Althusser, Miliband and Poulantzas, and even the brief overview of their main ideas presented before, shows that the importance of separation of power holders within and from the state has not become central in the mainstream of Marxist thought. Like Marx, then, many modern Marxists, too, have been left without a clear conception of the mechanisms that might limit the overbearing tendencies of the state, and lead to democratic socialism.

This, moreover, is not of merely academic significance. For Marxism is not just another theory for students to memorize, but a most potent ideology as well. And the fact that Marxism (as a theory) has practically disregarded the autonomy of elites has led Marxism (as an ideology), however inadvertently, to give a rationale for the Communist regime.

To be sure, modern Marxists cannot be held responsible for a regime which came into being before they did. But many of their writings have had the indirect effect of granting *post factum* intellectual absolution to this regime.

This has been expressed for instance in the well-known fact that Western Marxism has been lenient in its evaluation of Communism. While it has been highly critical (though not entirely dismissive) of capitalist democracy, it has either disregarded the repressive tendencies of Communism, or has dealt with them but sparingly (see Bowles and Gintis, 1986; Herman and Chomsky, 1988; Parenti, 1986). And this lenience has continued to be apparent in several Marxist writings even recently. To my mind it is only because of the Marxists' disregard of the importance of the autonomy of elites and sub-elites that their laxness towards Communism could entrench itself so deeply as to resist change even after Communist leaders themselves have been admitting to the long-time viciousness of their regimes.

## Marxism and the collapse of Communism

This, in turn, is related to the Marxists' share of intellectual responsibility for the collapse of Communism. Through the omission from their thought I have described, Marxists have also given an (unpremeditated) absolution to a type of regime which has not been open to struggles initiated by social protest movements. As I will argue at greater length below, in Western countries the relative autonomy of social movements and their leaders and activists has long served as the yeast for the dough of their regimes. It has promoted their gradual change, while helping to prevent their collapse. Under Communism social movements have not been able to fulfil this autonomous, adaptive role.

By failing to highlight the importance of the autonomy of elites, Marxists have thus inadvertently helped to justify a political structure in which few such movements could emerge and survive, and which therefore lacked internal mechanisms for reformist changes spurred from below. To the extent that the Marxist theory/ideology has contributed – though only by default – to the entrenchment of a system which has become compulsively rigid and self-defeating, this theory/ideology has also indirectly contributed to its downfall. By contributing to the rigidity of the Communist regime, Marxist theory has thus had an additional effect. Inadvertently and by default, it has helped prevent more gradual changes, induced by social movements, changes that might have led precisely to the type of socialist democracy which Marxists claim to advocate.

## The delegitimatory effect on democracy

The fact that the conception of the struggles and the relative autonomy of elites has been largely missing from Marx's and Marxist theories has had implications for the West as well. It is true that the concept 'relative autonomy' has been used by contemporary Marxists in their analyses of capitalist regimes. But, as we have seen, the Marxist conception of relative autonomy is almost the mirror image of that of the liberal democratic elite theory. While the liberal tradition has emphasized relative autonomy *from* and *within* the state, Marxist theory has emphasized the relative autonomy of the state. Still lacking from Marxist theory, therefore, is a conception of the autonomy of elites and sub-elites as a mechanism of limiting state power in Western regimes.

It is in the light of this that the dearth of Marxist critique of Communism, combined with its heavy strictures of and ambivalence towards capitalist democracy, should be looked at. Because of it, this imbalance has had certain implications that have not worked in favour of democracy. As such, critique is legitimate for both capitalism and Western democracy. Both, moreover, have much to be criticized about. But because of the absence of the principle of elite checks and balances from their theories, Marxists have lacked an appropriate criterion or measuring rod by which communism and capitalist democracy could be compared.

It is this lack of a standard for comparison that has mystified the issue of democracy. It has led Marxists to underestimate the difference between the Eastern bloc, in which the autonomy of elites and sub-elites has been largely repressed, and the West, where it has been – however imperfectly – implemented. It is for that reason that the Marxist critique has helped delegitimize not merely the subversions of Western democracy caused by capitalism, but democracy itself.

## Recent developments

Latterly there has been a shift in Marxist thought. In a recent book Mandel (1989) finally presents a scathing critique of the Soviet regime. Miliband (1989b) goes even further. He now reverts to the core idea of liberalism: the importance of checking power by power, this being something which the Communist regimes, to their detriment, have spurned. The problem, however, is that when Mandel and Miliband ponder the ill-fate of Communism, they refrain from relating it to the omissions of Marxism. Miliband, for instance, castigates Communism for having spurned the checking of power by power without admitting that this mechanism of checks and balances has long been if not spurned, at least disregarded by Marxist theory as well.

This should not be taken as a call for Marxism to discredit itself. On the contrary: realizing an omission may well signal a new vigour. Incorporating the liberal idea of checks and balances into Marxist thought, may well signal the beginning of a considerable Marxist contribution to both the theory and reality of democracy.

## Public-centred theories of democracy: critique and complacency

In contrast to Marxism, which has diverged from liberal thought, public-centred theories have followed this tradition in some respects. In line with the liberal tradition, they have put the chief emphasis on the liberty of the *populus*, or the public. Yet they, too, have neglected to highlight the main mechanism advocated by liberal thought for ensuring this liberty.

These theories include populist-participatory theories of democracy, which have argued that although Western democracy is not government by the people, it ought to be. They also include pluralist theories of democracy which, in their most simplistic version, have contended that it already is. Thus these two theories take different stands towards extant democracy in the West: the one is critical of it, while the other is rather complacent about it. Both, however, have not done justice to the idea of countervailing power, or the relative autonomy of elites.

### Participatory theories of democracy: a critical approach

Having their origins in the writings of thinkers such as Jean Jacques Rousseau, Alexis de Tocqueville and John Stuart Mill, participatory discourse overlaps with liberal thought. For it, too, seeks to limit the power of governments. It seeks to do so, however, not via agents of countervailing power, but by maximizing the direct input by the public. Such public participation is to be guided by the principle of majority rule – duly restrained by the counterprinciple of minority rights.

Represented by theorists of the calibre of Carole Pateman (1970), Benjamin Barber (1984) and H.T. Wilson (1984), this school of thought has rightly criticized Western societies for the sparsity of public political participation in them. In Wilson's view, Western industrial societies are characterized by the ascendancy of legal-rational authority and of expert dominated, formally rational bureaucratic structures, epitomized by bureaucracy. Because of these structures, and because of their emphasis on individual material achievements, Western societies entice people away from active political participation. Hence Western representative institutions are in decline, and there is growing political apathy among the public.

Similarly, Barber disparages liberal democracy for being a 'thin' democracy, since its 'minimalist' values undermine the very democratic practices on which the rights of individuals rest. Individual liberty in its extreme manifestation – as stressed in liberal democracy – spells atomism, isolation, hence anomie. This may render democratic societies vulnerable to takeover by totalitarian leaders. In view of this, this theory's call is to move the system on the path to direct democracy, beginning with the level of local government, the workplace and education. This, in turn, is to serve as a preparatory ground for more direct democracy at the level of central government.

Important as public participation is for democracy, and beautiful as the theories that call for such participation may be, the problem is that they have little to say on how Western democracy actually works. What they do have to say concerns the presumed ills of modern society in general, and the connection of these to the problems of democracy. But there is not enough on how democracy – as a political system with its own processes and mechanisms – operates, and much on how it ought to operate. Or, as Sartori put it, whenever they are at a standstill they resort to an 'ought' (1987, p. 153).

Being but marginally concerned with what happens in political reality involves an additional problem. Participatory theories of democracy fail to make a clear distinction between public participation orchestrated from above – which is one of the most effective tools that ever existed for totalitarian rule – and participation that comes genuinely and independently from below. They also fail to identify the democratic mechanisms through which the former may be prevented while the latter may be fostered.

*Pluralist theories of democracy: a complacent approach*

Another offspring of the liberal tradition is pluralism, whose popularity peaked in the 1950s and 1960s. As the older pluralist theories (such as those of Dahl, 1956; Lindblom, 1965; Riesman, 1961) saw it in the West, and particularly in the United States, the political system was an intricate balance of power. In it power was increasingly diffused among a plurality of overlapping interest or pressure groups. Each group was held to exercise a certain influence on the policy-making process, but none was seen as possessing a decisive share of power, since the different groups all checked and counterbalanced each other. Through this plurality of interest groups all major parts of the public could make themselves heard in the decision-making processes of Western democracies.

Thus no distinct group of power holders was discernible, and the idea of such an elite was held to be more fiction than reality. The government, to be sure, was vested with power. But in order to keep itself in office it must respond to multiple pressures so as to keep everybody reasonably happy. Looked at in this light, the power of the government was limited by multiple interest groups. Hence other key power holders had no special role to play in ensuring the curbing of government power and the proper workings of democracy. This turned out to be an overly complacent view which even several prominent pluralists – including Galbraith, Lindblom and Dahl – later abandoned.

Another version of pluralism, sometimes referred to as the pluralist elite theory, has put more emphasis on contending power holders (rather than merely on contending groups) as limiting government power in a pluralist setting. Its prominent spokesmen have been Galbraith (1952), Truman (1971) and Dahl in some of his (but not in his most recent) writings (see 1961, 1967, 1971). More recently they have included Bealey (1988), Polsby (1985) and Sartori (1987). Their approach has been more guarded, sophisticated and convincing than that of simple pluralism. Some of their ideas, particularly the emphasis on the existence of countervailing and contending power holders in democratic societies, are not different from democratic elite theory.

Yet, like pluralists in general, and unlike democratic elite theorists, they perceive a considerable fragmentation of power in Western democracies. Galbraith (1952), for instance, believes that in the modern capitalist state both business people and government are major power holders. But the power of large business is countervailed by the support given by the government to a variety of groups. These include farmers, labour, white collar workers and others, in fact any group that cares to organize itself. Although the world of countervailing power is imperfect, it redresses the position of weaker groups and leads to a decentralized decision-making process, governing the economy.

Dahl, for his part, asserts that in the democratic systems he refers to as polyarchies, oligarchy has given way to multiple power centres. This, moreover, holds for both the local and the national level. In his study of a typical American community (1961), he concludes that the previous power elite has been replaced by variegated patterns of power and influence. Leaders have come to include both public officials and private individuals, who reflect conflicting interests of different segments of the community. What has emerged is thus an intricate conglomeration of chieftains, holding independent sovereignties and spheres of influence, sometimes in confrontation and sometimes in coalition with each other.

As Dahl (1967, 1971) sees it, this is the case also on the national level, where multiple power centres represent varying interests. These vie with each other and prevent each other from becoming wholly sovereign. Thereby they also lead to a wide sharing of power. In a similar vein Sartori writes: 'democracies *are* characterized by diffusion of power . . . by a multiplicity of criss-crossing power groups engaged in coalitional maneuverings' (1987, pp. 147–8).

From the viewpoint of democratic elite theory I would say that these scholars are right in holding that there is a multiplicity of power centres and elites in Western democracies. But several of them have not sufficiently emphasized that there are elites of elites – some elites which are significantly more powerful than other elites. Lacking is a clear distinction between key elites (such as those of the government, of the major opposition parties, of the bureaucracy, of business and trade unions), with their seconds in command, on the one hand, and the elites of lesser pressure groups, action groups and the like, on the other hand. The former are relatively few, while the latter have recently proliferated into the hundreds if not into the thousands. The former are relatively powerful and central actors in the political arena, the latter are greatly heterogenous and some may be quite marginal.

The lack of such an unequivocal distinction between key elites on the one hand and a multiplicity of pressure groups on the other hand still leads to an unrealistically optimistic conception of the dispersion of power in Western democracies. As pluralist elite theorists have considered power to be so widely dispersed, some of them have considered it to be sufficiently diffused already. Therefore they have shown a distinct lack of enthusiasm for greater public participation in the political process. Although shared by some democratic elite theorists (such as Berelson and Kornhauser) this lack of enthusiasm is not shared here.

## The neglect of the autonomy of elites

In addition, there is another respect in which both participatory and pluralist theories of democracy differ from democratic elite theory: they both fail to emphasize the importance of the relative autonomy of elites and sub-elites for democracy. They also fail to explore the relationship between the autonomy of elites and sub-elites on the one hand and participation and pluralism, respectively, on the other hand.

Participatory theories of democracy have criticized democratic elite theories as elitist, as having a profound disregard for the role of the public in a democracy. They themselves, however, have been remiss in having an equally profound disregard for the role of elites. They have failed to bring out that the autonomous power of elites and sub-elites and the autonomous participation of the public are related to each other: although the relative autonomy of elites, in itself, cannot ensure public participation, it is nonetheless necessary for it.

Theorists of participatory democracy, thus, have not done justice to the idea that even the public participation that takes place in the West today (however inadequate it may be) could not have come about were it not for independently powerful elites such as those of opposition parties and the media. For it is only these elites that are capable of encouraging the formation of independent public opinion, which is the *sine qua non* for such participation. And they are motivated to do so because without such public opinion their own positions would be much more vulnerable, if not altogether untenable. These ideas will be extended further on.

Pluralists, too, have not accorded elite autonomy the attention it deserves. Older theories of pluralism have belittled elites, while pluralist elite theories have given them more recognition. Both, however, have still put the main emphasis on the *plurality* of power groups (besides competitive elections), rather than on the relatively *self-sustaining* power of even a few such groups, as the main mechanism sustaining democracy. They generally refrain from stressing that, beyond a certain minimum, it is not primarily the number of pressure groups and power centres but the degree of their separation from each other and from the elite of the government that counts. They have not brought into sufficient relief that pressure groups and their elites, no matter how plural they might be, cannot promote democracy unless they have some independence of resources from those they are attempting to pressure and from each other. This idea, too, will be further developed below.

Also, by contrast to democratic elite theorists, several pluralist and pluralist elite theories have stressed the importance of 'criss-crossing' power groups, and thereby have implicitly discouraged the mutual independence of pressure groups and elites. For some time it was almost an article of faith among many pluralist scholars that democratic grovernments could not survive unless the main cleavages among interest groups were cross-cutting, unless the groups were overlapping and their leaders had multiple group affiliations. Such cross-cutting cleavages were supposed to produce interconnected loyalites, which moderated extremism and conflict, and thereby encouraged compromise and stability. As against this, mutually reinforcing cleavages were supposed to produce such intense conflict as to destabilize the regime and make the workings of democracy impossible.

Some democratic elite theorists still adhere to this view. Thus Polsby (1985) still considers large numbers of groups with *overlapping* memberships as an indicator of democratic pluralism. And as noted before, Sartori (1987) considers a multiplicity of *criss-crossing* power groups as a basic characteristic of democracy. Yet if leaders of pressure groups overlap, it is difficult for them to be separate, let alone autonomous from each other in their control of resources. And if the members of pressure groups also overlap, and if the leaders of these groups derive their power from the support of their members, this, too, detracts from their mutual autonomy. So, while there is pluralism among pluralists and pluralist elite theorists, it is in defence of a plurality of pressure groups and power holders, rather than in defence of their autonomy that this theory can most easily be mobilized.

Another point neglected by these theories is that the relative autonomy of elites is a necessary – though by no means a sufficient – condition for pluralism. They have not adequately clarified that some powerful elites have an interest in suppressing interest groups, when those groups' aims contradict their own. But by the same token some power holders have an interest in defending the independence of a plurality of interest groups. This is so because, in order to defend their own autonomy, elites must defend the meta-principle of autonomy.

And by doing so, they necessarily defend the autonomy of less powerful groups as well.

Pluralists have stressed that bureaucratic agencies are often in league with interest groups because their own power depends on support from these groups. But they have not sufficiently stressed that without the support for their autonomy by elites, the (less powerful) pressure groups might well have been swallowed up by the state. What pluralists have failed to stress, then, is that unless the autonomy of elites is ensured, whatever pluralism exists in the West today cannot be ensured either.

## Civil society: a catch-all concept

There is yet another version of the public-centred approach. It is to be found in the recently revived focus on the concept of 'civil society'. This concept has its origins in liberalism: as Miller (1990a) vividly describes, it can be encountered in the eighteenth-century writings of Adam Ferguson, who was anxious to ensure freedom of citizens' associations in the face of growing state power. Thereafter the concept became best known for its use in Friedrich Hegel's, and subsequently in Marx's, theory. For Hegel it represented the partial interests of society as against the state that represented the general interest. For Marx it reflected the partial interests of the property owning class.

Subsequently the concept went into something of an eclipse until it was revived by Gramsci. Gramsci conceived of civil society as the sum of social activities and institutions which were not part of the government and the state. Afterwards the concept went into a decline once more until it was revived in the 1970s by intellectuals in the Eastern bloc. These envisaged civil society as the realm of free social and cultural space to be carved out of the domination of the Communist party-state.

The idea of civil society was also revived in the 1970s among Western radicals, and here it was directly related to the upsurge of interest in the writings of Gramsci. This was noticeable among the eurocommunists as they searched for alternatives to Soviet-type Communism. For the other radicals, the renewed interest in civil society came via the reformulations of the concept in Habermas's and kindred theories (Miller, 1990a).

Today the idea is used by a variety of scholars who wish to stress the role of the public in a democracy (see Keane, 1988; Frentzel-Zagorska,

1989; Miller, 1990b; Rigby, 1990a). Through their use of the term, it has now assumed a more positive connotation than that with which Hegel and Marx endowed it. It has been variously defined as embracing communities, organizations, professional associations, social networks, enterprises, social movements, and an array of other structures, processes and activities through which individuals interact in freedom from state control.

Yet the concept of civil society casts its net too widely. It is a catch-all concept, and therefore also an attention-catching term which, right now, is quite fashionable in intellectual circles. But by catching so much, it catches very little. It refers to a whole hodge-podge of social patterns and manifestations, indeed to all social phenomena or processes that are not part of the state. These vary greatly in the degree of their centrality for democracy. To be sure, the autonomy of all these processes is part of the fabric of democracy. But only the independence of the processes in which elites and sub-elites are involved can organize and defend that of all other micro-processes of interaction – without which the formal procedures of democracy would have little value.

Thus, in the notion of civil society – as in the notion of interest groups – the distinction between elites, sub-elites and the public is blurred, and the focal role of the autonomy of elites is, once again, relegated to the back of the stage. Consequently – I believe – it is necessary to introduce into the analysis a distinction between the elite and the public component of civil society. When the elite component is teased out from the more general concept of civil society, it can be seen to refer to the autonomy of elites, which is what democratic elite theory is about.

## New combinations of previous themes

In the social sciences today, theories are responses to other theories. Much as they are engaged in mutual disputes, they still fertilize each other's thought. It is not surprising, therefore, that recently some theories have come into being that forge new combinations of themes already existing in previous theories. Their very uniqueness and strength – as well as their weaknesses – lie in the particular manner in which they have been able to reshape and combine elements from existing theories to suit their purpose. These theories include quite prominently neo-pluralism.

## Neo-pluralism: on capitalists and politicians

Some highly influential erstwhile pluralists (such as Galbraith, Dahl and Lindblom), now known as neo-pluralists, have subsequently changed their views. They are pluralists in that they still pay attention to electoral, party and a plurality of interest group politics. But they now see them as confined chiefly to secondary issues. Manley (1983) correctly states that these theorists have not become Marxists or neo-Marxists: while they criticize Western democracy, they still wish to preserve its essence. But they have clearly been influenced by Marxism. In line with Marxist critiques, they point a (justifiably) accusing finger at the excessive power of capitalists. And they show increasing concern with the manner in which such capitalists impair democratic processes. Intentionally or unintentionally, they have thus been working towards a convergence between Marxism and pluralism.

Approaching the topic from an economic perspective, Galbraith, for instance, suggests that – pluralist pressure groups notwithstanding – large-scale corporations enjoy a privileged position (1967). They demand and obtain from governments stability in the regulation of the business environment, and government and capitalist activities become interdependent if not unified. As Dahl and Lindblom (1976) and Lindblom (1977) concur, business people play a role in politics that is qualitatively different, and much more powerful, than that of other interest groups. The power of capitalists is also greater than that of trade unions, since the former can withdraw investments while the latter cannot (in the long run) withdraw labour. So much so that the American political economy is controlled by business more than it is by government.

Lindblom (1977) moves even further on the road to Marxism by suggesting that Western democracy works in favour of capitalist interests precisely because it has the outer appearance of pluralism. It does so, also, because the legitimacy of the system itself is never put before democratic judgement. The logical sequel to this is Dahl's contention (1982, 1984, 1985) that the economic power of business elites runs counter to the very essence of democracy, which says that we vote through the ballot box and not through the pocket book.

Forging an alliance not only with Marxism but also with participatory theories of democracy, Dahl (1985) goes on to say that to attain real democracy, public participation must be greatly enhanced. There must be democratic participation in economic enterprises. And in order for that to happen, there must be a substantial equalization of ownership and control. In addition, there ought to be more effective public participation in the political arena, with the *demos* controlling the political agenda.[2]

In spite of their just critique of the excessive power of capitalists, it is regrettable that neo-pluralists have put even less stress than previously on the existence and importance of the autonomy of elites in the West. For they take adequate account only of multiple and diffuse interests (the influence of which they see as limited) and of political and especially business elites (the influence of which they see as overwhelming). Dahl (1982, 1984) also emphasizes the importance of the autonomy of organizations. At the same time the issue of the autonomy of elites *qua* people (rather than of organizations), and of key elites other than capitalists and politicians, is skipped over too lightly, and in some cases is practically ignored.

### The state-centred view: on autonomy of but not from the state

Pluralists of whatever variety have not put major emphasis on the state: they have acknowledged the power of governments but have seen it as counterbalanced by others. Pluralist and pluralist elite theorists have seen it as counterbalanced by multiple pressure groups, and neo-pluralists as counterbalanced first and foremost by capitalists. Recently there has been a tilt in a different direction by some other scholars who have been more state-centred in their views. Following a considerable timespan in which the state was somehow lost from sight, they have refocused attention on it. They regard the state as a major centre of power, a trend Almond (1988) refers to as a statist movement.

While this statist approach diverges from pluralism, it incorporates elements from Marxist, elitist and Weberian strands of thought, synthesizing them into a novel perspective. Scholars such as Skocpol (1979), Nordlinger (1981), Tilly (1981), Giddens (1982b), Mann (1984, 1986), Block (1987), Birnbaum (1988), Levi (1988) and March and Olsen (1989) follow the Marxist perspective in speaking of the relative autonomy of the state. These scholars put greater emphasis on this idea, pushing it further than Marxists have. They speak of the potential, the almost complete, or even the complete independence of the state from classes and other forces in society. But they still adhere to the main Marxist conception that it is the state that gains (whatever degree of) autonomy from other forces in society, rather than the other way around.

At the same time the proponents of the state-centred view speak of 'state managers' who are not much different from what elite theorists refer to as governmental or state elites. Also in similarity to elite theorists, they conceive of such managers as having and promoting interests of their own. Some of these theorists also stress the political capacity of state managers and the contradictions and struggles within different branches of government. And following a Weberian perspective they highlight the structured power of the state bureaucracy. They also refer to the diverse ways in which the state penetrates society and structures social action. Or else they focus attention on how political institutions affect the flow of history.

An example of this view is presented by Block (1987) who accords state managers a greater autonomy from capitalists than Marxists had generally acknowledged. He considers that there is a three-sided conflict among state managers, capitalists and the working class. Similarly, Giddens (1982b) emphasizes the contradictory character of the state: while constrained by capitalism, its policies are also influenced by the power of the working class, exerted through its right of the collective withdrawal of labour. Thus he recognizes that the state has more scope for exercising its own discretion than Marxists proper would be willing to grant it.

Another good example of this view can be found in Birnbaum (1988). Birnbaum makes the point that political outcomes (such as collective action and political ideologies) can best be explained by political inputs (particularly the strength of states). Using historical illustrations from nineteenth-century Europe and from the United States, he argues, for instance, that strong states have more autonomy from other forces in society than weak ones. But he contends that they are also more likely to call forth radical, oppositional ideologies focused on the state itself.

One distinct advantage of these theories lies in the fact that by refocusing attention on the independent power of the state, they (intentionally or unintentionally) focus attention also on the dangers to liberty and democracy inherent in such power. Still, valuable as these scholars' contributions are, and convincing as their arguments may be, they are concerned primarily with the impact of the state on society and the independence *of* the state *from* society. Thereby, and in difference from democratic elite theory, they too fail to do justice to the importance of the obverse factor: that of independence of other forces, particularly elites, *from* the state.

## Corporatism: on governments and peak associations

Another theory that has become popular in recent years is corporatism, also known as neo-corporatism. This theory, too, is the outgrowth of a cross-breeding between different schools of thought: traces of pluralism, in conjunction with elite theory, state-centred theory and (in some cases) Marxism are clearly perceptible in it. The result is a rather powerful hybrid creature. Or, as McLennan put it, it 'carries the promise of a productive synthesis' (1989, p. 225).

Like pluralists, corporatists believe that there is more than one single centre of power in the modern polity. Like elite theorists, they believe that with respect to the most fundamental issues there is an interlocking set of such centres: a few small groups of power holders that determine more or less unilaterally what happens, particularly in the sphere of economic policy. Like state-centred theorists, corporatists believe that in determining major outcomes the state plays a central role. Like Marxists, several corporatists believe that among the interlocking power centres the capitalists have the upper hand.

A seminal work in this school of thought was an essay by Stein Rokkan (1966), arguing that votes count, but resources decide. Today's most prominent corporatists include Schmitter and Lehmbruch (1979), Crouch (1979), Cawson (1983, 1986), Lehmbruch (1985), Grant (1985). For them, the situation is one of a political exchange which is limited to few participants and insulated from external pressures. The state has an interest in minimizing the number of groups it has to deal with on economic policy. It confines such dealings primarily to state-selected 'associations of associations', or 'peak' associations. These are particularly business or employer associations and confederations of unions or major labour unions (some authors mention quasi-governmental organizations as well).

The state legitimizes the select few by granting them a representational monopoly, and by making them part of the economic policy-shaping process. In return, it obtains their support for its policies, and expects the main organizations to deliver the compliance of their member organizations with the dictates of these policies. Most commonly this works in the form of compromises among the government, the main capitalist organizations and the major representatives of trade unions. These arrangements generally bypass parliamentary, democratic procedures. At the same time, corporatist arrangements do not concern peripheral issues, which may be dealt with through pluralist arrangements.

According to this view, corporatism was the established practice in most European countries in previous centuries. It found expression in the extensive influence of traditional associations, mainly guilds, which were exclusive and monopolistic. During the first part of the nineteenth century most European countries moved towards the abolition of guild monopolies. But around the latter part of the nineteenth century they moved towards a resurgence of associations and towards the emergence of hierarchies among them.

In the twentieth century this came in conjunction with tendencies towards monopolies, oligopolies and cartels in the economic marketplace. It was expressed in the emergence of employers' peak associations and of centralized trade union confederations, and in growing state intervention in the economy. The most prominent example of corporatism developed under Fascism and Nazism, but it was by no means confined to those regimes. In the United States corporatism did not develop to the same extent as it did in Europe. However, in Western Europe, the tendencies towards corporatism were accelerated after the Second World War and reached their fullest development during the 1960s and 1970s.

In recent years, corporatist (or neo-corporatist) arrangements have involved the further integration of central trade union and business organizations into the process of economic policy formation. In practice (while the form varies widely from one country to another) they have found expression in a set of consultative bodies and arrangements encompassing both labour and capitalist peak organizations, such as conciliation and arbitration boards, wage determination boards, tripartite state–labour–management agreements and the like.

According to some corporatists, such as Grant (1985) or Schmitter (1985), none of the interlocking groups participating in these arrangements clearly overwhelms its partner. Other corporatists, for instance Crouch (1979), Jessop (1978, 1979), Panitch (1981), Cawson (1986), contend that corporatist arrangements work as an aid to the ruling capitalist class in subjugating the working class. In Western capitalist democracies they do so by incorporating organized labour into the political process, in return for its willingness to submit itself to the requirements of the capitalist system.

In either case, it is chiefly the power of the political elite, the capitalists and trade unions that is emphasized, while the autonomous power of the other (no less important) elites is underestimated. In addition, the formation of policy is seen as a concerted effort, it alone is emphasized, and the relative autonomy of elites thus, once again, drops into the background.[3]

## Conclusion

This chapter has presented a brief overview of various theories which all have made major contributions to our understanding of power and politics in modern societies. Yet, and despite the great differences among the various theories, there is one respect in which democratic elite theory is at odds with them: they all, to various extents, neglect the point which forms this theory's main focus – the relative autonomy of elites. Since it is these theories that hold hegemony over the intellectual scene, the whole issue of the institutionalized separation of elites, its advocacy and defence, and its importance for democracy, has been relegated to the margins of intellectual discourse. While this may appear to be of negligible significance, it is not.

Granted that this may be far from anyone's intent, nevertheless disregard of the issue of elite autonomy helps create a certain intellectual climate. This is a climate in which differences between autocratic and democratic regimes are not sufficiently emphasized, in which democracy is consequently devalued. It is an intellectual climate which may well lend inadvertent justification for attacks on elite autonomy. It is a climate which is not favourably oriented to supporting elites in defending their self-determination whenever it is threatened. Even in Western societies, moreover, such threats are not unusual or insignificant, as will be shown below.

The task of the following chapters is to present my own analysis, which further develops democratic elite theory. The task is to show how this theory can be applied to the analysis of actual historical and contemporary processes, for the benefit of a better understanding and defence of democracy and for further democratization.

## Notes

1  Western Marxism only is dealt with.
2  The last two points are based on an analysis of the ideas of Lindblom and of Dahl by McLennan, 1989, ch. 3.
3  For a more detailed analysis of the theories reviewed in this chapter, see Held, 1987, and McLennan, 1989.

# PART III

# THE DEMO-ELITE
# PERSPECTIVE

# 5

## *The autonomy of elites and democracy*

As noted before, in the social sciences today there is a mutual fertilization of all theories. Indeed, any theory that did not take account of other theories would be hopelessly out of date. Nonetheless, differences among theoretical viewpoints are still visible. It is in view of this that the demo-elite perspective assumes its stance. While it has affinities with several of the theories reviewed, it also differs from them.

### The demo-elite perspective within the broader theoretical spectrum

Before the main tenets of the demo-elite perspective are presented, I would like to clarify its position within the broader theoretical spectrum. It is important to stress that, as part of democratic elite theory, the demo-elite perspective follows in the footsteps of some of the theories reviewed in the previous chapter. But it also develops it in new directions and thus diverges from them in some important respects:

- Contrary to some other elite theories and contrary to corporatist theories, it sees the distinctiveness of Western democracies in the fact that in them (with some exceptions) elites do not form concerted power structures.
- In contrast to Marxist theories which have disregarded the import-

ance of checking state power by power, it reverts to the original liberal tradition in putting particular emphasis on this point.

- Contrary to Marxist and state-centred theories which have emphasized the relative or complete autonomy of the state from other forces in society, it emphasizes relative independence from and within the state.
- In distinction to the emphasis which proponents of the concept of 'civil society' put on the autonomy from the state of organizations, communities and a whole array of processes, it emphasizes the autonomy of elites and sub-elites (whether atop or outside organizations and communities); for it views relatively self-propelled holders of power and influence *qua* people (and not abstract structures and amorphous processes) as sustaining democracy.
- While pluralist and pluralist elite theories focus attention on pressure groups as mouthpieces for the public, and on elites mainly inasmuch as they represent such pressure groups, the demo-elite perspective re-shifts attention to elites and sub-elites, whether or not they have pressure groups to back them up.
- In dissimilarity to pluralist and pluralist elite theories that tend to view all pressure groups as a single phenomenon, this analysis makes a clear distinction between a few powerful pressure groups (whose elites are among the key power holders in Western democracies), on the one hand, and lesser interest groups (whose numbers have recently proliferated into the thousands and some of whom may be quite marginal), on the other hand.
- Contrary to pluralist and pluralist elite theories, it sees power, even in the West, not as widely dispersed among the diverse pressure groups, but as primarily in the hands of the key elites and sub-elites.
- In contrast to pluralist and pluralist elite theories, its aim is to show that although a further dispersion of power among large numbers of groups and elites may be highly desirable, (beyond a certain minimum) what counts primarily for the preservation and further democratization of democracy is not their number. It aims to show that what counts is not the pluralism of elites but their relative independence from government in terms of the control of resources.
- As distinct from the above theories it makes a clear and major distinction between established elites (including the elites of well-entrenched interest groups) intent on perpetuating the status quo, and the non-established leaders and activists of social movements as the only elites in society whose *raison d'être* is the push for change.

# The demo-elite perspective within democratic elite theory

While it differs from the other theories, the demo-elite perspective picks up where liberal philosophy and previous democratic elite theory has left off. This theory has recently suffered neglect, and it is in urgent need of invigoration and elaboration. It is to such an elaboration that this perspective is devoted. It resumes the threads of this theory, but it reweaves them and develops this theory further so as to draw out its implications for both historical analyses and the contemporary world:

- Liberal philosophy and democratic elite theory speak of the separation and autonomy of power agents, but only in general terms. The present analysis spells out what such autonomy entails specifically in terms of the control of several types of concrete resources.
- Liberal philosophy relates the separation of powers only to liberal (and not to democratic) governance, and democratic elite theory relates the autonomy of elites to democracy, but again only on a high level of generality. The present analysis spells out the connections between such autonomy and the commonly accepted principles of democracy.
- In this context it puts special emphasis on the informational role not only of the media but of a relatively independent opposition, judiciary, state comptroller, public accounts committee, and similar elites (whose specific forms vary in different democracies), generating the type of adversary public discourse without which the electoral and other principles of democracy could not be implemented.
- By contrast to its forerunners, only few of whom had something to say on this topic, this analysis attempts an initial exploration of the relationship between the relative autonomy of elites and sub-elites and their cooperation within a working political system.
- The present demo-elite analysis adds depth to democratic elite theory by exploring not merely the contemporary relationship between relative elite autonomy and democracy, but also the historical/causal relationship between the two. This is done by pinpointing the mechanisms through which lack of elite autonomy may hinder the emergence and stabilization of democracy, while the previous evolution of such relative autonomy may encourage both the stabilization and development of democracy.

– A further contribution of the present analysis lies in drawing out the theory's implications for the contemporary world. This is done by relating the historical analysis to recent developments in Eastern Europe and also by calling attention to the dangers for democracy that emanate from threats to elite and sub-elite autonomy in the Western world today.

– Finally, the demo-elite perspective contributes to democratic elite theory by giving it an egalitarian bent. This is done through the definition of elites as including not only bastions of the establishment who defend existing privileges, but also leaders and activists of social/protest movements who push for their abolition. It is also done by analysing the latter's unique contribution to making democracy more democratic and egalitarian.

In the end, the test of this perspective lies not in where it stands in relation to other theories, or even to previous democratic elite theory, but in the contribution it can make to our understanding of Western democracy. This contribution should become clear from the presentation of its main elements and tenets (in this and the following chapter) and from the application of its tenets to concrete historical and contemporary analyses (in the rest of the book).

## Elites, resources and sub-elites

Like all elite theory, the demo-elite perspective revolves around the concept of elites. As noted, elites are defined as those people who have an inordinate share of power, on the basis of their active control of resources. Resources are simply those things which are scarce, which affect people's lives, which at least some people require or want, and for which there is more demand than supply.

These include resources of physical coercion, such as the barrels of guns as well as prisons. They include organizational-administrative resources, or the ability to organize people and control the resulting organizational structures, such as bureaucratic organizations. They further encompass symbolic resources such as knowledge, information and the ability to manipulate symbols in constructing reality for others. And they include material-economic resources such as capital, means of production and exchange, and economic enterprises. Finally, they include psycho-personal resources of charisma, time, motivation and energy. These resources are all interconnected with each other, and they are frequently used in various combinations.

It has also been noted that the concept of elites does not necessarily entail a dichotomous division of society into those who hold power and influence and those who do not. Instead a trichotomous division of elites, sub-elites and the public is being used here. By this division, elites are those who are located at the very top of power and influence structures. Sub-elites come next, and occupy the middle ranks of power structures. The public occupies the lowest rank in this constellation. But – as here conceived – it is by no means powerless, as will be argued in greater detail below. Following Putnam (1976, pp. 8–12) it must be admitted that deciding on a cut-off point between the echelons of power is, in the end, a matter of judgement. This, however, does not necessarily invalidate the division.

Using such judgement, then, we may say that in modern societies elites include the holders of top political positions, such as members of governments, members of powerful parliamentary or congressional committees, and top bosses of government and (where they exist) of major opposition parties. Other elites include the top echelons of the bureaucracy, the military, the police and the judiciary.

To this must be added the business (or economic) elite, made up of active owners and top managers of large-scale enterprises, and the upper echelon of the labour or trade union leadership. These, by the way, are also the leaders of modern societies' most prominent interest groups. Also included are the media elite, composed of senior staff of major (both electronic and printed) media organizations, the academic/intellectual elite – encompassing the most senior academic staff of major universities and the most prominent publicists, writers and the like – and the central leadership of major social/protest movements.

Including in the definition of elites the top leadership of major social movements holds special theoretical significance. It means that, by this definition, elites are not only some of the most advantaged, but also the *most active men and women among the disadvantaged*, or those who champion the interests of the disadvantaged. Elites therefore include those who are the most active in preserving inegalitarian, elitist structures, that is, the status quo, but also those who are anti-elitist and struggle for change towards greater equality.

Sub-elites are less powerful, and in the political sphere they include, for instance, backbench or rank-and-file members of legislatures and leaders of sizeable, but not the two largest, interest groups. In the economic sphere they include middle management of large enterprises and top ownership/management of somewhat smaller ones. In addition, they include those occupying middle echelons of the bureaucracy, the military and the police, leaders of smaller social movements, holders of middle-ranking or even junior judicial, media and academic positions, and officials or activists (as distinct from leaders) of labour unions and social movements. The public, for its part, is composed of the rest of society. Subdivisions within it with respect to power and influence could easily be discerned, but they will not be taken up in this analysis.

By this definition, some sub-elites are seconds in command to elites in the same organizations. In these cases, the position of sub-elites may be that of representing elites before the rank and file, or vice versa, or both. Their position may thus be that of the meat in the sandwich, so to speak, and in some cases that of the buffer zone, or mediator, between the elite and members of the rank-and-file public. Looked at in this light, the autonomy of sub-elites from their own elites, those that stand at the helm of their own organizations, may be no less significant for democracy than the autonomy of those elites from other elites. Hence it would be of interest to explore the degree of that autonomy.

As against this stand other considerations, however. The autonomy of sub-elites from the elites in their own organizations is a matter of internal organizational democracy more than it is is a matter of democracy in the overall political arena. Micro-democracy in organizations and macro-democracy in the overall polity are not unrelated to each other, but they are separate variables, with their own separate contexts. Furthermore, the relationship among these factors is highly complex, as well as variable. Some sub-elites have a greater degree of autonomy than others. Some countervail the power of 'their own' elites, some countervail the power of other elites but have no autonomy from their own elites, while still others are merely seconds in command, bolstering the power of all those at the top.

Such multiple relations deserve a detailed analysis of their own, supported by historical/empirical illustrations (and this I intend to attempt in the future). To incoporate this here, however, would merely derail the present analysis and distract it from its main purpose. This purpose is one of exploring the role of the relative autonomy of elites together with their sub-elites from other elites, and particularly from the elite of the government, in a democracy.

# What is the relative autonomy of elites

## *What the relative autonomy of elites is not*

Before the relative autonomy of elites and sub-elites is defined, it is important to explain what it is frequently mistaken for, but is not. First, it is not elite pluralism. Elite pluralism has to do with the numbers of elites; elite autonomy has to do with the distribution of resources among them.

Second, the autonomy of elites and sub-elites is not the autonomy of organizations. As noted before, an elite is a group of people wielding power on the basis of its control of a disproportionate share of society's resources, and a sub-elite is next in line in the magnitude of its resources. It is true that in modern societies most resources are generated in organizations. This is true in particular with respect to coercive, material and administrative resources. Still, resources are generated outside organizations as well. Some economic resources, for instance, may be accumulated by individual enterpreneurs. Some symbolic resources, too, are created by individuals, who may be members of elites on their own, with freelance writers and artists as prominent examples. The same is particularly true with respect to resources of motivation, energy and charisma. These may be the main assets of leaders and activists of (only partly organized) social movements.

As some elites and sub-elites work outside organizations by freelancing on their own, or by leading only partly organized groups or movements, it follows that the autonomy of elites and their aides must be kept analytically distinct from the autonomy of organizations. Even within organizations, moreover, the autonomy of elites is not identical to the autonomy of organizations. The fact that an organization's elite has autonomy does not necessarily imply that the same is true for the rest of the organization as well. For, as noted, organizations are usually hierarchies. And organizational elites that are autonomous from the power of others may well deny such autonomy to their own sub-elites and other subordinates.

The autonomy of elites must also be distinguished from the autonomous power of the public: while interrelated, these two types of autonomy are not identical. And only when kept analytically distinct can the relationship between them be explored.

## The relative autonomy of elites and resources

The autonomy of elites and sub-elites may now be explicated on the basis of the autonomy of resources on which elite power, and hence elite position, is based. The following types of such resources are especially important in this respect:

*Resources of physical coercion*   An elite or sub-elite will be considered as autonomous, first, if it is not subject to repression through the coercive resources of others. It will also be regarded as autonomous when such repression, though attempted, is not successful, as the members of the affected elite and sub-elite mount successful resistance to it. Absence of coercive repression is frequently connected either with absence of repressive legislation, or with legislation that explicitly protects from repression, such as legislation for freedom of the press, freedom of assembly and the like. Needless to say, no less important than legislation is the manner in which it is (or is not) implemented in practice.

*Material resources*   An elite or sub-elite is autonomous, second, when it is not dependent on the material resources of others. It is also autonomous when it is in charge of material resources that are not subject to the control of others and cannot be affected by their actions. For example, we may speak of the autonomy of an elite or sub-elite when the budget with which it operates, the salaries or the capital and profits of its members cannot be influenced from outside its own boundaries.

*Administrative/organizational resources*   An elite or sub-elite is autonomous, third, when it is not controlled by the administrative/organizational resources of others. It is also autonomous when its own organizational resources cannot be determined or influenced externally. Thus we may speak of the autonomy of an elite or sub-elite when its members are not supervised from the outside, and are not obliged to follow instructions that emanate from outside its own boundaries. We may also speak of such autonomy when an elite or sub-elite functions outside an organizational structure, heads a separate organizational structure or has the means to function as a separate entity within a larger organization.

*Symbolic resources*   An elite or sub-elite is autonomous, fourth, when it is not dependent for its activities on the symbolic resources of anyone outside its own boundaries. It is also autonomous when other people's symbols are not imposed on it, and when its own symbolic resources are not constructed and controlled by others. For instance, we may speak of the autonomy of an elite when the information it requires to perform its tasks cannot be externally controlled, or when the ideologies that inform its activities are not forged from the outside.

*Combined resources*  Autonomy may also be based on various combinations of autonomous resources. For instance, appointments and promotions involve both material and administrative resources. An elite or sub-elite may be considered autonomous when its members' appointments, promotions and tenure cannot be influenced from outside its own boundaries.

Given that in any sociopolitical system the major resources ultimately are drawn from a common well, and given that some elites control more resources and are more powerful than other elites, it is recognized that elite and sub-elite autonomy can never be absolute, only *relative.* An elite or sub-elite will thus be regarded as *relatively* autonomous when, although some of its resources are controlled from the outside, it still has significant resources that cannot be controlled, or can only marginally be controlled from outside its own boundaries. An elite will also be regarded as relatively autonomous when its autonomy is significantly greater than the autonomy of the same elites in non-democratic regimes.

## How the relative autonomy of elites may be recognized

It is therefore clear that the autonomy of elites is not an either–or proposition, but a matter of gradations. And the dividing line between an elite's subjection to the control of others and an elite's relative autonomy cannot be set with mathematical precision. This dividing line cannot be established quantitatively any more than it is possible to quantify the boundaries between, say, alienation and the absence of alienation, or the precise point at which hegemony turns into non-hegemony. The same, moreover, would be true for a large number of phenomena referred to by other concepts that lie at the core of the social sciences. To establish whether relative autonomy of an elite (or alienation, or hegemony, etc.) exists or does not exist, a certain amount of interpretative analysis, or judgement, will probably always be necessary. But the historical-empirical cases analysed below show that whenever relative elite autonomy does appear, it is clearly recognizable.

Frequently, the relative autonomy of an elite or sub-elite is manifested externally in the manner in which it uses its resources. For the relative autonomy of elites in the control of resources implies relatively separate, and frequently opposing, interests with respect to those resources. Employing resources and acting in a manner that does not promote, or works against, the interests of others, thus attests to an elite's relative autonomy from those others.

For instance, an elite or sub-elite may show its independence from others through the generation and use of symbolic resources. It may do so by developing conceptions or ideologies which do not promote subservience to those others, or even ideologies which undermine those others' legitimation. It may manifest its independence by revealing damaging information about those others, or by publicly criticizing and vilifying them. In a nutshell, the relative autonomy of elites is usually manifested in lack of symbolic subservience to others, and frequently (though not always) in friction with others. Elite confrontation may thus serve as a useful, though not as the sole, indicator of relative elite autonomy.

## Autonomy from whom?

If an elite or sub-elite has relative autonomy, the next question is, from whom is it relatively autonomous? In principle, the answer is: from anybody. In practice, those who might encroach on an elite's and sub-elite's autonomy are generally other elites, whose disproportionate power or control of resources may lend them the ability to control the resources of others as well. While all elites may invade the domains of other elites, some are particularly 'imperialistic'. These include those who stand at the top or close to the top of the power structures of the state, who, by virtue of their monopoly over the main means of coercion, may exert repressive control over other elites. On top of this, these people have disproportionate control of administrative-organizational and material resources, which may also enable them to gain ascendancy over the resources of other power holders. At the same time, the business (or economic) elite may also encroach on other elites by virtue of the 'persuasive' power of its purse (material resources).

An elite or sub-elite is thus relatively autonomous if it is to a significant extent exempt from control of its resources by other elites or sub-elites, including the elites (or sub-elites) of the state, and the business elite. But the main focus of this analysis is on the relative autonomy which other elites and sub-elites have been able to carve out from one major state elite: the government, or the governing elite. It is the mutual autonomy of elites, but even more so this latter type of relative autonomy, countervailing and limiting government power, which is a major requirement for democracy, and which has developed in Western democracies more than in other regimes.

## The central tenets

The first central tenet of the demo-elite perspective is that what makes the difference between non-democratic and democratic elites and sub-elites is that which has been advocated by liberal philosophy and democratic elite theory: their relative autonomy from each other, and the relative autonomy of some other elites from the elites of the state and the government. This relative autonomy of elites is thus an important requirement for democracy: without it, the principles of democracy can neither exist nor persist.

The second central tenet of the demo-elite perspective is that to a certain extent this relative autonomy has actually come to be institutionalized in Western democratic regimes. For although Western democracy has not generated political or economic equality, it has nonetheless had some accomplishments. One of the most important of these is that in it, more than in any other regime, elites and sub-elites – for instance those of opposition parties, trade unions, the media and business – have gained relative independence from the state. And within the state itself, some elites – for instance the judiciary and (in some democracies more than in others) the bureaucracy – have gained significant autonomy from the government.

The autonomy gained by elites and sub-elites from state and government in Western democracies is never complete, always imperfect. Moreover, it is highly variable from one elite to another, and from one democracy to another. Yet I argue that we can still speak of the relative autonomy of elites in Western democracies as a distinctly recognizable phenomenon, because such autonomy is considerably greater than it is in non-democratic regimes. This should become clear in particular in chapter 8, where the lack of autonomy of elites in Communist regimes (as an example of autocratic regimes) is discussed.

These tenets are firstly descriptive ones, claiming to analyse what is empirically a condition for democracy, and to depict a certain feature that actually prevails in Western societies. But there is also an assumption – which is best made explicit – that Western-style democracy is to be promoted and defended. This being the case, the above tenets are also prescriptive (or normative) ones: if elite autonomy is crucial for democracy, and if democracy is worth promoting and defending, then elite autonomy is worth promoting and defending as well. In other words, these tenets also advocate the relative autonomy of elites and sub-elites from state and government.

It is worth noting, and has been pointed out before, that most theories, whether pluralist, elitist, Marxist or whatever, have this duality in them, even if they do not always make it explicit. Therefore Weber's well-known call for the separation between analysis and evaluation is no longer considered realistic by many social scientists today. When we come right down to it, it probably never was realistic, even at the time it was made by Weber. Indeed it was probably not regarded as realistic even by Weber himself. For, as for instance Held has pointed out (1987, p. 164), some of Weber's own work has clear normative implications to it. Thus the combination of descriptive and normative elements in one theory should not necessarily be viewed as a drawback.

If it be said, however, that elite autonomy both exists in, and is crucial for, democracy and that democracy is worthy of being defended, does not this simply supply a legitimation of the status quo? Is it not, as Pateman in her critique of the pluralist perspective once put it (1970, p. 16), in effect just saying that 'the system that we ought to have is the very one we do in fact have'? My answer to this possible query is negative. For although (considering past and present alternatives) Western democracy deserves to be preserved, this does not imply that it deserves to be preserved in its present state. Much of the discussion in the final part of the book is devoted to detailing some of what is going amiss in Western democracy today, and what the mechanisms are that may lead to its change. As will also become clear there, the autonomy of elites and sub-elites is itself a mechanism that may lead to democratic change.

# How the autonomy of elites relates to the principles of democracy

It has been argued that the thesis on elite autonomy, since it has to do with countervailing and thus limiting government power, can amount to a theory of liberalism, but not to a theory of democracy. The following analysis, however, is meant to demonstrate that there is a close relationship between the autonomy of elites and the principles of democracy, and that the theory on the autonomy of elites is therefore also a theory of democracy.

The principles of democracy – by which democracy is commonly defined – include as their centrepiece the gaining of the power to govern via free, competitive elections on the basis of universal and equal suffrage. They also include civil liberties such as freedom of speech, of information and of association (or organization) – without which free elections would not be possible – and a separation of powers within the state.[1] The more concrete rules of democracy then flow from these general principles.

There is a certain paradox here: these maxims are not couched in terms of the autonomy of elites, and make no explicit reference to it. Indeed, if the principles of democracy were to refer explicitly to the immunities of elites, they would be considered undemocratic. Yet, the autonomy of elites forms an over-arching meta-principle, which is a large part of what these principles sustain, and what sustains them. In other words, the relative autonomy of elites forms a large part of what the principles of democracy are really about.

Thus democratic principles sustain elite and sub-elite autonomy in the following sense: when the principles of free elections and of freedom of organization and speech are implemented in practice, they confront the governing elite with a recurring threat of replacement. Thereby they provide the rationale and mechanism for the autonomous activity of its potential replacers: oppositional political parties and their leaders, activists and officials. In other words, without freedom of elections and of organization there can be no institutionalized independent opposition. If this sounds like a truism, this is because free elections are so intimately related to opposition as to be practically inseparable. It becomes less of a truism if we consider what it implies: the most democratic of principles makes possible the autonomy of an elite and sub-elite.

The implementation of the principles of freedom of speech and organization also defends the relative freedom of the media. This, too, sounds like a truism until we consider that the media are controlled by a group of highly influential people: publishers, editors, journalists. So once again, democratic principles defend an elite and sub-elite. The principle of the separation of powers between the legislature, the executive and the judiciary, and within the executive between the elected government and the appointed bureaucracy – wherever it exists, and however imperfectly implemented – has an equivalent effect. It safeguards the relative autonomy of the various echelons of the judiciary and of the bureaucratic elite and sub-elite, top and high-ranking officials, respectively.

Organizations are accumulators of resources, and most resources, we have said, are accumulated in them. The principle of freedom of organization thus also spells freedom to amass resources, including economic resources. The implementation of this principle thus entails *inter alia* economic or business elites (albeit not necessarily capitalist ones) that have at least a partial immunity from state intervention. The principle of freedom of association further guards the relatively independent power of the trade union and some other associations' leaders and activists.

Relative elite autonomy, for its part, sustains democratic principles. For the elites and sub-elites whose independence is championed (and legitimized) by democratic principles then have an interest in preserving those principles. They also have the power to do so. They thus tend (albeit to varying extents) to sustain these principles on which the perpetuation of their own special position depends. Thereby a circle of mutual protection between the principles of democracy and the meta-principle of the autonomy of elites is generated, and constantly regenerated.

There is a further sense in which the relative autonomy of elites sustains the principles of democracy: it forms a mechanism without which the principles of democracy could not be implemented in practice, or would soon atrophy. Thus not only the principle of freedom of information, but even the principle of free elections could not be implemented in practice without a relative autonomy of elites. For the process of such elections requires that the public have information, whose content is exempt from government control. Only in this way can informed, adversary public discourse develop and be sustained. And only on the basis of such discourse can the public make an informed choice between the government and the opposition. Such independent information on the performance, and possible lack of performance, or wrongdoings, on the part of the government can only be supplied to the public by elites and sub-elites who are relatively exempt from government control.

The best known of these are the elites and sub-elites of the media. But also important from this viewpoint are the academic/intellectual elite and sub-elite, the opposition, the judicial elite, the elite of the state comptroller/auditor general/inspector general, the public accounts committee, and various types of commissions of inquiry, and their senior staff. These elites and sub-elites are generally, and justly, seen as countervailing the power of the government, thus limiting its power. But *they also fulfil an important electoral role, through the information they supply to the public* and the relatively informed public discourse they thus make possible.

The academic elite engages in research about reality, and interpretation of reality (including sociopolitical reality). To the extent that the output of its endeavour filters through to the public through students, textbooks, public lectures, popularization in the media and the like, this forms a reservoir of information on which the public can draw to form views on social reality in general, and politics in particular. The output of the academic endeavour, especially in the humanities and the social sciences, is frequently rent by internal controversy. But this is itself a boost to the adversary public discourse necessary for democracy.

The opposition, by virtue of its location at the hub of the political arena, gleans information about the government which is not intended to be available to anyone except the elite of the government itself. If this information should shed a negative light on the government, the opposition generally has an interest in bringing it to the attention of the public, for instance through speeches in the legislature or elsewhere, and/or through the media. The information disseminated by the opposition is not necessarily objective. But if independent from government control, it forms an important balancing mechanism to the information supplied to the public by the government itself. And precisely because it is not objective, there is special importance in the information furnished to the public by additional relatively independent elites.

Thus the judicial elite, through verdicts having to do with cases of judicial review, actually informs the public of possible wrongdoings by the authorities, information which can then become the basis of political discourse and electoral decisions. The same is true of reports of the state comptroller/auditor general/inspector general, public accounts committee and committees of inquiry. These reports are frequently brought to the public's knowledge by the media elite. And the informational task of all these elites and their aides, which is so important for the electoral process, can only be carried out if they have relative autonomy from the governing elite, or the government, about which they transmit information to the public.

By way of an example, it is worth noting that the role of countervailing government power and of supplying information to the public by the judicial and state comptroller elites has become especially important in safeguarding Israel's democracy in recent years. Perhaps this is so because of some deficiencies in the autonomy of other elites. A thorough explanation of these processes, however, deserves a separate discussion and is beyond the scope of the present one.

A similar case for the relationship between elite autonomy and the electoral principle of democracy can be made with respect to the autonomy of the bureaucratic elite: research has shown that when the bureaucracy is politicized, this results in electoral corruption which may practically invalidate the electoral process. And only a relative autonomy of the bureaucratic elite can safeguard the electoral process from such corruption (Etzioni-Halevy, 1985). Similarly, a politicized police elite can disrupt the electoral process by harassing the opposition; therefore a relatively autonomous police elite is also required for a proper electoral process. And similar arguments can be made with respect to other elites as well. What it boils down to, then, is that relatively independent elites have both the interest and the power to sustain democratic principles, although neither the power nor the interests are totally impermeable.

## The power of the public

The argument that elites and sub-elites and their autonomy are central for democracy does not imply that the public is not crucial as well. The importance of the public lies, first, in that it is the progenitor of elites. As Pareto has pointed out, there is a circulation whereby members of the public join elites and vice versa. Pareto viewed this process as the circulation of elites. It is equally important to view it as the circulation of the public. This is merely the mirror image of the same process. But it has its own claim for attention, because it entails the opposite, bottom-up perspective.

At times the circulation between the public and the elites flows freely and at times it is blocked. Pareto aptly emphasized that this has important implications for the dynamics of society: free circulation leads to gradual changes, blockage to abrupt ones. Pareto further believed that the openness versus blocking of mobility into the elite depended on the character of the elite. But contrary to Pareto's view, this blockage may originate in the public as well. When the public is docile and apathetic (at times, to be sure, but not always because of elite repression), the chances for the free circulation between elites and the public are decreased. In this situation elites can perpetuate their power with less fear of replacement, and they become progressively more separated from the rank-and-file members of the public in their interests and mentality. The chances that elites will successfully conduct struggles with other elites on behalf of the public are thus substantially decreased.

Conversely, when the public is well informed and closely monitors elite actions, the chances that some of its members will join the elites are increased. In this manner the probability for the renewal of elites grows, and the elites that are constantly rejuvenated from the public are more inclined to represent its interests, or those of a sizeable part within it. Seen in this perspective, the achievement of democracy lies in that it provides some institutionalized channels for, and thus facilitates, the circulation between the public and elites. This does not ensure that elites will struggle for public interests. But it provides a supportive framework for such struggles.

While this is important in itself, the power of the public in a democracy goes far beyond it. It derives from the fact that relative elite autonomy and the democratic role of the public go hand in hand. Only where there is an independent opposition can the public fulfil a democratic role through free elections. And only where free elections lend the public the ability to vote the elite of the government in and out of office, where the power of the opposition thus hinges on public electoral support, can an opposition be independent in its resources from the government. Furthermore, only where the government can be voted out of office by the public, and only where an independent public opinion arises, is there any real significance in the media and other elites asserting their independence by acting as watchdogs on the government. Conversely, only where the elites of the opposition, the media, etc., are independent from the government and can thus speak out can an independent public opinion arise. The autonomy of elites thus depends to a large extent on the democratic role of the public, and vice versa.

The ultimate test of the importance of the public in a democracy is its ability to make elites responsive to its own wishes. Here, too, the autonomy of elites and the role of the public are closely intertwined. Elite autonomy cannot ensure such responsiveness. But the elite rivalry it entails increases the likelihood that elites will need the support of the public for the maintenance of their positions and for the achievements of their goals. Hence the increased likelihood that public opinion will have at least *some* influence on what they do or do not do.

As Lipset has clarified (1981, p. 278), and notwithstanding disclaimers from elite theorists (see Dye and Zeigler, 1987), this is evidently the case with respect to the government and the opposition. An effective opposition and vigorous electoral competition may not lead to the public being the arbiter of policy issues. But it certainly gives the public a greater say on policy than would otherwise be the case. This is also the case, for instance, with respect to the media elite. At least that part of the media elite and sub-elite which is independent from government funding must compete with other members of that elite and sub-elite for public patronage, and hence cater to what it perceives the public's taste to be.

By the same token, a private enterprise economy may no longer be based on a cut-throat competition between capitalists. But non-government production, entailing the relative autonomy of the business elite from the state, still leads to greater competition and more catering to consumer preferences than does production sponsored by government or governing party. Anyone who has visited a supermarket or a department store in the erstwhile Communist bloc and compared it to its counterpart in the West would readily attest to the truth of this statement. In short, several elites and sub-elites that are not dependent, and cannot depend, on government sponsorship are forced to be more competitive among themselves than dependent elites, to vie for the favours of the public as voters, readers, listeners or consumers, and thereby to be more responsive to its wishes.

## Note

1   The principle of the separation of powers within the state is basically a liberal principle. But, as noted, certain liberal principles have become democratic principles as well.

# 6

# *Elite autonomy versus cooperation and the historical development of democracy*

Returning now to the autonomy of elites as such, it can be seen that in some respects it also has problems involved with it. These problems have to do with autonomy versus consensus or cooperation of elites.

## Elite autonomy versus cooperation

Some scholars have argued that elite cohesion and consensus on the rules of the political game are as important a requirement for democracy as elite autonomy. Eisenstadt, for instance, has posited that elite conflict contributes to the successful operation of a democratic political system, but only if it is counterbalanced by elite solidarity and consensus on some basic values or on the basic rules of the game. Dye and Zeigler have also argued that elites in stable (including stable democratic) regimes share a consensus over basic norms and rules (1987, p. 4).

I would like to introduce a slight variation into this theme. Adopting the distinction which Dahrendorf has made between social integration and social harmony (1967, p. 195), I argue that a similar distinction needs to be made between elite cooperation on the one hand, and elite solidarity and consensus on the other hand; and further, I suggest that it is in fact chiefly elite cooperation (rather than elite consensus on rules or elite solidarity) which is necessary for the proper functioning of any political system, hence also of democracy.

For any political system to operate, it is obviously necessary that the government have the power to govern. This requires a measure of cooperation by other elites and sub-elites with the government. The operation of a political system also requires a degree of collaboration among the other elites and sub-elites themselves. Without such elite cooperation, the other elites would constantly obstruct the government and each other, the system would be in a perpetual stalemate, and would eventually self-destruct. And since democracy is a type of political system, it cannot persist without a modicum of elite cooperation either. In other words, without elite cooperation, there can be no democracy. But without elite autonomy, there can be no democracy either.

This raises the question whether elite cooperation, for its part, is not necessarily based on elite solidarity and consensus, and whether, therefore, there is no inherent contradiction between the manifestation of relative elite autonomy and elite cooperation. Relative elite autonomy, we have said, is frequently manifested by elite conflict. Is elite conflict, then, necessarily incompatible with, or can it coexist with, elite cooperation?

My reply would be that if we define elite consensus procedurally, to mean actual adherence to democratic rules and procedures, then by definition the cooperation of elites and sub-elites in the maintenance of democracy requires such consensus. But if consensus is defined as signifying that elites and sub-elites share beliefs, values or norms with respect to the rules of democracy, then the question of whether elite cooperation requires such consensus becomes an empirical one. And a look at empirical reality in various democratic countries shows that elite cooperation may well require *some* solidarity and consensus, but the required consensus is minimal. In other words, such cooperation may exist with but the thinnest thread of consensus.

Elite and sub-elite cooperation in a democratic regime may well require some consensus about the desirability of democracy through free elections and civil liberties as such. What is clear, however, and research (see below) in various democratic countries has shown, is that elite and sub-elite cooperation may exist without consensus on the actual, concrete, rules by which the electoral process and other democratic conflicts are to be waged, and by which civil liberties are to be implemented. The rules that do exist, moreover, are frequently inconsistent, hazy and ambiguous – there is no necessary consensus on their interpretation, and they are thus frequently controversial.

If the cooperation of elites and sub-elites were necessarily based on pervasive consensus among them, this would in fact preclude elite conflict. Since, however, this is not the case, the elites' and sub-elites' cooperation is not incompatible with conflict and struggles among them, which in turn is a manifestation of elite autonomy. Moreover, research has also shown that not merely elite dissensus but even elite conflict on the rules of democracy is not incompatible with elite cooperation, hence is not necessarily destructive of democracy.

Thus, my comparative research on bureaucratic elites (Etzioni-Halevy, 1985), on national broadcasting elites and sub-elites (which may be seen as pertaining to the media and the bureaucracy at one and the same time) (Etzioni-Halevy, 1987) and on parliamentary elites (Etzioni-Halevy, 1990, and see also chapter 9 below) has shown that the various elites and sub-elites profoundly disagreed over, and gave different interpretations to, various inherently inconsistent and ambivalent democratic rules. They were also engaged in various struggles with each other over those rules so as to make the rules suit their interests. They all nonetheless cooperated with each other over the maintenance of their respective systems.

The same point may also be illustrated on the basis of some recent developments in Israel. For several years now, elite and sub-elite conflict in Israel has been waged on the issue of whether or not Israel should have a written constitution and a bill of rights. For several years elite and sub-elite conflict has also been waged over possible changes in the rules of the electoral system: whether representation should continue to be proportional or whether it should be transformed into a first-past-the-post system, or into some combination of the two. Finally there has been elite conflict on the system of government: whether it should continue to be parliamentary, or be transformed into a semi-presidential system, with the prime minister elected directly by popular vote. This conflict, however, has not precluded elite cooperation in perpetuating the present system, and hence has not been destructive of but, if anything, has invigorated Israeli democracy.

If elite cooperation is not necessarily based on pervasive consensus, what then are its possible bases? And is it not possible that the other bases for elite cooperation are contradictory to elite autonomy? This issue can be clarified when we look at these bases.

Apart from deriving from solidarity, the cooperation of elites and sub-elites may derive from their common interest in the preservation of the system on which their resources and elite positions depend. Such cooperation may also be based on the government's ability to use its resources, the resources that lend it power, in order to infringe on or threaten other elites' resources, when cooperation on their part is not forthcoming (the stick method). Conversely, elite and sub-elite cooperation may also derive from additional resources offered to them by other elites, particularly the government, in return for such cooperation (the carrot method).

This being the case, elite cooperation may well be contradictory to absolute elite autonomy. But, as noted in the previous chapter, such absolute autonomy is in any case precluded by the fact that all elites draw their resources from, as it were, a common well. All this, however, does not preclude *relative* elite autonomy, as long as the elites and sub-elites that cooperate do not become dependent for the lion's share of their resources on other elites and are still in charge of significant resources over which others have little or no control. It does not preclude the relative autonomy of elites as long as their resources make it possible for them to continue and maintain their elite positions even when they refuse to cooperate with the government or with other elites.

For instance, a potential opposition party elite may enter a coalition agreement which induces it to cooperate with the government in return for a share of government power. This does not contravene the relative autonomy of that oppositional elite – as long as it has independent financial, organizational and symbolic resources which enable it to resume an oppositional stance at any time. Likewise, trade union leaders and activists may be induced to cooperate with the government with respect to the moderation of industrial action, in return for a share of power in determining economic policy. This, too, does not contravene the trade union elite's relative autonomy as long as it can still maintain its trade union based power even if it refuses to cooperate with the government, and if it can resume industrial action at any time.

At times, however, a government may bear down on other elites and sub-elites to elicit their cooperation in a manner that infringes on their relative autonomy in the control of resources. Or else elites and sub-elites may voluntarily cooperate with each other through exchanges that infringe on their own, or on each other's relative autonomy in the control of resources. As already noted, the boundaries between elite dependence and relative independence cannot be set with mathematical precision. Hence the limits between eliciting the cooperation of elites in a manner that does not infringe on their relative autonomy, and elite cooperation which does infringe on that autonomy cannot be set with precision either.

The best that can be done is to identify these boundaries with the aid of the principles and rules of democracy (which defend elite autonomy): as long as elite cooperation is elicited in a manner that does not contravene those principles and rules, relative elite autonomy is safeguarded as well. It is only when elite cooperation is brought about in a manner that contravenes these rules that relative elite autonomy is infringed on.

Henceforward, the practice of a government eliciting the cooperation of other elites and sub-elites by bearing down on them in a manner that infringes on or threatens their relative autonomy in the control of resources and contravenes the principles and rules of democracy will be referred to as the *subjugation* of elites and sub-elites. And the practice of elites and sub-elites cooperating with each other by developing close interconnections for the exchange of resources in a manner that infringes on or threatens their mutual autonomy in the control of resources and contravenes the rules and conventions of democracy will be referred to as the *collusion* of elites.

As we have seen, however, and as will be be argued in greater detail in chapter 9, the rules of democracy are frequently inconsistent, and controversial. Therefore some practices of a government bearing down on other power holders, or of those developing close interconnections, may be legitimate by some democratic rules yet illegitimate by other democratic rules. They may also be located on the borderline between what the rules of democracy condone and what they condemn. Or else they may be in line with democratic rules accepted by some people but contrary to the democratic rules adhered to by others. It will be argued in chapter 9 that less than fully legitimate practices of this sort may also be seen as subjugations and collusions of elites. Several examples of such practices will be discussed.

In sum, then, elite cooperation stands in a problematic but not necessarily in a contradictory relationship to the autonomy of elites. In a democracy, elite cooperation which does not encroach on the relative autonomy of elites and sub-elites contributes to the functioning of the political system, hence to democracy. On the other hand (as I will argue and illustrate below) elite cooperation which infringes on relative elite autonomy or puts it under siege (the subjugation or collusion of elites and sub-elites) jeopardizes democracy. Eliminating or minimizing cooperation of this latter kind is thus essential for the survival of democracy.

## How the relative autonomy of elites came about

From the previous discussion it follows that both elite and sub-elite cooperation and their relative autonomy are necessary for democracy.

But I argue that it is the requirement for, and the actual development of relative *autonomy* that is distinctive of Western-style democracy.

Here the question may well be raised as to what the relative autonomy of elites itself derives from. Certainly the present claim is not that it is a completely independent phenomenon: its emergence in the West was obviously influenced by prior developments. For instance, it may well have been encouraged by the prior development of a certain intellectual climate of liberalism, tolerance and the like. It probably has also depended on a certain level of economic development and affluence, within which liberalism and tolerance would have been more likely to flourish. Additionally, it may have been promoted by the even earlier development of an independent landed aristocracy before the advent of the central state. But these factors, in turn, are the result of other factors, and a single analysis cannot be expected to decipher the entire causal chain of the development of the autonomy of elites and thus of democracy.

In this context, my claim is that the evolution of the relative autonomy of elites is a democratic achievement which was probably influenced by, but was not an automatic outcome of, previous processes. Historically in the West the evolving elites and sub-elites had to take matters into their own hands and deliberately struggle quite persistently for their self-determined power. These elite struggles for autonomy – which lasted several centuries, and reached their peak in the nineteenth and the beginning of the twentieth centuries – were thus a factor in its own right, without which democracy could not have come about.

At times the elites and sub-elites conducting those struggles represented the interests of classes or groups from which they themselves originated, at times they represented classes other than their own, and at times they represented no one but themselves. In any case, their struggles resulted in a dual process: their successive incorporation into existing power structures, and the granting of progressively more autonomy to them.

Thus the political elites of the aristocracy – which in the old regime mostly monopolized political power – were forced to accept into the establishment, first the political elites and sub-elites of the upper bourgeoisie, then those of the extended middle class, and finally those of the working class. Simultaneously the newly admitted groups also gained increased self-determination from and within the establishment. This took the form of the gradual development of clearly demarcated political parties, revolving round their leaders and activists, some of whom formed relatively independent oppositions to the government. It was also expressed in the development of relatively independent trade unions with their own leaders and activists. It was further expressed in the evolution of relatively free enterprise economies and their (businesss) elites, and in the emergence of relatively autonomous bureaucratic, judicial, media and academic elites and sub-elites.

In the process of struggling for power and autonomy, some of the participants genuinely also struggled for and achieved certain benefits for the classes or groups whose interests they purported to represent. Mostly they did so only as long as the interests of those classes or groups coincided with their own; in some cases they subsequently abandoned them. Moreover the reforms they helped bring about came slowly and belatedly; they were piecemeal and hesitant. Thus the achievements they 'delivered' to those classes or groups were frequently much smaller than was initially expected. Yet eventually their struggles still led to the reshaping of the existing political and social structures in a more egalitarian fashion (though not, of course, to the abolition of inequalities).[1]

Whether those who struggled truly intended to promote democracy, or whether they were concerned only with their own power and privileges, is a moot question. In any case, in retrospect, their struggles can also be seen to have been struggles for the development of the principles of democracy. And they were, in fact, interconnected with the gradual (though imperfect) development and implementation of those principles as we know them today.

## The historical relationship between elite autonomy and democracy

This still leaves open the question of the causal, or the historical relationship between the evolution of the relative autonomy of elites and sub-elites and the evolution of the principles of democracy. This is not merely a chicken-and-egg problem. Establishing it is of prime importance for understanding how democracies evolve and stabilize or break down.

I suggest that while the relative autonomy of elites and sub-elites is part and parcel of democracy, it also serves as an important historical condition for its development and stabilization. This is not to say that it is the sole condition, or even the sole important condition, for its development. Other theories have focused on other circumstances which foster the development of democracy, and these circumstances may well be important, too. I merely argue that the development of relative elite autonomy is *an* important historical condition for this development.

Thus some theorists explain the development and stabilization of democracy chiefly in class terms (see Moore, 1969; Therborn, 1977; Stephens, 1989). Even among elite analyses, not all focus on identical factors. Recently it has been argued that it is elite settlements, or compromises, which pave the way for stable democracy (O'Donnell and Schmitter, 1986; Morlino, 1987; Burton and Higley, 1987; Diamond et al. 1989-90; Higley and Burton, 1989), while the fragmentation of elites makes democracy susceptible to breakdowns (Linz, 1978; Lepsius, 1978; Herz, 1982). Or else it has been argued that either elite-sponsored accommodations or elite-sponsored violence lead to the consolidation of democracy (Schmitter, 1988, p. 95).

These other analyses have to do chiefly with splintering of elites, with the degree of dissensus as against consensus and cooperation that develops among them, or with the violence they do or do not engage in. By contrast, the present analysis concerns the degree to which non-governmental elites and sub-elites have resources that are immune from government and each other's intervention. Therefore it is not in contradiction to the above analyses, but focuses on a different dimension of elite structure.

As argued before, so long as cooperation does not flow from iilicit encroachment on their resources, elites and those close to them can reach settlements, enter into cooperation, and still be relatively independent from each other. And both cooperation and independence may well be important historical conditions for the rise and stabilization of democracy. One may even go as far as to argue that in one respect the two factors complement each other: *if there were no independently powerful elites prior to the development of democracy, there would be no one with whom it would be necessary to reach a settlement.* And democracy being a complex structure, its unfolding and persistence are most likely to be the result of a variety of historical developments. Here it is merely submitted that the relative autonomy of elites and sub-elites is one of the most important of these.

Diamond, Linz and Lipset (1988) have also made the point that ruling elites which allow for autonomous structures and associations (including independent media) form an important precondition for democracy. Of the various analyses on the emergence of democracy, this one seems closest to the present one. I still prefer to focus on the autonomy which non-government elites and sub-elites gain for themselves – whether through the goodwill of rulers or by other means – rather than on the autonomy of structures and associations. For I view relatively autonomous elites *qua* people as (intentionally or unintentionally) working in favour of the evolution and persistence of democracy.

In sum, there are various factors that are responsible for the development and stabilization of democracy, and I do not purport to be able to do justice to all of them. All I hope to accomplish is to isolate one important factor in the complex constellation of social causes and consequences, and show that it does help explain pertinent developments better than we could understand them if this factor had not been taken into account. This is what I claim for the relative autonomy of elites and sub-elites when I say that it is an important precondition for the development and stabilization of democracy.

This claim makes it necessary to identify the mechanisms through which the previous autonomy of elites and sub-elites encourages the development and stabilization of democracy. This presupposes the obvious distinction betweeen the mere emergence of democracy and its stabilization. Following the previous characterization of democracy, we may speak of its appearance when free elections and universal suffrage have been put into place and civil liberties have been instituted. Following Lipset (1967), we may speak of stable democracy when two phenomena converge. First, democracy has been in existence, without disruption, for a lengthy period – as a rule of thumb we may say, for at least fifty years. Second, there are no major disruptive forces which threaten it in the foreseeable future. The criteria of stabilization, thus, are evidently more restrictive than those of emergence. The latter has occurred in a variety of countries all over the world. It is no great revelation to say that the former has occurred in only a few, so far mostly in the West.

My argument, then, is in the first place that the previous relative autonomy of elites and sub-elites serves as an important condition for the stabilization of democracy. The mechanism through which previously instituted relative elite autonomy works for the stabilization of democracy is simple: given the intimate relationship between elite autonomy and the principles of democracy, autonomous elites and sub-elites have an interest in defending and perpetuating these principles which serve as a basis for their independent power.

Therefore, once elites have developed a tradition of standing up for such principles, they are likely to do so even against forces that endeavour to destroy them. Once democracy has been disrupted and a despotic ruler takes over, he can apply physical coercion to silence even the most autonomous of elites. But the point is that previously autonomous elites can defend the principles of democracy early on, when the forces working to disrupt democracy have not yet gained the upper hand. They can thus decrease the chances of such a ruler coming to power in the first place.

Conversely, in the absence of previous elite autonomy, democracy, if it develops, is a form without a substance. Lacking elites and sub-elites that by defending their own autonomy would also defend democracy, it is much more vulnerable to the onslaught of non-democratic forces. Hence it would have difficulty in stabilizing itself. All this will be illustrated in chapter 7 through a historical comparison between Britain and Germany towards the end of the nineteenth and the beginning of the twentieth centuries.

Without the advent of democracy, however, there can be no stabilization. I argue, in the second place, that the autonomy of elites is also an important condition for the mere arrival of democracy. Here, too, the mechanism leading relative elite autonomy to promote the development of democracy is simple. As long as no relatively auto- nomous elites and sub-elites develop in an autocratic regime, there is likely to be little push for such a regime from outside the ruling elite itself. Other established elites, such as the magnates of the economy, of trade unions or of the media, would have no interest, would be too intimidated by, incorporated into, or rewarded for their loyalty by the ruling elite to institute a serious push for such change. If another established elite – such as that of the military – hoped to take over government on its own, it would stand a better chance of doing so by instigating a coup, rather than through lobbying for multi-party elections. In the absence of relatively independent non-established elites of social movements, such a regime would also not be prone to pressures for democratic change from below.

Only the rulers themselves could thus initiate changes towards democracy, and in the absence of outside pressures, and barring some exceptional circumstances (such as imminent collapse of the system in any case), they would obviously have little motivation to do so: such changes would most likely jeopardize their own power. Even if they felt compelled to institute some changes, they would be likely to give preference to limited changes over substantial ones, to changes heralding a semblance of democracy over changes leading to actual democracy.

By contrast, if relatively autonomous elites and sub-elites develop in a non-democratic regime, this may be the outcome of self-imposed limitations of the despotic rulers, or of forces over which they have no control, that is, of their weakness. In either case, such relatively autonomous people become instrumental in weakening the regime, or in weakening it further, by mounting various sorts of opposition to it. For opposition, which is institutionalized in a democracy, is something a non-democratic regime is ill-equipped to cope with.

In addition, once relatively autonomous elites and sub-elites develop in a non-democratic regime (and given the intimate relation between democratic principles and relatively autonomous elites), they have an interest in pushing for democratic principles, so as to enhance their own independent power. And by playing a role in the unfolding of democracy, they help democracy along to the stage where it *can* be stabilized. It is precisely this that budding elites have done in the Western world. Also, this argument will be illustrated through a historical/contemporary comparison of developments in the Soviet Union and Poland (see chapter 8).

As the autonomy of elites forms a large part of what the principles of democracy are about, ostensibly the claim that such autonomy furthers democracy merely means that democracy at a previous stage reproduces democracy at a later stage. This would be interesting in itself for, in principle, things might well have been different. After all, and despite the popular maxim that nothing succeeds like success, it is by no means self-evident that early success of an endeavour leads to its later success as well. It might well have been that early success of democracy leads to subsequent stagnation or failure.

But there is more to it than that. For the argument is that some elite and sub-elite autonomy in the control of resources can develop in a non-democratic regime, before democratic principles, and particularly free elections, have been put into place. This can happen simply because of the inablity of the rulers to master and control all major societal resources, or because they are reluctant to do so. And further, that this relative autonomy then becomes important in paving the way for democracy. Conversely, the lack of such autonomy before the transition to democracy impedes this transition.

Also, if the preceding argument on the stabilization of democracy is correct, this shows that the meta-principle of elite autonomy is more important in stabilizing democracy than the explicit electoral principle of universal suffrage. Moreover it is only democratic elite theory which assigns such a core role to the autonomy of elites in both the appearance and perpetuation of democracy, while other theories do not. Demonstrating the role of this autonomy in stabilizing and even in promoting democracy should thus bring out the distinctive contribution of the demo-elite perspective in the analysis of this regime. This is done in chapters 7 and 8.

## Conclusion and discussion

The foregoing two chapters have presented the chief tenets of the demo-elite perspective, and have outlined its contribution within democratic elite theory. The chapters have shown this contribution to lie in explicating elite and sub-elite autonomy in terms of the distribution of resources, and in some initial exploration of the relationship between relative elite autonomy and elite cooperation. They have also shown this contribution to lie in pointing to the possibility of the subjugation and collusion of elites even in a democracy, and in exploring the causal or historical relationship between the relative autonomy of elites and sub-elites and the development of democracy (themes that will be further developed in the next two parts of the book).

In addition, one of the aims of the chapters has been to show that the implicit meta-principle of relative elite autonomy has come to be interwoven not merely with liberalism, but with the explicit electoral and other principles of democracy. A further aim has been to demonstrate that the same meta-principle is interwoven with the democratic role and the power of the public: it does not ensure elite responsiveness to the public, but it makes such responsiveness more likely than would otherwise be the case.

Like elite theory, liberal theories and democratic elite theories have been criticized for disregarding or denigrating the public and for being inegalitarian. In addition, they have been criticized for being complacent about Western regimes. And, indeed, liberal thought has focused on liberty at the expense of equality. Initially, liberal thought recoiled even from democracy, because the latter had egalitarian elements in it. Later on, when liberalism incorporated some democratic themes, it became scared by its own courage, withdrew from the logical conclusions of its own assumptions, and failed to advocate full democracy through universal and equal suffrage.

Even later on, when such univeral suffrage came to be accepted in the – by then – liberal democratic tradition as a matter of course, liberalism could still be dubbed as inegalitarian: it did not include adequate provisions for the redistribution of wealth. Later on again, when liberalism came to be wedded to the doctrine of the welfare state, it could still be seen to have inegalitarian elements. For welfare states are designed to mitigate inequalities and not to abolish them. Within the social sciences proper, those heirs of the liberal tradition who came to be identified as democratic elite theorists could also be stigmatized as inegalitarian. They were accused of using the mantle of democratic theory to lend legitimation to the exploitative capitalist regime.

The fact that other theories such as Marxism have lent indirect legitimation to even more inegalitarian regimes is irrelevant in this respect. It must not make us oblivious to the element of truth in this critique. It ought not to blind us to the fact that the separation of powers advocated in the liberal tradition was meant to sustain political rights, not economic equality. And the emphasis on the relative autonomy of power groups in the democratic elite tradition of Weber-Mosca-Schumpeter-Aron was meant to help us in understanding and sustaining democracy within a basically unequal economic system.

In this context, the final aim of the foregoing chapters has been to show that in its present version democratic elite theory is not complacent about existing democracy, or opposed to equality. Indeed, it can be developed in a critical and egalitarian fashion. In this manner, it can help not only in showing up the shortcomings of Western democracy, but also in understanding how democracy may be encouraged to breed a more egalitarian democracy as it goes along. This claim is substantiated in the final part of this book.

## Note

1   For a detailed discussion of these developments see Etzioni-Halevy, 1989a, chs 3 and 4.

# PART IV

# THE AUTONOMY OF ELITES AND THE SUCCESS (OR FAILURE) OF DEMOCRACY

# 7

# *Stabilization versus breakdown of democracy: the cases of Britain and Germany*

If the thesis on the role of the autonomy of elites in stabilizing democracy is well founded, it should be possible to find support for it in actual historical developments. This can be done by deriving an expectation from it. Thus, in countries which subsequently developed a stable democracy, there should be evidence of the relative autonomy of elites and sub-elites *before* democracy matured. Conversely, in countries which experienced some democratic developments followed by a democratic breakdown, there should be evidence for the lack of such autonomy *before* the breakdown occurred.

## A historical comparison between Britain and Germany

Illustrative support for this thesis comes from a historical comparison of relevant developments in Britain and Germany towards the end of the nineteenth and the beginning of the twentieth centuries. During these timespans both countries underwent processes of democratization. But while in Britain these processes matured, in Germany they were, of course, disrupted. As expected, it was the case that in Britain there was a clearly recognizable development towards the elites' and sub-elites' relative autonomy from government interference, before democracy was fully in place. Conversely, in Germany, *before* the collapse of democracy, their counterparts had not gained a similar degree of independence.

Interestingly, if the formal definition of democracy and its central explicit principle – competitive elections by universal suffrage – alone is taken into account, in some respects the transition to democracy in Germany preceded this transition in Britain: in Germany universal male suffrage existed from unification in 1871, while in Britain it was introduced only in 1918. Universal suffrage was introduced in Germany in 1919; in Britain it came about only in 1928.

True, in Germany the electoral laws were devised so as to give over-representation to the wealthy. But to a certain extent this was the case in Britain as well, through the mechanism of plural voting. In any case, in Germany this obstacle was not insuperable: by 1912 the German (working class) Social Democratic party (SPD) had become the largest party in the Reichstag, the German parliament.

True, in Germany the government was responsible to the monarch and not to the elected parliament as in Britain. But the government was still dependent on the elected Reichstag for the passing of legislation and for ratification of the budget, without which (formally at least) it could not govern. So, if the electoral criteria of democracy alone are taken into account, Germany had a headstart over Britain. Yet it is in Britain that democracy stabilized while in Germany it was later disrupted.

The final blow to democracy in Germany was inflicted by the ascent of Nazism, which did not occur in Britain. But the fact is that the disruption of democracy in Germany occurred during the Weimar republic, even *before* the Nazi takeover, and only because of this did Nazism have such a smooth path to power. By contrast, it was precisely at this time that democracy was consolidating itself in Britain. It is this difference prior to the Nazi takeover (rather than the takeover as such) which the issue of the previous autonomy of elites and sub-elites helps us to explain.

I do not claim that there are no additonal factors that help explain this difference. It has been noted (chapter 6) that some scholars have related democratic stabilization to elite settlements or cooperation, and democratic breakdown to elite fragmentation. Some of these have used the Weimar republic as a case in point. The breakdown of democracy in Germany has also been explained by the effects of the First World War, and the constitutional problems of the Weimar republic. However, as we have seen, elite cooperation may coexist with elite autonomy, just as elite fragmentation may coexist with elite dependence. And factors peculiar to postwar Germany do not obviate more general factors such as elite autonomy versus dependence. Hence the present analysis deals with a separate variable, and is not in contradiction to the previous ones.

Further, it will be argued below that the variable I focus on was itself related to other factors. It was connected in particular with the different stature of the state and the different intellectual climate and social philosophies that predominated in the two countries. These, in turn, may well have been influenced by a whole chain of other factors. My claim, however, is that the prior weakness in the autonomy of elites and sub-elites – although not the only or ultimate factor – was an important factor in its own right in the breakdown of German democracy. Conversely, the relative and growing strength of the same autonomy in Britain was an important factor in the stabilization of democracy there.

How do we know that relative elite autonomy is indeed an important factor in contributing to these differences? Ideally, the countries compared should have been identical in every way, with only the degree of elite autonomy differentiating between them. If it should then turn out that democracy subsequently stabilized where this autonomy was strong and broke down where it was weak, our confidence that the above thesis had found empirical support would have been very high indeed. The reality, however, is that such perfect experimental settings for historical-comparative analysis rarely materialize. Societies usually differ on clusters of, rather than on one or two variables only. As Lipset put it 'given historical situations are determined by a multitude of factors and . . . it is impossible to perform the methodological operation of holding other factors constant, or randomizing them, as can often be done when studying large numbers of individuals' (1968, p. 51).

This does not mean that comparative-historical studies to test theory-derived expectations must be abandoned. As Lipset adds, 'there is no necessary clash between developing general sociological hypotheses and taking historical specificity into account.' Such specificity merely means that comparative-historical analysis must also rely on reasoning and interpretation. In the present case, for instance, the confidence we may have in the thesis is strengthened by the following reasoning.

First, the thesis is not an ad hoc one, made to measure for this particular comparison. Rather, it is derived from a broader theory, developed without those cases in mind. Second, the theory does not produce the thesis as a rule of thumb. Rather, it clearly specifies the mechanisms through which elite autonomy encourages stabilization of democracy while its absence encourages democratic breakdown. These mechanisms have been presented in general terms in chapter 6. And they can be seen to have been clearly at work in the cases compared.

Thus the German elites and their aides, having previously lacked autonomous resources, had not acquired the ability to defend their positions – and thereby the institutions of democracy – against anti-democratic forces. And, in fact, they did little to defend those positions when (even before the advent of Nazism) they were attacked. Conversely, as the British elites and sub-elites did struggle for, and gain, relatively more independent resources, they could then use them to gain further independent power, and in the process they aided democracy. Seeing these concrete mechanisms at work in actual (historical) practice thus strengthens the theoretical argument.

As noted, the argument is that the weakness of German elite autonomy facilitated the decline of democracy before the ascent of Nazism to power. But although this is not the main point of the argument, it is interesting that the lack of previous elite autonomy had ramifications after the Nazis came to power as well. At that point, the regime could have overrun any resistance (had it occurred) by force in any case. But the fact is that at that time, too, resistance was sparse: the elites and sub-elites that had previously lacked autonomy certainly did not have the resilience to resist the Nazi apparatus once it was in control. All this is illustrated through a brief delve into the histories of Britain and Germany during the relevant timespans.

These histories have been extensively studied already. This analysis – by a sociologist – is not designed to uncover hitherto unknown historical facts. Rather, the purpose is to show how the facts (which have been established by a whole variety of both old and new historical scholarship),[1] support a thesis derived from a demo-elite theoretical perspective. This is done below with respect to four elites and sub-elites: those of trade unions, of business, of the media, and with respect to the academic/intellectual elite.[2]

With regard to each category, its degree of relative autonomy (or lack thereof) is examined with the aid of the criteria set out in chapter 5. These criteria include lack of its successful repression or suppression through the coercive resources of the the state (usually connected with absence of repressive legislation, or with legislation which protects from repression). They also include relative absence of control over it through the government's administrative, material or symbolic resources. Finally, they include the relative lack of government or state control over its own administrative, material and symbolic resources.

Relative autonomy by these criteria can be most easily recognized through an elite and sub-elite developing symbols of resistance and conflict, and its actual willingness to stand up to the government. This manifestation of relative autonomy (or lack thereof) will be examined as well.

## The business elite and sub-elite

Several theorists (see Moore, 1969) have made the connection between the development of a free enterprise economy, the rise of the bourgeoisie and the evolution of democracy. From the viewpoint of the demo-elite perspective, however, what is important is a free enterprise economy not as a basis for the ascent of the bourgeoisie as a class, but as a basis for the autonomy of the most active and powerful element of this class: the business elite and sub-elite. It is this group which, by countervailing the power of the state, protects democracy. Hence the importance of the evidence which shows that in Britain relative economic freedom developed earlier and more thoroughly than in other Western countries, while in Germany it never took off.

### In Britain

Mercantilism, or the administrative subordination of the economy to the state, prevailed in Europe from the beginning of the seventeenth century up until the end of the eighteenth century, and encompassed both Britain and Germany. But in Britain business people struggled for independence from state interference through the latter's resources of administrative regulation. Moreover, their struggles were crowned with relative success: the old economic order, with its elaborate restrictions and local taxes, was broken down before 1770 (except for the more restrictive situation in the wool industry). Also, freedom to engage in the economic activity of one's choice already existed in Britain in the latter part of the eighteenth century to an extent unknown on the continent before the French revolution. The industrial revolution in Britain was thus spearheaded by a relatively independent business elite.

In the nineteenth century the business people who had emerged from the industrial revolution (including leaders of industry, manufacturers, ironmasters, merchants, retailers, shipowners, bankers and their staff) were all 'jostling with each other' (Bédarida, 1991, p. 50) as well as struggling for independence from hampering administrative regulation of economic activities. From the beginning of the century many British urban large and smaller capitalists, voiced the demand that the state stay out of the regulation of wages. Subsequently the struggles for economic freedom were also expressed as struggles for free trade. These entailed opposition to the protectionist Corn Laws, and were led by the Anti-Corn Law League activists. Following these struggles and a bad harvest in Ireland (which led to a famine), the Corn laws were repealed in 1846.

The desire for economic freedom, which on the practical level was manifested by the business people's struggles against government interference, was expressed on the symbolic level by Adam Smith and his fellow classical economists. These theoreticians taught that maximum freedom for the play of economic forces would further the economic interests of all. By furnishing the rationale for the laissez-faire economic system, the classical economists thus became the ideologues of the business representatives' struggle for independence. And their teachings were partly implemented in the economic policies and practices of the nineteenth century.

These practices, which culminated towards the middle of the century, did not imply an absence of government intervention in the economy. But many traditional administrative restrictions on economic activity (such as restrictions on freedom of movement and on shipping) were now absent, free trade measures were introduced and state interference was significantly reduced. Many of the laws and regulations which did exist, moreover, were geared primarily to prevent the intervention of non-economic forces in the economic sphere. They were thus geared to protect the autonomy of those in charge of business activities.

As a consequence, business people asserted themselves further, taking charge of the economy. 'With the levers of power in their hands the bourgeois set themselves up as the promoters of the economy. They gambled heavily on the system of unlimited competition and sanctified the race for money, power and advancement' (Bédarida, 1991, p. 53). Their economic independence and power made it possible for business people to struggle for political power as well.

At the beginning of the nineteenth century political power had still been largely monopolized by the elite of the landed aristocracy and gentry. But the creation of social movements, headed by the elite and sub-elite of the bourgeoisie, and the waves of revolt they initiated during the first part of the century, led to the incorporation of large scale capitalists – bankers, big industrialists – into the top ranks of power. These then endeavoured to stabilize their power by gradual (though not full) extension of the franchise. The democratic power struggle was thus greatly expanded.

As Bédarida further shows, the struggle for exemption from state control in economic activity was practically inseparable from the struggle for exemption from state control in all other areas of human activity. And this was so both on the philosophical and on the practical level. The development of economic liberties, the free enjoyment of one's property, was therefore closely intertwined with the development of personal liberties, the freedom of one's body, movement and expression. These, in turn, were but the other side of the coin of political liberties that (by definition) are of the essence of democracy. All this, moreover, stood in stark contrast to the authoritarianism of some of the regimes in continental Europe. In this manner, leaders and lower level politicians drawn from the bourgeoisie managed to attain a share of political power. Concomitantly they also consolidated achievements of liberalism and certain, though intentionally limited, advances towards democracy.

After 1880 freedom of business came to be hampered by a number of complex factors, and in the twentieth century government intervention in the economy increased again. But by that time democracy had been well established and, moreover, intervention never reverted to its previous level in the mercantilist era.

## In Germany

By contrast, during the same era in Germany, practically all economic activity was regulated through the administrative power of the state. Methods of production were strictly prescribed, with public inspectors exercising control. Sales, too, took place under strict official supervision. These conditions obviously did not provide a fertile soil for the development of an independent business elite. Also, industrialization in Germany was belated: it peaked only in the 1870s, 1880s and 1890s. Therefore, to catch up with other European nations, Germany had to industrialize quickly and thoroughly. It was thought that this could best be accomplished through state guidance. As Mathias and Pollard point out (1989, ch. 21), such guidance was not the result of a rationally conceived policy. Rather, it consisted of a set of arbitrary measures, that were yet clearly interventionist.

Government involvement in the economy was achieved in part by the state's own participation in economic activity. This was done through mixed private and public entrprises, and through the holding of state property. Apart from the powerful state banks and the nationalized railroads, coal mines and blast furnances were owned by the state as well. Thus the state was the largest single economic entrepreneur, and the management of economic enterprises was frequently in the hands of civil servants and others dependent on government agencies. The state thus had direct administrative control of economic activity.

Non-government enterprises were not absent, and capitalist entrepreneurs of various magnitudes were granted the ability to make profits. But they, too, were controlled through the administrative resources of the state: in return for being allowed profits, they had to submit to the dictates of the state bureaucracy. Thus much of what the business people wanted in material terms was provided not by their own efforts but by the state from above (Blackbourn, 1987, pp. 68–73). Hence, neither the economy, nor its elite and sub-elite, attained the autonomy the parallel group attained in Britain.

Significantly, as Blackbourn further demonstrates, this was connected with the fact that German business people, and the German bourgeoisie in general, never developed the push towards liberalism which was characteristic of their British counterpart at the time. Further, 'the science of economics ... provided more scholarly justification and support for the claim of the state to intervene in the free market economy ... in Germany than anywhere else in the industrialized world' (Mathias and Pollard, 1989, p. 753). In this manner the theoretical foundations for liberalism that were well established at the time in Britain were also lacking in Germany. All this meant, as we further learn from Blackbourn, that the businessmen, while they did not capitulate to the aristocracy, nevertheless did not engage in political struggles. They thus forfeited their political muscle. Instead they were voluntarily tied to the machinery of government through their role in semi-public organs of self-administration, such as the chambers of commerce and commercial courts.

Industrialization from above and state participation in the economy also meant that, right from the beginning, there was a high centralization of economic enterprises. It took the form of syndicates, cartels and trusts. This was not only tolerated, but encouraged by the state. The German economy thus passed directly from the feudal stage to the stage of state-sponsored, oligopoly or monopoly capitalism. This cartel structure, as well as state control over the economy, was perpetuated under the Weimar republic. It was supplemented by a system of corporatism, in which big business was tightly organized in trade associations, or Verbände. These culminated in national peak organizations or Spitzenverbände: the Vereinigung der Deutschen Arbeitsverbände (union of employers) and the Reichsverband der Deutschen Industrie (National Industrial League). This organizational structure, too, facilitated state control of the economy. All this meant that those activating the German economy were, once again, administratively controlled from above.

This fact later assumed prime importance for the collapse of democracy. Big business leaders used their money and political contacts in enthusiastic support of chancellor Von Papen, who planned to revise the constitution in an authoritarian direction. Having been accustomed to a system in which the state had paternalistically controlled the economy and their own activities, they had no problem in supporting an increasingly authoritarian regime. This regime, then, was instrumental in dismantling democracy and it eased the transition to Nazism.

There is some dispute as to whether the big business elite consciously supported the Nazi rise to power. But there can be no doubt that important segments of the business and heavy industry elite and their senior staff backed the Deutschnationale Volkspartei (DNVP). This was an authoritarian party which cooperated increasingly closely with the Nazis after 1928. Also, even before its ascent to power (as early as 1930) the Nazi party had not concealed its plans for a state-controlled, corporatist economic order. Yet the business magnates – who had been accustomed to some elements of such an order already – did not put up any concerted opposition to it.

In 1933, moreover, the Reichsverband der Deutschen Industrie voluntarily dissolved itself; its remnants, along with those of other industrial organizations, were swallowed up into the Nazi-sponsored, state-controlled Reichsstand der Deutschen Industrie. Having been previously incorporated into a state-dependent corporatist structure, the business elite subsequently experienced no great difficulty in fitting itself into the Nazi system of enforced corporatism.

## The elite and sub-elite of trade unions

It is my argument that an autonomous elite and sub-elite of trade unions provides a protective shield for democracy. Importantly, therefore, the evidence shows that although the labour unionists in both countries were reformist and politically moderate rather than revolutionary, there were some significant differences during the period examined. In Britain this group of people gained relative (though certainly not total) independence, while in Germany repeated attempts were made to suppress it. Although these were not successful, the group was made docile, and eventually turned into a helping organ of the state.

## In Britain

In Britain, repression of trade union elites through the coercive resources of the state – aided by repressive legislation – was not absent. But it gradually shrank, and virtually disappeared, as legislation was changed to protect them from such repression. Trade unions began to be formed in 1816 and, in the wake of legislation in 1825, repealing previous repressive laws, they greatly expanded. New unions were formed, and they could now conduct their business more openly than before. It was at this time that trade unions began the practice of collective bargaining for working conditions. But unions did not as yet gain full legal recognition, and they were still subject to repressive measures by the government. Possibly in part for that reason, their scope was still limited, and their leadership unstable.

However, as a result of protracted struggles, between 1848 and 1870 the principle of freedom of association gradually gained acceptance. Accordingly unions were given greater legal recognition – and thus greater protection from repressive measures – by the state. By 1871 they were given legal protection for their funds and for their methods of collective bargaining, and they won full legal recognition in 1876. Nonetheless, unions' legal rights were not fully determined until the Trades Disputes Acts of 1906 and 1913. Even thereafter, attempts were still made to repress unions, though overall such attempts diminished.

After 1871, growing legal recognition in conjunction with economic expansion brought about the growth and proliferation of trade unions. These factors also led to greater manifestations of the relative independence of the leadership of the unions through their instigation of industrial strife. Previously unions had been chiefly craft unions, preoccupied mostly with mutual help and mutual insurance. Only sporadically had their representatives organized strikes to back up demands for improved working conditions. But what Middlemas (1979) terms 'new unionism' took over. Union leaders and functionaries began to enlist the masses of the less skilled workers into union ranks, and they increased agitation among those unskilled workers. They thus became considerably more active in struggling for workers' rights and conditions.

During the same period, the union leadership's struggles forced employers gradually to moderate their repressive measures, and grudgingly increase their recognition of unions. Middlemas recounts that in 1897-8, for instance, a strike and a climactic battle between the Employers' Federation of Engineering Associations and the Engineers' Union resulted in a humiliating defeat of the latter. The defeat, however, elicited further militancy by the union activists. This, in turn, resulted in a more compromising attitude on the part of the employers' association. Although it retained its harsh confidence in public, by 1911 it was willing to reappraise the role of trade unions, if only because by then it could no longer afford the price of prolonged strikes like that of 1897.

Even beforehand, the trade union leadership, together with other popular movements and associations, had been pressuring for social and political reforms. They had done so through lobbying the existing parties and playing them off against each other. This had led to a number of reforms, including the further extension of the franchise and the establishment of the secret ballot in 1872. In 1900 the various labour and socialist groups combined with the trade union movement in setting up a Labour Representation Committee to return workers' representatives to parliament. This signalled the birth of the Labour party, formally established in 1906.

As Middlemas (1979) clarifies, at that time trade union leaders and activists were beginning to compete aggressively for recognition in the political as well as in the industrial sense. On the political front, and in conjunction with the Labour party, they were also relatively effective in pressuring for legislation which further improved working conditions and social welfare, although the achievements were not as far-reaching as the demands. They were also instrumental in pressuring for the further extension of the franchise to include the working class, with universal male suffrage introduced in 1919.

Thus, in combination with the Labour party elite, those in charge of the growing and increasingly well-organized trade union movement came to be a formidable power in British politics. 'Given the outbreak of dissent, at political and industrial level after 1909, it was hardly surprising that the parties responded, seeking not only votes ... but incorporation of the organized working class, in order to ensure their future access to permanent power' (Middlemas, 1979, p. 38).

In sum, as freedom of association was increasingly recognized and incorporated into legislation, state repression declined, unions grew and proliferated, and their elite and sub-elite manifested its relative independence by increasingly organizing industrial conflict. The union movement leadership, which came to be interrelated with that of the Labour party, had its basis of power in the support of the membership from the working class. Therefore, if only to augment its power basis, it also pressured for, and was increasingly successful, in leading to democratic reforms which extended the franchise to (the males of) that class. Thereby it helped widen and invigorate the democratic power struggle and move Britain further along the path to democracy.

## In Germany

In Germany, as in Britain, the industrial age had brought with it a growing proletariat organized in expanding trade unions. These were related to the growing Social Democratic party (SPD). But in Germany the coercive resources of the state were used to a much greater extent than in Britain in an attempt to repress and suppress the labour movement. Trade unions were legalized by the North German Federation in 1869, but in unified Germany, under the Reich, Bismarck endeavoured to suppress unions through anti-socialist legislation. Such legislation, which placed a ban on socialist meetings and on the distribution of socialist literature, was passed in 1878, and renewed in the 1880s, before it died in 1890.

The anti-socialist legislation could not eradicate, but severely hampered the unions and their leadership. Even afterwards, attempts by the authorities to suppress the labour movement by coercive means continued. The SPD was subjected to constant harassment. Although the party was no longer illegal, its activities were continuously monitored and supervised by the police, which broke up many of its meetings and imprisoned its activists on the slightest pretexts. The related trade unions and their organizers, too, continued to be tampered with. Their activities, and particularly strikes, continued to be circumscribed by a set of legal restrictions. Using administrative intervention, trials for *lèse majesté* and the like, the state went on creating difficulties for them.

According to Roth (1963, pp. 307–8), Bismarck's attempt at suppressing the labour movement ultimately failed, and the government eventually gave up any serious attempts at suppression. This gave evidence of the continuous vitality of the movement. But while the government did not succeed in suppressing the movement, nonetheless, through its attempts to do so, the labour activists were pushed into a corner: they had to be careful not to provoke the intensification of repressive policies and the crushing of the movement.

It is perhaps partly for that reason that, while the labour movement did much to bring about improved working conditions as well as democratic rights – including equal suffrage and fair representation – its leaders manifested a degree of subservience to the state and the government that was unknown in Britain. This was evident, first, on the level of symbolic resources. On the one hand the labour leadership developed a confrontational rhetoric. But on the other hand, it also manifested a Hegelian, legitimatory ideology, if not a docile attitude to the state, which Dahrendorf termed 'a fatal love of the state' (1967, p. 190).

The union leaders also tried to avoid actual conflict with and within the state, and they considered industrial disputes to be open to arbitration by the state to a much greater extent than did their counterparts in Britain. Although strikes did occur, and although they grew in numbers and importance in the 1890s (though many of them failed), the vast majority of labour disputes were settled primarily through the industrial courts. In some respects (as in their action against the May Day strike) those in charge of the major unions even gave in to state pressures to the extent of siding with the state against the radicals within the labour movement.

From the 1890s and onwards, and at the beginning of the twentieth century, trade union leadership put great emphasis on moderation. 'Analysing the Wilhelmine working-class movement, some historians have pointed to its moderation . . . and indeed there can be little doubt that those who wished to turn everything upside down remained in a small minority'. Even so, power holders shunned reforms that might have given the labour movement more power. Instead they continued to rely on 'the Army, the police and the bureaucracy' (Berghahn, 1987, p. 23).

Union leaders reacted with more moderation, as they moved unions increasingly away from industrial and political struggles and in the direction of friendly society, or mutual insurance activities. According to both Berghahn and Pachter (1978) they also put great emphasis on non-political cultural activities. In conjunction with this, they 'very soon concentrated upon organizational strength rather than upon agitation, for the top leaders' strategy [was one of] "self-maintenance"' (Roth, 1963, p. 310). Similar tendencies were shown by the SPD: the party had a revolutionary ideology, but it also 'gave employment to thousands of editors, printers, organizers, and "labor-union secretaries" – a new profession – who would not wantonly expose their offices and homes to the risk of police raids' (Pachter, 1978, p. 30).

In terms of organizational resources, the unions' officials became involved in public administration: they organized the election of workers' representatives on the trade and arbitration courts. Thereby they involved the trade unions in social policy and forced them into a measure of collaboration with the representatives of the employers and of bourgeois parties.

This tendency was strengthened under the Weimar republic. At that time, the state's administrative resources were used in order to incorporate the unions' higher echelons into existing state and institutionalized structures. Compulsory state arbitration for labour disputes was established, and heightened the administrative control of the government over the union leadership. A law of 1920 encumbered the workers' councils in their enterprises with the double task of representing the workers while also supporting the employers in the successful running of those enterprises. The labour leaders and their representatives were also appointed to positions in bodies such as the labour courts or the national coal council; thereby they were transformed into semi-administrative personnel. Thus the state's attempt to suppress the unions during the Bismarck era had now given way to an (even more successful) attempt to turn their representatives into a helping organ of the state. In both phases they were denied the degree of relative independence which their counterparts had gained in Britain.

It may be thought that during the later years of the Weimar republic the labour movement, or the more radical parts within it – particularly the communists – in fact manifested too much autonomy in the sense of being overly oppositional and thus disruptive of the system. However, consider what one of the most prominent historians of this period, Arthur Rosenberg, writes on this issue: 'the KPD, since 1925, had no serious political programme which ran counter to the day-to-day framework of capitalism – it, too, was one of the factors in the German stabilization system, and within its restricted framework, it became possible for it to utilize the conditions of stabilization' . . . 'It emerges that, since 1925, the KPD was no more than the shadow of the German Republic, and it disappeared with the disappearance of the body itself' (1943, pp. 279–80).[3]

In view of all this, and particularly since a large part of the trade union elite and sub-elite was already incorporated into, and thus dependent on the state, it is not surprising that later on – in the last stages of the Weimar era – it acquiesced in chancellor von Papen's plan for a fully authoritarian state, which was to perpetuate its dependence, and also dismantle democracy. This plan was also the pathbreaker for the Nazi regime. There was hardly any reaction from the labour leadership to Papen's dismissal of the Prussian government, led by social democrats, in 1932. This passivity (together with that of other elites) contributed to the downfall of the Weimar republic.

Although this is not the main point of this discussion, it is of interest to note that even after the Nazi ascent to power, a large part of the union leadership attempted to accommodate to it. It is true that in 1933 the representatives of the SPD opposed Hitler's 'Ermächtigungsgesetz' which, in practice, abolished popular representation. But the labour leadership was helpless in the face of the Nazi attack on itself: there was no effective resistance in 1933, when the SPD was prohibited and trade unions were dismantled. There was thus no difficulty in replacing them by an over-arching, state-controlled organization: the Deutsche Arbeitsfront (DAF), which served as an instrument for the Nazi indoctrination of workers.

True, during the years 1932 to 1934 there was resistance, and later underground resistance, to Nazism by labour (SPD and Communist) leaders. But it was fragmented, only a small number of people participated in it, and there was little that it could accomplish. Thus, as the labour elite had already been made relatively docile, and then largely incorporated into the state, it was relatively easy for the Nazi regime – as it took over the state – to overrun it.


## The elite and sub-elite of the media

Freedom of speech and of information are considered as basic democratic rights of all citizens. From a demo-elite perspective, they are important *inter alia* because they protect the autonomy of the media elite which, together with its sub-elite, is crucial for democracy. Once again, as expected, in Britain such freedoms did, in fact, develop during the nineteenth century – while in Germany they did not take root.

## In Britain

In eighteenth-century Britain, the concept of freedom of speech and of the press had not as yet been introduced. At the time, the rulers insisted that the press support all their deeds. By the beginning of the nineteenth century such freedoms came to be considered as legitimate. But their actualization did not come all at once: laws limiting them were only gradually reformed, and coercive repression of editors and journalists was thus only gradually alleviated. The Reform Bill of 1832 attenuated some of the previous restrictions, but overly stringent limitations on the publication of libel, obscenity, treason and so on continued. Only the struggles of journalists and editors, leading to further laws clarifying the legal meaning of these phenomena, reduced the incidence of legally aided repression. The last legal restrictions on the press were removed in 1869, and coercive repression of the press thus ceased.

All this coincided with journalists increasingly manifesting their independence on the symbolic level by criticizing the government and opposing its policies. Under the auspices of steadfast editors, journalists even began publicizing the inside machinations of the establishment. They also wrote of the intrigues, corruption and other disreputable facts concerning the ruling political elite. Thereby they managed to raise public indignation to such an extent as to force resignations, dismissals, and even trials of leading politicians.

For instance, *The Times*, which had previously been the semi-official organ of the government, changed towards the middle of the nineteenth century. Under a new editor, it established itself as a social and political power in its own right. Its staff managed to uncover many unpalatable facts about politicians and many official secrets. Their critical reports of British management of the Crimean War helped bring down the government in 1855. Although these reports infuriated the government there was little it could do about them. For legally aided repression had become increasingly difficult, and eventually impossible, to apply. Those running the paper had also built up its independent power through a wide following among opinion leaders throughout the country, who were willing to stand up for its autonomy. Thereafter, although *The Times* came to be the paper of the establishment, it infused British politics with the idea that the press was to be geared towards an informed public opinion, and independent from the government. The newspaper itself followed a policy that maintained a large degree of such independence.

The *Manchester Guardian* was founded by a reform movement activist in 1821. His staff manifested its independence by aiding the cause of liberalism, consciously battling for liberty whenever possible. It also became a proponent of radical and dissenting public opinion. It favoured a wide array of sociopolitical reforms by democractic methods. Towards the end of the century it supported Irish home rule and during the First World War it supported pacifism, both against the policies of the government. As Merrill (1968) stresses, its independence thus became a true affliction to the powerful.

The *Yorkshire Post*, on the other hand, was a Tory newspaper. Yet during and after the First World War the paper editorially rebuked Conservative leaders, 'an indication of the independence that characterized [its] editorship' (Merrill, 1968, p. 83). Indeed, The *Post* repeatedly criticized the prime minister for the government's appeasing attitude towards the increasing threat posed by Hitler and Mussolini.

The British editors, journalists and reporters of both the left and the right thus gave ample evidence of their relative independence from the government. Together they put before the public relatively reliable (and sometimes damaging) information about the government, a set of widely differing approaches and interpretations of political reality and a variety of critiques of government policies. Thereby they aided the formation of diverse and adversary public opinion, without which the electoral struggles and the periodical changeovers between government and opposition – following elections by a gradually widening electorate – would not have been possible.

## In Germany

In Germany, on the other hand, earlier prospects for media elite independence were not realized. The Prussian constitution of 1849 had contained a bill of rights guaranteeing freedom of expression. In the wake of the revolutionary events of the mid-nineteenth century, liberal newspapers had sprung up all over Germany. But in 1863, Bismarck persuaded King Wilhelm I to issue an edict denying the newspapers the right to criticize the government. The Bismarckian constitution adopted by the North German Federation in 1866, and taken over with only minor changes under the Reich, contained no bill of rights. A law abolishing restrictions on the press was enacted in 1874, but legally aided repression was renewed under Bismarck's anti-socialist legislation of 1878.

In practice, before unification, Bismarck coercively suppressed the writings of Prussian journalists. In the Reich, Bismarck accused some journalists of attacking and maligning him on a regular basis. But he overcame problems such as these by regularly bribing them into making propaganda for his policies. Their independence was thus limited by the fact that some significant part of their material resources accrued from the government.

Under Bismarck's successors, coercive control over the press was loosened. By the turn of the century the German press was as exempt from coercive control as any other European press. This independence, however, was not manifested on the symbolic level. For the latter part of the nineteenth century saw the rise of a 'Massenpresse' or a 'Parteilose Presse', that is to say, a non-partisan press for the 'masses', which sought to be completely apolitical and whose representatives 'studiously avoided editorial comment on political questions'. (Altschull, 1975, p. 232). Thus, even during the short period in which the press enjoyed immunity from coercive repression, its representatives did not utilize it: they showed a marked lack of an oppositional stance towards the government.

This virtual absence of a tradition of press elite independence was reflected in the Weimar republic. The constitution reverted to the doctrine of 1849, affirming freedom of expression. But in practice this right was severely restricted. In the early years of the republic the leftist press was suppressed. In the mid years of the republic the situation improved, but the liberal press became more and more apolitical or politically tame. In the later years of the republic, liberal journalists were dismissed from major newspapers which (with some exceptions) 'had grown soft' (Altschull, 1975, p. 229) or moved more and more to the right. By their 'softness', or docility, many of the press people contributed to the situation in which no major voices were raised loudly and publicly when democracy was being dismantled. They thus contributed to this dismantling by default. Towards the end, in 1930–2, both Communist and Nazi publications were suppressed.

In view of this record of suppression of the press elite and sub-elite and little willingness on their part to stand up to the government, or subservience to it, the rest was practically a foregone conclusion. When it came to power, the Nazi regime had no difficulty in taking over the existing press (consisting of no fewer than 2,483 daily and weekly newspapers) since the press immediately 'rolled over and died as Goebbels took control' (Altschull, 1975, p. 229).

## The academic/intellectual elite and sub-elite

Like freedom of speech, academic freedom is generally considered as integral to democracy. From the viewpoint of the demo-elite perspective this is so because it protects the autonomy of the academic-intellectual elite and sub-elite, which serves as another safeguard for democracy. Interestingly, therefore, although the conception of academic freedom had first developed in Germany, the phenomenon eventually took much firmer root in British universities.

### In Britain

At the beginning of the nineteenth century, the only two existing universities, Oxford and Cambridge, were under the administrative control of the Anglican church. Many of the college fellows were its ordained members, and dissenters were prevented from graduating and from being appointed to the faculty. Moreover, the virtual monopoly of the church over the universities was perpetuated by the state, which had the power to confer university charters.

Tory rule, and an intimate association between the church and the state, at first seemed to preclude the possibility of reform. But the prevalent philosophy among British intellectuals was entrepreneurial-liberal – as epitomized by the classical economists and the utilitarian and liberal philosophers. As liberals, they put major emphasis on the call for limiting the power of the state and the official authorities. In conjunction with this, they forcefully argued for the wresting of control over universities from the church and the state.

This led, in the first instance, to the foundation of University College, London – planned from 1825 onward – as a secular institution, not under church control. Such pressures also led to the establishment in the 1850s of royal commissions to investigate the two old universities. They also led to reforms, enacted in the middle of the century, that eventually abolished the Anglican monopoly in them. But Oxford and Cambridge were thought to have remained bastions of

Toryism. This encouraged the establishment of yet other universities that were to be independent of both the church and the state. This took place gradually towards the middle of the century and onwards.

Once the church's monopoly was broken, state intervention in higher education, too, was minimal. For in the nineteenth century British universities were based on a system of private finance (although this was supplemented by some limited government grants). This meant that the lion's share of the universities' material resources did not derive from the government, and were not controlled by it. This was also one of the factors that lent their staff immunity from administrative government control. For it would have been contrary to the British tradition for the government to intervene within a private and largely self-supporting institution.

Also, following a tradition which had its origin in the Middle Ages, British universities (or colleges in the case of Oxford and Cambridge) were self-governing, that is, organizationally independent institutions. In all universities (except Oxford and Cambridge) ultimate sovereignty resided in a governing body in which academic staff did not form a majority. But only rarely did such a body deprive academics of the privilege of managing their own affairs. The scientific revolution, far from making this system obsolete, increased its importance. For academics of various ranks came to enjoy liberty not merely in teaching – those engaged in scientific research also gained the freedom of inquiry necessary for this pursuit.[4]

The modern system of government finance of higher education did not take shape until after the First World War, when Oxford and Cambridge first accepted government grants. Even then state grants constituted only a third of university finance, and it is only since 1945 that such grants came to dominate university finance in Britain. Although university staff thus came to be dependent on economic resources accruing from the government, they were protected from government control of these resources – and thus from government interference – by the University Grants Committee.[5] The system of British universities as self-sustaining bodies which developed during the nineteenth century, was thus perpetuated well into the second half of the twentieth century.

Academic staff of various ranks were therefore in a position to develop and disseminate a variety of bodies of knowledge and ideas. Among those were liberal ideas which legitimized limitation of state and government power. As Perkin observes, 'in the late Victorian and Edwardian age [the university became] a source of new ideas on how society should be organized, preserved and reformed, and of young men eager to put those ideas into practice' (1989, p. 87). The push for sociopolitical (including democratic) reforms that was evident on the British political scene thus also came in part from the (by then relatively autonomous) academic elite and sub-elite.

## In Germany

In Germany, on the other hand, the ideal of academic freedom was not realized in practice: there was a formal as well as a *de facto* dominance of the state over the universities. By contrast to the situation in Britain at the time, in nineteenth-century Germany the state controlled the universities' finances. That is, it controlled their economic resources, a fact which gained in importance towards the latter part of the nineteenth century. The universities were also administratively controlled by the state: the state intervened in the testing of students (Jarausch, 1982, p. 134). Similarly, a law of 1898 laid down that the promotion of social-democratic purposes was incompatible with university teaching. Consequently, Social Democrats were not allowed on German faculties before the Weimar period (Ringer, 1986, p. 156).

State dominance over universities also prevailed in matters of appointments in general. Professorial appointments to newly created positions were made by the government, while such appointments to existing positions could be – and in quite a few cases were – vetoed by the government. The government-appointed or government-approved professors, in turn, controlled the more junior appointments: lecturers were not likely to obtain their licences to teach unless they won the approval of the professors. This being the case, the government also exerted indirect control over the universities' teaching and research, that is, over their symbolic resources,

Not surprisingly, academic staff, who had constituted strongholds of struggles for liberty in the middle of the century, towards the end of the century no longer manifested such a conflictual stance, and developed increasing submissiveness to the state. Universities became training institutions for holders of public office, and members of the academic elite served the ruling elite as experts. By the beginning of the twentieth century, professors and other teachers 'in addition to being public servants economically, shared the attitude of civil servants' (Pachter, 1978, p. 23).

Accordingly, and in contrast to the situation in Britain, the dominant trend among the intellectuals (both inside and outside universities) was accommodation to state power. On the symbolic level, three modes of such accommodation may be discerned. First, a minority of intellectuals were critical of the government and the state. In the use of their symbolic resources they thus showed independence from the government. But their virulent critiques sometimes led to expulsion by the authorities, and in some cases critical intellectuals accommodated the authorities by emigrating voluntarily. The numbers of independent intellectuals in German society were thus significantly depleted. Second, a larger group of intellectuals withdrew from society into the realm of the spiritual, and became apathetic to politics. Their symbolic resources thus were not used in subservience of the state, but neither did they stand up to it, or adopt a conflictual stance towards it.

Third, an even larger group of intellectuals, including most academics, supported the ruling order and the state's claim to ultimate authority. They idolized the state, and in the wake of the highly influential Hegelian philosophy developed ideologies which served to legitimize its power. Their symbolic resources thus served to promote subservience to the state. In the words of Pachter: 'The majority of intellectuals, too, had adopted a civil service mentality. They were sensitive to the viewpoint of state and nation and often looked . . . up to the symbols of the state. The government was seen as standing above the interests of the various classes and representing the national will' (1978, p. 23). For instance, the dominant direction within the prominent Social Policy Association favoured a paternalistic bureaucracy which was to maximize the welfare of the nation. The independent, critical intellectuals who actually remained in Germany were thus hardly noticeable among the majority of intellectuals who, in one way or another, submitted themselves to the power of the state.

Under the Weimar republic the universities remained state institutions, as the government refrained from restructuring higher education. Appointments continued to be government controlled. Contrary to the situation in the Reich, the government, in which social democrats now participated, intervened in appointments in order to prevent discrimination against candidates with non-conservative leanings. In several cases the government effected professorial appointments against the wishes of the faculty, most of which perpetuated its previous, conservative stance. Until the last years of the republic, government intervention was thus applied most prominently to counteract the previous bias against social-democracies, and to promote left-leaning candidates.

Since the government was now democratic in its form, the academic elite was able to oppose it publicly, denouncing the entire republic as incongruous with the German spirit. It was also able to protest publicly against government intervention in academic affairs, as it had not done under the Reich. Despite its supervision of appointments, the government thus was unable to eliminate opposition to itself. But although slackened, government control of academia through appointments was not eliminated.

The continuing German tradition of state control over universities fitted in with the predominant ideology of German academic intellectuals. As in the days of the Reich, they continued to idolize the authoritarian state. Their ideology also legitimized German chauvinism and heroic leadership. This ideology, in turn, was well suited to legitimize the authoritarian character of the state during the last years of the republic, when democractic institutions were being gradually disposed of. By promoting this anti-democractic, authoritarian line, the academics-intellectuals – wittingly or unwittingly – contributed to the fragility and eventual downfall of German democracy. They also helped prepare public opinion for the ascent of Nazism (Dahrendorf, 1961; Bleuel, 1968).

The tradition of servility of German intellectuals towards the authoritarian state was perpetuated under the Nazi regime: this regime encountered only few voices of protest from among them. Despite its initial suspicion, it had no difficulty in controlling the universities. And, as Weinreich (1946) has extensively documented, large numbers of intellectuals of both high and lower standing in various fields of learning became willing accomplices of Nazi rule and deeds, by providing the ideology which lent them justification.

## Conclusion and discussion

The contention that the relative autonomy of elites forms an essential condition for the transition to stable democracy has been largely (though only illustratively) supported through a historical comparison between Britain and Germany. It could be seen that in Britain, where democracy subsequently stabilized, the four elites and sub-elites analysed had struggled for and eventually gained a significant degree of autonomy from the government. Such autonomy was never absolute, but relatively speaking, in comparison to what had been the case before, it was considerable.

In Germany, on the other hand, where democracy subsequently broke down, there was not one elite which (together with its sub-elite) truly gained relative autonomy. Here the elites, and those immediately below them in power and influence, were partly suppressed by the state, and even when such repressive measures in the end proved unsuccessful, they had the effect of making them especially careful to avoid being crushed. Or else they were administratively controlled by the state and were prevented from gaining significant resources (such as appointments) that were immune from the government. Alternatively, they had – or gained – power, which was partly incorporated into that of the state. They thus, in one way or another, remained partly subjugated by the state, and many of their members (though not all) were more subservient to the state and more docile than their counterparts across the Channel.

These differences between the two countries in elite autonomy, in turn, were related to the different stature of the state in the two countries. In Britain the state had grown relatively strong by the sixteenth century, but thereafter its power was gradually checked. This process found its legitimation in liberal philosophy, which sought the limitation of state power in order to foster individual rights and civil liberties. By contrast, in Imperial Germany the state enjoyed a degree of power that was unequaled in Western countries. The supremacy of this super-state, the 'Obrigkeitsstaat', was legitimized by the prevalent Hegelian philosophy, which proclaimed the state as the locus of the highest morality and the guarantor of freedom.

While all this is well known, it is important to emphasize that in Britain the gradual checking of state power went hand in hand with the transition to democracy not only because it was interrelated with individual rights and liberties. It was also important for the stabiliza-tion of democracy because it was encouraged by, and in turn encouraged the development of the relative autonomy of elites, which guarded those liberties. In Germany, on the other hand, the state's supremacy was an impediment to stable democracy not only because, as is commonly argued, it imposed an overall authoritarian political structure and culture on German society; it also impeded democracy because it was intertwined with the weakness of the autonomy of elites, which therefore could not promote and defend democratic liberties.

The historical overview in this chapter demonstrated how in Britain each of the elites and sub-elites discussed, while increasing its autonomy in the control of resources, also encouraged the organizational settings, symbolic systems and public discourse which helped stabilize democratic liberties and procedures. Conversely, in Germany the deficiency in the independence of the same elites and sub-elites impeded the development of the resilience which might have helped these groups defend democracy by fending off the onslaught on their own bastions of power. Consequently those groups furnished active support, or passive justification, for the dismantling of democracy throughout the last years of the Weimar republic.

This analysis was neither intended, nor equipped, to determine how the British elites and sub-elites would have reacted had they been faced with a phenomenon like Nazism. Importantly, however, in Germany the attack on democracy and the onslaught on the elites' power began well before the advent of Nazism, and led to a pre-Nazi decline of democracy. And it is only because the elites, and those close to them, were not able to defend democracy even before the Nazi takeover that it was so easy for Hitler to demolish its last remnants.

This conclusion is important not for the benefit of scoring points in a theoretical controversy, but for the benefit of democracy. For the argument is not merely that the autonomy of elites is an important part of democracy, but that it is an element of democracy which is *capable of defending the other elements in it*. And it is this that the historical analysis has illustrated. For it was not for lack of a multi-party and competitive electoral system, but – at least in large part – because of deficiencies in previous elite immunity that human rights were crushed and millions of human lives were later extinguished under Nazi rule, a lesson that we will do well to remember.

## Notes

1 The principal sources consulted for the analysis were the following. For Britain: Bédarida, 1991; Hobsbawm, 1962, 1968, 1975; Middlemas, 1979; Perkin, 1969; Thompson, 1980. For Germany: Abraham, 1986; Blackbourn, 1987; Dahrendorf, 1961, 1967; Fraenkel, 1964; Jäger, 1910; Kehr, 1965; Lamprecht, 1904; Mathias and Pollard, 1989; Rosenberg, 1928; 1943; Stern, 1972. On Bismarck: Bismarck, 1889–1919, 1943; Eyck, 1958; Palmer, 1976. On the labour movement: Cole, 1950; Evans, 1982; Grebing, 1985; Ritter, 1981; Roth, 1963. On economic development: Hobson, 1917; Knowles, 1932; Turner, 1985. On the media:

Altschull, 1975; Merrill, 1968. On universities and intellectuals: Bleuel, 1968; Jarausch, 1982; Liedman, 1986; Perkin, 1989; Peterson, 1952; Vaughan and Archer, 1971; Weinreich, 1946.

2   As there may be some lack of clarity on this, it is worth noting that by the academic/intellectual elite I refer to the group of people whose power and influence rests on the creation and dissemination of symbolic resources. It includes – apart from academic university staff – writers, publicists and artists. It is to be distinguished from the overlapping, but much broader category of the intelligentsia, the highly educated, engaged in various non-manual occupations.

3   The text cited is in Hebrew; the translation is my own.

4   In the seventeenth and eighteenth centuries research had taken place in other organizations, such as the Royal Society. It was brought into the universities in the nineteenth century.

5   On this, see chapter 9.

# 8

# *Problems of transition to democracy in Eastern Europe: the cases of the Soviet Union and Poland*

One area in which this lesson may be relevant is in our understanding of the momentous events heralding the collapse of Communism in Eastern Europe. In the West, these events initially called forth a gush of euphoria with respect to the prospects of the Communist bloc's transition to democracy. This was then increasingly intermingled with misgivings. On the basis of the demo-elite theory, I say that as things looked by the beginning of 1992, overall, the euphoria was premature and the misgivings were justified.

## Why misgivings are justified

I base this assessment on a diagnosis of the state of the autonomy of elites and sub-elites in Eastern Europe, both in the past and at the time of writing. This autonomy was long hindered by the pervasive power of what is commonly referred to as the Communist party. According to a well-known anecdote, a Communist dignitary once said to his American counterpart: 'We have so much trouble with one party. How do you ever manage with two?' In truth, however, even this was an overstatement, as the Communist regimes did not have even one party in the Western sense. What is known as the Communist party was, in fact, an over-arching super-elite – with its own sub-elite of apparatchiks and activists – which had seized state power and ruled East European countries. It was not only a gigantic conglomeration of power but, like a jealous deity, did not tolerate any other conglomerations of power besides itself.

Hence, even though some East European countries introduced multi-party elections, while others were on the verge of doing so, this necessarily raised a question mark. The question was whether in some countries these changes might not turn out to be the mere imposition of a superstructure of democratic procedures on an undemocractic base of centrally controlled elites.

This is not to say that the autonomy of elites cannot be achieved in Eastern Europe. But this might not be an easy process, for several reasons. First, although there have been great differences among East European countries, in several of them the repression of elites under Communism was merely an exacerbation of trends that had existed there even before the ascent of that regime. It was thus entrenched in a longstanding tradition. Traditions may change. But tradition-imbued phenomena are obviously more difficult to eradicate than temporary ones.

Tradition aside, the autonomy of elites and sub-elites requires (by definition) that they have control of some resources – including material, organizational and symbolic resources – that cannot be interfered with from above. In the past, resources were concentrated mainly at the top and the centre, and from there flowed downwards and outwards at the discretion of the super-elite. Thus to gauge the evolution of democracy in these countries, to hold our finger on the pulse of this fledgeling, so to speak, what we ought to monitor is not so much declarations and legislation; rather we need to look at the undercurrent of the flow of resources – where they are coming from, where they are going, and who is controlling their flow.

Neither lofty resolutions nor legislation on its own may be expected to bring about an instantaneous decentralization of resources. To be sure, struggles by evolving elites for the control of resources could well be crowned with relative success, as has been the case in the West. But Western experience shows that as a rule an elite does not relinquish resources easily. And the struggle over their control in Eastern Europe may be expected to be more devious than the struggle over multi-party elections as a formal procedure.

One reason for this is that, by 1992, in some East European countries, the people who had staffed the apparatuses of the previous Communist establishment were still in many key positions in the state bureaucracy and in other organizations. Although in some cases the party itself was defunct, and although the erstwhile party position holders had been demoralized, they still had control of existing organizations. They also had inside information on how the system worked. Hence it was easier for them than it was for other people to control the system's material resources and to pull the strings that activated it. So, even if they were no longer as powerful as they had been, and even if they decided to lie low for tactical reasons, this did not necessarily mean that they would voluntarily relinquish the advantages with which these resources endowed them, in favour of newly independent elites.

For democracy to stabilize, we have said, one elite that must gain autonomy is the economic or business elite. In Eastern Europe this would have to happen through the privatization of the economy. This would herald the introduction of new inequalities (to replace the previous ones), but it is nonetheless a condition for democracy. By 1990 there had, in fact, been moves towards a market economy. But these were fraught with major difficulties, and hence 'remain[ed] partial and precarious' (Rigby, 1990a, p. 3). The main barrier to this process was the grandiose dimensions of the property of which the East European regimes had control. This included land, energy resources, quarries, the major means of air, surface and sea transport, the means of communication, the media and infrastructure, in addition to all branches of agriculture and industry. Self-divestment from these holdings would necessarily be a complicated process.

Moreover, even if the states were willing to shed their assets, the question was, who would acquire them? By 1992 some people in the erstwhile Communist hierarchy had managed to accumulate business assets, and some other business people, too, had begun to emerge. In some individual cases they amassed fortunes quickly. But most business people, initially, would probably have to work on a relatively small scale, thus becoming a sub-elite rather than an elite. It would probably take time before they accumulated sufficient capital to acquire the enormous state resources, and thus become a fully fledged business elite.

Provided there was a favourable international climate, there would probably be foreign investment. But while such investment may be capable of participating in the creation of a private sector economy, it is not capable of generating an indigenous, independent business elite. Some budding indigenous capitalists might become attached to foreign firms. But initially they would have to fulfil a satellite role, becoming local representatives of foreign investors. In the short run, they were unlikely to be able to take on large-scale industrial production on their own. Initially they, too, were thus likely to develop into a sub-elite in search of an indigenous elite. Not only the divestment of assets but their acquisition, too, and the creation of a relatively independent business elite, would thus be likely to be a prolonged process.

To be sure, all this could come to pass. But unlike multiparty elections it is difficult to legislate into existence. The intentions of those who introduce competitive elections may be pure and noble. But as long as other elites and sub-elites are not freed from the control of state elites breathing down their necks, even meticulously correct multi-party elections can amount to little more than strewing flowers over a heap of dung.

Thus, although by 1992 some of the countries in Eastern Europe might have been in the throes of a genuine quest for democracy, this did not mean that they all were on the verge of reaching it. Taking account of the substantial differences among the various countries, it has to be said that in some cases their quest might well lead them into a long trek through the wilderness.

## Not all transitions are equal: the cases of the Soviet Union and Poland

While, at the time of writing, in all East European countries a *stable* democratic outcome was still a hope rather than a reality,[1] nonetheless there were differences. Some countries were clearly closer than others to this state. I cannot provide a general explanation for the political transformations in Eastern Europe,[2] nor for the degree of stability or otherwise of the various regimes. But if the thesis on the role of the autonomy of elites as a precondition for the emergence of democracy is well founded, it should be possible to derive an expectation from it. The expectation is that in countries in which the advances towards democracy were more successful, there should be evidence for the relative autonomy of elites and sub-elites *before* democracy emerged. Conversely, where advances towards democracy have been less successful, there should be evidence for the lack of such autonomy *before* the development of democracy began. In other words, it should be possible to explain differences among various East European countries in their advances towards democracy, in part, by the extent of the previous autonomy of elites in them, both before and during the Communist era.

Two countries are being looked at: the erstwhile Soviet Union and Poland. In both there had been some steps towards democracy. In both, these processes were interlinked with traumatic upheavals, they were fragile, and their perpetuation was far from assured. Still, there were disparities between them, and at the time of writing Poland was further advanced on the road to democracy than the Soviet Union had ever been, and it subsequently collapsed before it had implemented the basic procedures of democracy.

## Overtures towards democracy in the Soviet Union

In the Soviet Union,[3] competitive (but not multi-party, and therefore not totally free) elections were introduced in 1989 under Mikhail Gorbachev. Hundreds of political prisoners were freed, and prosecution for political views was ended. In the spring of 1990 the Supreme Soviet abolished the constitutional superiority of the Communist party. Subsequently it also passed a law allowing for freedom of association through multiple parties.

By then, several parties had appeared. The largest of these was the Russian Democratic party, whose stronghold was in the Russian republic. By that time, too, a multitude of new political movements had come into existence, ranging from royalists to greens. Yet multi-party elections were not in the offing yet. Also, a marked lack of stability was noticeable. This was the result of various republics rejecting Soviet rule, with some of them then gaining independence. It was also a result of the collapsing economy.

Moreover, the August 1991 coup of Communist hardliners gave evidence of strong anti-democratic forces and interests still at work in the country. The coup was defeated by Boris Yeltsin, the elected president of the Russian republic, supported by thousands of champions of democracy. This also led to the suspension of the activities of the Communist party and to its collapse. But at the time of writing it is not yet clear whether the anti-democratic forces have been truly defeated. Even after the disintegration of the Soviet Union, the situation continues to be wrought with instability, and it is not clear either whether the newly forged looser union among the republics will be maintained. Importantly, Yeltsin himself seems to have overstepped the powers with which his election endowed him: while the Soviet-Union still existed he issued decrees pertaining not only to Russia but to the rest of the country in general.

## Overtures towards democracy in Poland

In June 1989 a semi-free election took place in Poland: the Communist party and its allies were assured of 65 per cent of the seats in the Sejm, the lower house, while the remaining seats were filled by a free election, as were the seats in the (less powerful) senate. The Solidarity movement, which had previously been legalized, developed a political arm – the civic committees. These became the only legal oppositional organization allowed to stage a full-scale electoral campaign. Nonetheless, many oppositional groups with differing political persuasions were active in the campaign, including a Freedom and Peace movement and other radical student groups.

Despite the limitations of the election, the Communist party suffered a major defeat, which was also a sweeping victory for Solidarity. The ensuing government was a coalition, with Solidarity controlling the cabinet, and with a president from the successor of the Communist party, the Social Democratic party. By the end of 1990, Solidarity had divided itself into two parties, and a free, competitive presidential election took place. In the autumn of 1991 there was a multi-party election for both houses of parliament. The vote was split among many parties, and the elected president, Lech Walesa, had difficulties in forming a government. Nonetheless, Poland's transition to democratic electoral procedures had been practically completed.

Overall, of course, it would be foolish to attempt any predictions of future developments. However, at the time of writing, the overtures towards democracy have been far more advanced in Poland than they have been in the Soviet Union. And since the latter country's disintegration, several of its erstwhile parts – now newly independent states – have been in a near chaotic situation. Poland, on the other hand, despite various crises, has passed the threshold of full electoral democracy.

## An explanation of the differences

My argument is that one major explanation for these differences may be found in the extent of the previous autonomy of elites and sub-elites in the two countries. In line with this argument, it transpires that although neither in Poland nor in the Soviet Union did elites and sub-elites enjoy relative autonomy in the Western sense, nonetheless, from the end of the nineteenth century onwards, their autonomy was much more visible in Poland than it was in the Soviet Union.

I do not claim that this is the sole explanation for the differences in the two countries' advances towards democracy. Both countries have had long and convoluted histories, interspersed with a variety of convulsive transformations, struggles and instabilities. There were also various clear divergencies between them. In Russia the state had been exceedingly powerful. Poland, on the other hand, for long streches of its history had been split up and under foreign occupation, and so had little chance to develop a powerful indigenous state. In the Soviet Union, Communism was an indigenous development; in Poland, it was a foreign import. In the latter country it thus had to face greater hostility from the public, based *inter alia* on national identification. Hence, the Communist party in the Soviet Union enjoyed greater power, compared to its counterpart in Poland. All these differences may themselves have been related to differences in elite and sub-elite autonomy in the two countries. And they may well have left their imprint on the different degress of receptiveness towards democracy in the two countries.

My argument, however, is that the difference in this autonomy in the two countries is an important factor in its own right, which cannot be explained away by the other factors. And it, too, helps to explain the greater success of democracy in Poland compared to the Soviet Union. As in the case of the comparison presented in the previous chapter, life would have been easier for the social analyst had the two countries compared been identical on all counts but elite autonomy. The argument that the source of their differential advancement on the road to democracy has lain in the differences in their previous elite autonomy, could not then have been put into question. However, historical reality was not shaped with the sole purpose of facilitating comparative analysis.

Hence (as in the reasoning which guided the analysis in the previous chapter) here, too, the argument on the relationship between the two variables must rest on demonstration of the mechanisms which relate the one to the other. And indeed, it will be shown that such mechanisms were clearly at work. In the Soviet Union, where elites and sub-elites did not develop a significant degree of autonomy, they were part of the autocratic regime's power structure and helped stabilize it through their complicity. Or else they were largely passive, and helped entrench and legitimize the regime through their very passivity, that is, by default. By comparison, in Poland, where the relative autonomy of elites was more highly developed, the relevant elites fulfilled an important role in furnishing symbols for, and crystallizing centres of opposition to the regime, and in serving as an avant-garde in the battle for human rights and political liberties, and thus for democracy. To substantiate the argument, these differences are surveyed below with respect to the elite (top leadership) and sub-elite (lower clergy) of the church, the leaders and activists of trade unions, and the academic/intellectual elite and sub-elite both inside and outside universities.[4]

Here, as in the previous chapter, the criteria for elite and sub-elite autonomy used are absence of its *successful* coercive repression, relative absence of control exerted on it through state and party administrative, material and symbolic resources, as well as lack of external control of its own administrative, material and symbolic resources. An elite and sub-elite's manifestation of autonomy by willingness to stand up to, as opposed to its submissiveness to the authorities will also be considered. As in the historical comparison of Britain and Germany, this survey is not designed to unearth unknown facts. Rather, the intent is to show how the already well-established ones support my argument.

## The elite and sub-elite of the church

### In Imperial Russia and the Soviet Union

Since Imperial times, the main church, the Russian Orthodox church, and its hierarchy have been administratively subordinated to the state. This was symbolized by the fact that the Tsar acted as head of the church as well. In the early seventeenth century the church had gained some strength, but in the early eighteenth century it was completely subjugated to the state by Peter the Great. After that time the church was administered by the Holy Synod, a directorial committee of bishops which itself was supervised by an 'overprocurator' appointed by the Tsar. The Tsar appointed bishops on the nomination of the synod, and they appointed the lower clergy. In addition, the authorities constantly interfered with the church, issuing administrative instructions on liturgy, the building of churches and the like. For its part, the church establishment reinforced the state by its own subservience, and by preaching submission to it.

Throughout the Communist era the church and its higher and lower clergy suffered varying degrees of repression by the secular authorities, and was utilized by them for their own political purposes. The church was coercively smothered in the 1920s and 1930s: by 1941 95 per cent of the churches and chapels had been closed down, the number of bishops had fallen from 130 to under ten, and the number of priests had been reduced from over 50,000 to less than 500. Many bishops and priests were executed or sent to perish in concentration camps.

The church was allowed to revive during the Second World War to help mobilize the population for the war effort. Subsequently it enjoyed a respite from severe persecution until 1959, when the Communist party resolved virtually to wipe out religion. From 1959 to 1964, under Khrushchev, thousands of churches and over two-thirds of Orthodox theological seminaries and monastic institutions were forcibly shut down. Under Brezhnev persecution was attenuated but the trend was not reversed: over a thousand Orthodox churches were shut down, and the clergy's activities continued to be surrounded by restrictions. New cities were built without churches, and dissident priests were silenced by force. The church hierarchy reacted by continuous submissiveness to its oppressors.

Smaller religious groups asserted themselves more vigorously. These included the Uniate church in the Ukraine, and the churches in Lithuania, Latvia, Estonia, Georgia and Belorussia, which came out in opposition to russification; they also included religious sects (such as Seventh Day Adventists and Baptists) that did not toe the line. Even within the Russian Orthodox church a grassroots splinter group developed, which protested the church's subordination to the dictates of the regime. But the leaders and activists of these groups were subject to even more ruthless persecution. Moreover, the main leaders of the Russian Ortodox church remained subservient to the regime.

Under Gorbachev there developed a more tolerant attitude towards the church, and some major concessions were made to it. But even then the church remained administratively controlled by the authorities, and a severe shortage of churches and clergymen in relation to the massive numbers of believers was maintained. There also continued to be other administrative constraints on religion. There were hardly any religious publications, libraries and the like through which religious symbols could be disseminated. Religious education for children, too, was still severely restricted. In 1988 religious people were still being dismissed from their jobs or demoted, and they were materially disadvantaged in the allocation of apartments and other benefits. The bishops of the Moscow patriarchate were still being handpicked by the party and vetted by the state security officials of the KGB. The church's activities, too, were still controlled by the party. In late 1990 the Supreme Soviet passed a law ensuring freedom of religion, but only with the folding up of the Communist party in the wake of the 1991 coup did its control of the church finally cease.

What had happened before, however, could not now be reversed. In consequence of the long-time subjugation of the church hierarchy to the state, and later to state-party power, its leadership and lower clergy had become largely passive politically. As such, it did not generate and disseminate symbols that could serve as an alternative to the official ones, those promulgated by the Communist hierarchy to legitimize its autocratic rule. In the same vein it also refrained from encouraging sociopolitical protest movements, and it did not stand up for human rights and political liberties. Thus, it became an accomplice to the existing non-democractic regime by its very silence, and it could not fulfil a role in pushing the Soviet Union towards democracy. This omission becomes clearer when the church in the Soviet Union is compared to its counterpart in Poland.

## In Poland

The main church in Poland, the Catholic church, played a totally different role. Not only was it not coercively or administratively subjugated by any regime, but it developed a tradition of opposition to oppression, and served as a rallying point for Polish nationalism under foreign rule. This was the case after Poland's partition at the end of the eighteenth century, when the church and its clergy became the backbone of national resistance. After the First World War, when Poland regained independence, the church leadership supported the government which in turn strongly supported the church and allowed it to gain much influence in politics. But the church reemerged as a bastion of opposition under Nazi occupation: great numbers of religious leaders participated in the underground resistance and many of them were executed or died in concentration camps.

Under Communism, too, the church was a focus of resistance to foreign instigated repression. Despite repeated attempts by the government to overpower the church, it was neither subordinated nor destroyed. From 1948 and up until 1956, the government tried to demolish the church as an independent institution. It did so, first, with respect to material resources: church estates were confiscated, most of its income thus coming under state control. It did so also with respect to symbolic resources: Catholic publications were regulated and religious instruction was practically eliminated from the schools. The government also applied coercion against church personnel who would not collaborate. Many bishops, priests and monks were imprisoned, and some were sentenced to death. Administratively the government gained command of all church appointments, most seminaries were closed and Catholic institutions of higher learning were placed under supervision.

Despite all this, a relatively independent church leadership survived. This leadership manifested its degree of independence by struggling against the restrictions imposed on it, although the struggles were occasionally interspersed by attempts at reaching a compromise. Church leaders were aided in their struggles by the fact that large numbers of Poles supported the church for political no less than for religious motives. Consequently, the regime attempted to manipulate the situation by means of a dummy Catholic organization named PAX. Established in 1945, composed of regime supporters and financed by it, PAX was expected to syphon off support from the church. With its aid, a nucleus of regime-supporting priests was created, with the same aim in mind. But these manipulative attempts to dissipate the church's power, too, were unsuccessful.

In 1956, with the return to power of Gomulka, the previously ousted party secretary, the government was in need of popular support and it sought to attain it with the aid of the church. In consequence, it sought some accommodation with it. It made several concessions to the church leaders, who in return did their best to unite the people behind the government. By 1959, however, when Gomulka had regained control of the situation, the church was exposed to new pressures; religious instruction in public schools (which had been allowed to revive) was curtailed again, as were the lay activities of the church. The church leadership protested, and despite periodic harassment, was able to preserve its position as an elite which was not subservient to the regime. Although the church was forced to yield on some of its earlier gains, its confrontations with the regime once again brought to the fore the pervasive support which it had among the public, and this bolstered its strength. One proof of the church's degree of independence was the continuous existence of the Catholic University of Lublin, the only university not administered by the state in Communist Europe.

In the 1960s the church manifested its independence by increasingly assuming the role of the champion of human rights: it raised its voice in protest against the persecution of various groups, such as student protesters. In the 1970–81 period, the church leadership continued to insist on the unhindered exercise of religious rights. Also, at that time, its emphasis on defending human rights became even stronger. It bolstered its support of workers and others who opposed the regime, thus 'gradually becoming an ally of democratic opposition ...' (Frentzel-Zagorska, 1990, p. 766).

In this, the church leadership was aided by the election of the Polish Pope, John Paul II. As Kennedy explains (1991, pp. 43–7), the increasingly independent stance of the church hierarchy was connected to the Pope's wide-ranging influence in Poland. In consequence of his initiative in this area, the symbolism of religion also became the language of political emancipation, human dignity and human rights. The religious message was also transfused into the Solidarity movement, which the church provided with both symbols of liberation and a model of self-organization.

Yet the church leadership also showed flexibility; it confronted the regime whenever it felt it necessary to do so, but always tried 'to keep at a safe distance from the brink' (Nowak, 1982, p. 12). Despite defending dissident groups, it maintained a distance from them. This oppositional but flexible stance strengthened the church, and it became a mediator between Solidarity and the regime. While strongly supporting the movement, it sought to influence both it and the authorities to avoid violent confrontation.

After the imposition of martial law in 1981, the authorities again launched a campaign of harassment against the church: several priests were imprisoned, religious activists were beaten and a priest was murdered. The church leaders protested, while maintaining their flexibility towards the state, a policy which strengthened it even further. By 1987, the authorities still did not fully recognize the church, but it had become more powerful than ever: new churches were being built, practising Catholics multiplied, and – on the symbolic level – even church access to the media, though still limited, was freer than before.

In autumn 1990 religious instruction was reintroduced into the schools. This, moreover, was but one manifestation of the flourishing of religion and thus of church power with respect to symbols. In addition, religious broadcasts were introduced into state television, and military units were participating in religious processions. Indeed, by then church power had increased to such an extent that some people worried that the boundaries between church and state might be breaking down, and that the church might be on the verge of taking control of the state.

Up until this point, however, there can be no doubt that the church leadership had been a major force in advancing Poland on the road to democracy. For not only had it been an important focus of opposition to the autocratic regime in its own right, but it had done more than that. It had supplied symbols, role models and encouragement to other focuses of opposition. In alliance with those, it had also struggled for human rights and political liberties which – by definition – are of the essence of democracy.

## The elite and sub-elite of trade unions

### In Imperial Russia and the Soviet Union

In Imperial Russia a workers' movement developed in the last decades of the nineteenth century. Secretly organized by revolutionary social democrats in the 1890s, it assumed the name of the Union for the Emancipation of the Working Class. Massive strikes followed in 1895–6. However, there was partial repression: police surveillance in the factories, the hampering of the union's work and the arrest of many agitators. In the period from 1905 to 1914 some legal trade unions were established. The failure of the 1905 uprising led to a decline in political strikes, but the number of economic strikes – for higher wages, shorter working hours and better working conditions – rose.

This period of bloom, however, was shortlived. Under Communism, the trade unions came to be subservient to the party and state. Those in control of unions did not manifest independence by defending workers' rights: although there were some minor labour disputes, those were not organized by trade unions. Themselves administratively controlled by the party, the unions served to control workers by selective allocation of material benefits such as housing, welfare and even places in kindergartens, with advantages going to the faithful. Under Gorbachev, the official unions persisted, but their abilty to control workers declined, because workers were no longer willing to accept them.

The most vocal in this rejection were the miners, who defied the official union by establishing organizations of their own. Many other workers, too, allied themselves with local groups against party bosses.

In 1989 and the beginning of 1990, hundreds of workers' clubs, strike committees and unofficial trade unions sprang up all over the country. These miners' organizations and their organizers instigated prolonged strikes in various districts, aimed at achieving higher wages and better working conditions. In May 1990 they set up an independent Confederation of Labour. They also organized a conference which called for the resignation of the government for failing to fulfil previous promises to miners. The official trade union tried to gain control of this movement, but this attempt proved unsuccessful. In the autumn of 1990 a countrywide independent trade union of miners was created.

Eventually, then, trade unions did become allies of democratic reforms. But this step was belated. During the heyday of Communism unions had been but an instrument of the regime, and they had contributed to the perpetuation of its power. Nothing could have been further from both their intent and their action than working for democracy. The situation in Poland had been entirely different.

## In Poland

Right from the outset, trade unions were more successful in Poland than they were in Russia. Here workers' movements, Proletariat and the Union of Polish Workers, were formed towards the end of the 1880s, and a national workers' organization was established as early as 1891. It gained mass support, and organized the first strikes in 1891–2. The Russian authorities tried to put them down with large contingents of troops and numerous shootings. In general, however, Polish unionists could organize strikes almost with impunity, and they were much less subject to police surveillance than their Russian counterparts. Thus, towards the end of the century, most of the strikes in the Russian empire took place in Poland.

In independent Poland, between the two world wars, trade unions were rather weak. A semi-offical union existed, all unions together encompassed only a relatively small proportion of the workforce, and they were not adamant in defending workers' interests. Strikes did occur, but they were unusual. Still, a plurality of unions of different political colours, some of them attached to political parties, did exist. And unlike the situation in the Soviet Union at the time, they were not totally controlled by the state.

With the entrenchment of Stalinist Communism in 1949, there was a purge of leaders and activists of trade unions. Socialists were weeded out, and the unions' role as defenders of workers' interests was abolished. A law passed by the Sejm made them officially independent, but in reality they were administratively subordinated to the party, replicating the structure of trade unions in the Soviet Union. Their new function was to mobilize their members for the increase of production. Following another ruthless purge of unions' committee members, the party and the government no longer had any trouble with the official trade unions after the autumn of 1950.

However, unlike the situation in the Soviet Union, the Polish regime did not succeed in eradicating oppositional workers' movements. The collapse of Stalinism was followed by the October Movement in 1956, which instigated workers' riots in Poznan and the spontaneous proliferation of independent workers' councils all over Poland. Thereafter, workers' self-organization continued for several years. Another wave of workers' strikes swept through Poland in December 1970 and January 1971, in reaction to price increases. New workers' protests arose in 1976, when an organized oppositional movement emerged, and it remained active until 1980. At that time it culminated in the establishment of an independent trade union, Solidarity.

Under the leadership of Walesa, this organization was created as both a labour union and a large-scale social movement against Communist rule. Solidarity remained legal for only sixteen months. But the 1981 imposition of martial law, aimed at crushing the movement by military force, failed to do so. It managed to limit the active participation of workers in it, but not to eradicate it. Eventually, internal opposition within Solidarity developed, and new working-class leaders emerged during the 1988 strikes. These leaders continued to head the confrontation with the ruling elite, although the official unions that replaced Solidarity after the imposition of martial law never ceased to exist, and today are quite radical.

By the beginning of 1990 interest in Solidarity seemed to be waning: it had only two million members, compared with nearly ten million when its preceding congress was held. Many of its best people went to the civic committees and obtained posts in the government. However, a new oppositional group within Solidarity was created. In this manner the forceful character of Solidarity was revived.

More important, however, was its previous role under Communism. Being but a culmination of workers' protest movements throughout the years, its leadership was among the most active elements in rallying Polish society around opposition to autocracy and around struggles for democractic rights and liberties.

In sum, then, once the rein of Communism was loosened, both countries developed relatively independent trade union elites. The crucial difference, however, was beforehand: in Poland union activists struggled for and achieved a degree of autonomy and helped push the country towards democracy; in the Soviet Union they did not.

## The academic/intellectual elite and sub-elite

### In Imperial Russia and the Soviet Union

In Imperial Russia, the situation of intellectuals was uneven and unstable. At the end of the 1850s the previous control of symbols with its stern censorship on the writings of intellectuals was relaxed, and the number of periodicals mushroomed. Oppositional views among intellectuals flourished, and some periodicals assumed an extremist, radical stance. Yet the government often applied punitive measures to publications, 'now weakening, now intensifying censorship' (Push-karev, 1966, p. 161) and several of them were shut down. In 1865 some intellectual publications gained exemption from pre-censorship, but this did not entail the abolition of punitive measures. From 1865 till 1880, 177 warnings and 52 orders to stop publication were issued. The publication of some periodicals was suspended and 'unreliable' intellectuals were arrested and punished.

All this did not prevent the remarkable flourishing of Russian literature in the latter part of the nineteenth century. And neither did it hinder the development of subversive ideas among intellectuals: from the 1880s many adopted the ideas of Marxism, at the turn of the century many were oppositional liberals, and intellectual organs critical of the government continued to be published. At the beginning of this century intellectuals organized, joined and led various oppositional and radical – including revolutionary – parties.

As for universities, in 1863 they enjoyed a measure of administrative independence: they were granted self-government and the right of the government curators to interfere in their affairs was abolished. In 1884, however, a new law restricted the administrative powers of university authorities. The curator of each educational region became the supervisor of its university. All senior university posts were filled by the various government authorities. An imperial decree restoring university self government was issued in 1905, but in 1908 academic liberties were restricted again. In 1915 academic autonomy was once more recognized by the authorities, though this was to benefit universities for only a short while.

In the years 1918–21 the new Communist rulers instigated a wholesale purge of the intellectuals who remained from before the war. Thereafter there were recurrent waves of coercive repression. During the entire Stalin era, the Stalinist apparatus terrorized Soviet intellectuals. Consequently, according to Feuer (1970), conformist mediocrities came to dominate the research institutes and editorial boards of journals. There were liberalizing tendencies in the first decade after Stalin, and at the beginning of the 1960s intellectuals seemed to be on the offensive. But this elicited another wave of repression by Khrushchev and his successors.

In the late 1960s disaffection was spreading among intellectuals, in particular among the young generation. A literary opposition developed, manifested mostly through clandestine publications, or *samizdat*. The total number of active protesters, however, remained relatively small: at that time 738 intellectuals, for instance, signed protests of various sorts (Feuer, 1970, p. 8). And in the estimate of Rigby (1990b, p. 19) there were altogether a few thousand dissidents. The content of *samizdat* publications reached a wide public through Western broadcasts to the Soviet Union. But the KGB kept suppressing the literary opposition by beating up intellectuals active in non-conformist literary circles, and by sending them to prison, labour camps or exile. Most literary intellectuals thus saw no choice but to succumb to pressures in silence.

The intellectual elite was also subjugated through party administrative control of higher education, which led to the controls of the symbols created and disseminated in the system. This was done by means of party bureaus in institutes and universities, reporting directly to the party apparatus. These bureaus supervised the activities of the Communist members of faculties and institutes, who were expected to be inculcators of Marxist-Leninist ideology. The bureaus also reviewed the work of university administrations and departments. Further, they engaged in various propaganda activities to disseminate their symbols, including the organization of seminars and private discussions with scholars so as to inculcate them with the proper dogma. Interference was severe particularly in the humanities and the social science departments, which were also required to carry out ideological work among students.

Not all academics completely succumbed to this political invasion. According to Joravsky (1977–8), there were various responses, ranging from acceptance to defiance. At one extreme were the scholars who made no attempt to uphold the integrity of their disciplines. At the other extreme were those few who manifested their independence in the control of symbols, not only defending their own disciplines but going beyond this to defend autonomous thought in other fields as well. Some of these also maintained channels of communication with the public through clandestine circulation of writings. They thus emerged as spokespersons of the scientific opposition. This led the party to use much of its strength to continue to subdue intellectual opposition.

The overwhelming majority of scholars, however, were inbetween. They tried to be true to their disciplines, while appeasing the authorities by verbal tricks, by avoiding sensitive topics or by other small concessions. Or else they placated the authorities by silence, while refusing to attack tenets that were contrary to those of Communism. Most scholars thus did something to defend their disciplines, but little more: extremely few became 'self-appointed prophets of truth, rather than licenced advisers on special topics' (Joravsky, 1977–8, p. 37). Moreover, the system effectively encouraged 'slack and conformist spirits' (ibid., p. 41). It could not 'nip all wrong-thinking in the bud', but 'by the early 80s the KGB had pretty well won its long war against the dissidents, most of whom were now either tamed, in the Gulag, in exile, or somewhere worse' (Rigby, 1990b, pp. 19, 16).

How much did all this change with *perestroika* and *glasnost*? According to Pittman (1990), literary journals mostly supported these reforms. But they differed in their views on the forms and the degree of success in their implementation. Thereby they became forums of debate between reformist and conservative factions. But despite the wide range of opinions expressed in them, it seems that they were still administratively under the auspices of the authorities. Gorbachev needed an efficient intellectual machinery to lend legitimacy to his programmes. This led to personnel changes in the Central Committee and the Ministry of Culture. There was also a new appointee as first secretary of the official Writers' Union, which had several journals under its auspices. In addition, new people were brought in as editors and editorial board members on a number of literary journals. The diversity of opinion expressed in them may thus be seen as a 'ripple effect' (Pittman, 1990, p. 111) of these appointments, rather than as a self-propelled development.

The failed coup of 1991 could be expected to have a major impact on the degree of autonomy of intellectuals in the Soviet Union. At the time of writing, however, it was still too early to gauge what this impact would be. What counts for the present discussion, however, is what had occurred before. Most intellectuals had, in one way or another, accommodated to the regime. Active dissidents had been highly significant, but they had remained a small minority. As even those had eventually been defeated by the regime, there was little that Soviet intellectuals could and did do to pave the way towards democracy.

## In Poland

In partitioned nineteenth-century Poland, particularly in the Russian-occupied part, cultural liberties were restricted, and universities were shut down.[5] In this situation, the intelligentsia, the highly educated, supplied ideologues and leaders to all political camps. There was, however, something which united them: the feeling of mission for national survival and independence. The intellectual leaders became the leading force in the fight for national identity by cultivating the symbols of the Polish cultural heritage as the link of the divided country.

The intellectuals' consciousness of a special responsibility persisted in independent Poland in the interwar period. At that time, universities enjoyed a degree of administrative autonomy through self-governing institutions responsible for appointments. The police were prohibited from entering university campuses except by special summons from university authorities. Censorship existed but was mild, and a degree of freedom of expression prevailed. This made it possible for academics and other intellectuals to perpetuate the previous tradition of joining and providing ideologies for various political camps. While many university professors abstained from politics and others supported the government, there were intellectuals both inside and outside of universities who assumed an oppositional stance on the liberal, the left, and the right side of the government. The opposition to the government found expression in social clubs, and in one case, at least, professors (at the Jagellonian University) protested against government maltreatment of prisoners.

With the advent of Communist rule, the old intelligentsia felt estranged from the regime, but a new one was rapidly produced by the party-controlled universities. Many of its members were administratively controlled by the fact that they found channels of mobility in the party, for the sake of which they were prepared to adopt its ethos. Even in the more narrow category of intellectuals proper, such as writers and university professors, the majority propped up the system by their professional activities. But although many intellectuals were willing to serve as a mouthpiece of the regime, the 'output of the ... regime's writers and artists was so bad and so widely ignored that finally party and nonparty intellectuals rebelled against producing it' (Nowak, 1982, p. 1), and widespread intellectual opposition developed.

Marxism-Leninism was always relatively weak in Poland, and the formation of an alternative, relatively independent intellectual elite began before 1956. Its emergence may be traced back to the Crooked Circle Club (KKK) of young intellectuals, formed in 1954, where many leading opposition figures began their activites. At that time, many renowned writers and scholars began to display some independence by denouncing the misdeeds of the 'preceding' period with a new bluntness. This trend reached its peak in 1956. By 1957 two critical intellectual periodicals were shut down, and later the Gomulka regime revived censorship and restrictions on state publishing houses. But the limitations were less rigorous than before.

Although the party exerted administrative control by maintaining vigilants in universities, academic freedom was substantially greater than it had been. Some professors previously dismissed for their political views were reinstated. This led to a relaxation of symbolic control as well. Gradually philosophers and sociologists whose works had not been published before gained the ability to publish officially. Adherence to Marxism facilitated an intellectual's career, and its outright critique was not tolerated. But intellectuals manifested partial independence by perfecting the art of veiled criticism, which the authorities tolerated.

Eventually attempts at coercive repression gained momentum: a drive was launched against discussion clubs and particularly the Crooked Circle Club, which was closed down in 1962. At that time a leading intellectual died while in police custody, the freedom of writers to travel abroad was severely restricted and there was a stiffening of repressive measures against intellectuals. In 1963 two Warsaw non-conformist literary weeklies were liquidated. But this repression was not really successful, as evidenced by the fact that the writers responded with an open strike against the periodical which was to replace them. Intellectual ferment continued to simmer, and some enclaves of (limited) independence in non-conformist groups of intellectuals, artistic and professional organizations, survived. This, despite the fact that their leaders periodically suffered arrests and other types of harassment.

Such independence was evident in particular in the revolt of students and intellectuals in 1966–8. This involved a protest against censorship and party attempts to limit academic freedom. It led to the dismissal of some professors. Yet ferment continued, with its centre shifting to Warsaw University. Acquiring the overtones of a political opposition, it gained momentum in the mid 1970s. At that time, unofficial journals and publishing houses proliferated, evading censorship. The political police organized hunts for printing presses and jailed those who participated in them, but it could not stop them.

The alternative intellectual elite became even more evident in the Solidarity Period, and after the imposition of martial law in 1981. After the early 1980s members of this elite acted in conjunction with Solidarity, or with other underground organizations, to spread non-conformist ideas and information. Some non-conformist intellectuals were more moderate, others were more radical – all enjoyed wide social support. Although they were still screening their activities from the police, they had more opportunities than before to make a living, and thus greater material independence.

Overall, the variety and durability of non-conformist intellectual activity in Poland, which had to be hidden from the authorities but could not be suppressed by them, was unequalled in any other Communist country. Thus, more than any other intellectuals in the Communist bloc, Polish intellectuals assumed the task of disseminating information and generating counter-symbols to those of the regime, and of thereby encouraging the type of public discourse that forms an essential (though not the only) condition for democracy.

## Conclusion and discussion

In this chapter I have argued that advances towards democracy in all East Europen countries are problematic because of longstanding deficiencies in the autonomy of elites in them. The opening up of the electoral process and, in some countries, multiparty elections entail relatively simple procedures that can be introduced in a short timespan. But their value and stability are doubtful without the evolution of elite autonomy. And the struggle for such autonomy may be more arduous than that for formally competitive elections.

It has further been argued that the more successful overtures towards democracy in Poland, as compared to the Soviet Union, may be partly (though not exclusively) explained by the differences in the previous autonomy of elites and sub-elites in the two countries: neither has spawned elite autonomy in the Western sense, but the independence of the relevant groups had been substantially greater in Poland than it had been in the Soviet Union. This has been shown with respect to three of those groups.

In the Soviet Union the repression of the main church was more successful than in Poland: the church's establishment had been subservient to the state, while in Poland it never succumbed to the regime. In the Soviet Union trade unions had been pliable instruments of the regime, by 1990 the official trade unions still existed albeit in a weakened state, and independent unions had just begun to develop. By contrast, in Poland there had been a long tradition of independent workers' organizations, leaders, and activists, and a fully fledged independent trade union existed from the early 1980s. In the Soviet Union intellectuals had long been repressed, with small networks of dissidents actively resisting this repression. In Poland, repression was milder and less successful, and there was much more formidable and widespread independent intellectual activity.

The relevant elites and sub-elites in the Soviet Union were thus on the whole (though with the significant exception of the small number of intellectual dissidents) either part of the autocratic system, or largely silent. Hence they helped the entrenchment of the regime simply by failing to stand up to it. They did little to give rise to opposition, to campaign for political rights and liberties, and therefore to further the emergence of democracy. The parallel elites and sub-elites in Poland, on the other hand, were much more active in generating opposition to the regime on both the symbolic and organizational levels, and in championing civil liberties. Thus they helped weaken the regime and set the foundations for democracy.

In part, at least, these differences may be explained through the strength of the Communist party in the two countries. In all of Eastern Europe the party has acted as a super-elite, which made it difficult for others to gain independent power. But there were differences. In the Soviet Union, the party's leaders used it as an effective instrument of control over other contenders for power. They did so by maintaining party cells in all major organizations, including the government bureaucracy, the military, the police, the secret police, and industry. Through them, these organizations' personnel were all subject to penetration and checking by the party hierarchy.

In Poland, too, the party leaders implanted their cells in various bodies such as factories and offices. Yet the Polish party was not as mighty as the Soviet one. Its ideology did not carry much appeal. Also, it had to confront an initially hostile population, which considered it as an agent of Soviet domination. Under these circumstances, it had to proceed much more cautiously.

Importantly, however, the differences in party strength, were themselves – *inter alia* – also the outgrowth of differences in elite autonomy: the relatively smaller stature of the party in Poland as compared to its counterpart in the Soviet Union can be partly explained by constant elite and sub-elite opposition to it, which sapped its legitimacy and strength. Whatever elements of elite autonomy existed in the two countries were thus in reverse proportion to the monolithic power of the party in them.

In general, then, the analysis has once again elucidated the importance of elite autonomy for democracy. In the Soviet Union, where the party was stronger and the autonomy of elites and sub-elites was proportionately weaker, the overtures towards democracy have lagged behind those in Poland, where the party was relatively weaker and the autonomy of elites and sub-elites was commensurately stronger. Like the lesson from pre-Nazi Germany this, too, is a lesson that we will do well to remember for the sake of the future of democracy. It is a lesson, moreover, which Western democracies either have not adequately memorized, or else are in danger of forgetting, as will be shown in the next chapter

## Notes

1  For a definition of stable democracy see chapter 3.
2  For such an explanation with respect to the Soviet Union, see for instance Rigby, 1990b.
3  The Soviet Union as an entity only is being looked at. The situation in the republics is beyond the boundaries of this discussion.
4  The main sources consulted for this analysis were the following. On Imperial Russia and the Soviet Union: Abramovitch, 1962; Fainsod, 1953, 1958; Kaiser, 1976; Keep, 1963; Pares, 1962; Pipes, 1989; Pushkarev,

1966; Rigby, 1990a; Schwartz, 1961; Seton-Watson, 1952, 1967; Smith, 1973; Thompson, 1990; Wallace, 1961; Wildman, 1967. On Poland: Barnett, 1958; Frentzel-Zagorska, 1989, 1990; Gamarnikow, 1967; Hibbing and Patterson, 1991; Leslie, 1980; Polonsky, 1972; Staniszkis, 1990. On the church in Imperial Russia and the Soviet Union: Bociurkiw, 1966; Dunlop, 1989. On the church in Poland: Nowak, 1982; Ramet, 1984. On the academic/intellectual elite in Imperial Russia and the Soviet Union: Feuer, 1970; Hans, 1964; Joravsky, 1977–8; Pennar, 1960; Pittman, 1990; Rigby, 1990b. On the academic/intellectual elite in Poland: Hirszowicz, 1978; Karpinski, 1987; Kennedy, 1991; Rey, 1957; Schneiderman, 1963.

5   This was not the case in Austrian-ruled Galicia.

# PART V

# MEANWHILE IN THE WEST: PROBLEMS AND POTENTIAL OF DEMOCRACY

# 9

## Elite autonomy under siege and problems of Western democracy

Suppose, for the sake of argument, that Communist regimes have completed their journey and have reached the promised land of Western-style democracy. What does this promised land look like? If and when they are ready to adopt democracy, will democracy be worthy of being adopted? On the basis of the analysis on the independence of elites, I now argue that Western democracies have some severe problems of their own in this respect. Although their achievements have greatly exceeded those of other regimes, they have been far from adequate.

Even in Western democracies, elite autonomy has never been securely locked in and impervious to attacks. There has never been a golden age in which powerful elites – particularly those of the state and the government – have refrained from using their resources in order to threaten or infringe on the autonomy of other elites and sub-elites in the control of *their* resources in a manner that does not tally with democratic rules (the subjugation of elites). Frequently, Western elites have also diminished elite autonomy by entering into non-legitimate, excessively cosy relations with other elites for exchanges that infringe on their mutual autonomy in the control of resources, and do not tally with democatic principles and rules either (the collusion of elites). And struggles have always been necessary to sustain elite autonomy even in its far from perfect state.

# An explanation

## The social context

Just as the relative autonomy of elites is not born in a social vacuum, so infringements of elite autonomy are not born in a vacuum either. The social context relevant to these phenomena includes, for instance, the broader economic and organizational structures within which individuals – including elites and sub-elites – operate and which channel the opportunities they may have to subjugate other elites or collude with them. It also includes general philosophies or ideologies such as those relating to the augmentation or limitation of state power, which may either legitimize or delegitimize the subjugation of other elites by the elites of the state. It further includes general achievement oriented norms commonly prevalent in modern societies, which may put more or less of a premium on success by whatever means. Finally it includes the general climate of public opinion, which may be more or less sensitive over the observance of democratic rules and therefore more or less permissive towards the subjugation and collusion of elites.

Although these social-contextual factors are important in explaining the phenomena under study, it would be incorrect to view them as determining those phenomena. For this context is itself interrelated with several factors which operate at the level of elites and sub-elites themselves, and which are no less important in shaping their actions in this respect. These include the elites' own interests, the balance of power among them and the norms and rules by which they themselves act.

## Interests and temptation

The interests, and hence the temptation, which the elite of a government has to subjugate other elites and sub-elites in an authoritarian manner has frequently been overwhelming. A government is not surprisingly irked by other elites that show their independence by opposing it, criticizing it, or in other ways jeopardizing its power. Since the government has both the interest and (to varying degrees) the ability – or the resources – to attack the power bases of other elites, much self-restraint on its part is needed to prevent it from doing so. And such self-restraint is often in short supply.

By the same token, there are also pervasive interests, and hence a constant temptation, for the collusion of elites. For one elite and sub-elite frequently controls resources which another elite and sub-elite requires or covets. Political party leaders and activists need material resources, such as funds for election campaigns. If they are unable to access state coffers for this purpose, they want monies which capitalists control. Capitalists need resources that are administratively controlled by politicians and bureaucrats – including contracts, subsidies, tax exemptions and the like. Bureaucrats of various ranks strive for administrative/material resources in the form of promotions, ever larger bases for empire-building, and post-retirement posts in the private sector, and some of these may be controlled by politicians or capitalists. Journalists and reporters cannot function without a type of symbolic resource that is partly controlled by politicians, namely political information, while politicians need a symbolic resource controlled by journalists, namely favourable exposure in the media. Hence the interest of elites and sub-elites in entering into collusions with each other to exchange resources, even in less than legitimate ways.

## The balance of power among elites

By themselves, however, and even within a wider social context, the interests which government elites have in subjugating other elites and sub-elites, or which these have in colluding with each other, cannot serve as an adequate explanation for these practices. For the interests are virtually always there, yet the practices do not always occur. Another explanation concerns the balance of power among the groups involved. A powerful elite, especially a powerful government, which already has control of major resources at the expense of other elites and sub-elites, will find it easier to gain control of the remaining resources which they still have. And elites or sub-elites that are deficient in the control of resources anyway will find it more difficult to defend their control over the remaining resources.

Among the resources that are important in this respect are personal resources of ambition and determination. A government, one or more of whose members are especially ambitious to perpetuate their power and determined to do so even by bearing down on other elites, and other elites whose members are especially deficient in determination to resist such attacks, are both likely to contribute to the subjugation of elites in their own political arena.

In a way, this explanation is circular. But a circular explanation is not necessarily a cardinal sin. Frequently, as in this case, it points to a vicious circle: government power leads to more government power. The other elites' weakness leads to their being subjugated even further. As has been clarified through the historical analyses in the previous part of the book, government and state power, in turn, is embedded in, or limited by, wider ideologies or philosophies that lend it varying degrees of legitimation. The lesson to be learned from this can be variously interpreted, a topic that will be resumed further on.

In the meantime, it is clear at any rate that power as such, and even in combination with interests, cannot serve as adequate explanations for the subjugation and collusion of elites: under certain conditions both may be restrained, at least to some extent.

## Contradictory rules of democracy

Restraint on the subjugation and collusion of elites is possible when the rules and conventions proscribing such practices are unequivocal. This generally goes hand in hand with clearly specified sanctions for their transgression. Thus people are more likely to adhere to restraining rules when they are crystal clear and when they are relevant for them personally by being enforced. In other words, elites and sub-elites are more likely to adhere to rules restraining them from infringement on the autonomy of other elites and sub-elites when the contravention of these rules carries substantial penalties. Particularly effective is the penalty of dismissal, which may jeopardize an elite member's material benefits and basis of power. Conversely, they are more likely to disregard the codes of conduct when, due to lack of clarity and sanctions, these codes have no teeth.

Hence a further explanation for the subjugation and collusion under study can be found in the fact that different principles and rules of democracy, pertaining in particular to the relations among elites, are frequently inconsistent, contradictory and controversial. As noted before, the central overt principle of democracy is the electoral principle. By this principle the power to govern derives from elections. The electoral principle also implies the ability of the elected government to carry out its policies. For this, the government must be able to elicit the – voluntary or forced – cooperation of other elites and sub-elites. This is also necessary in order to prevent a stalemate and hence the paralysis of the system. But then there is also the implicit meta-principle of the autonomy of elites (concretely expressed in democratic rules of freedom of association, of information and of expression). By this principle other – non-elected – elites are entitled to autonomous power. Yet these two principles are frequently on a collision course with each other.

Because of this, practices that are in transgression of one principle may be carried out under the mantle of legitimacy of the other principle. Thereby these practices are located on the borderline of what is legitimate and of what is illegitimate by democratic rules. And where rules are contradictory, they are also controversial: contradictory principles enable each group to promote practices that fit that rule which works in its own favour.

An elected government is apt to put major stress on the electoral principle. Endeavouring to carry out policies for which it believes it has an electoral mandate, it is apt to see attempts by other power holders to frustrate its purpose as illegitimate. The government may therefore feel that it has a right, indeed a duty, to make the system workable by overruling their opposition. At the same time, these others can invoke the democratic principles of freedom of speech and of association to back up their claim for autonomous power. And (based on the lesson of history) we know that unless they defend their autonomy, even the electoral principle – the very principle by which governments exert authority over other elites – is in jeopardy.

## Inconsistent codes of elite behaviour

In the wake of the life-work of Talcott Parsons, it has long been one of the stocks in trade of the social sciences that the modern world is distinct in the major emphasis it puts on norms of universalism, as against those of particularism. That is to say, rules based on criteria of objective entitlements predominate over norms based on criteria of personal or political connections, or on group solidarity. However, while objective codes are probably more institutionalized today than they were in the past, they are not all-pervasive. In some settings – including particularly settings in which elite relations are embedded – personal-political or group codes of behaviour persist, and they are applied side by side with objective ones. Occasionally they even overrule them.

This, for instance, is the conclusion one may reach on the basis of the famous study by Rosabeth Moss Kanter, *Men and Women of the*

*Corporation* (1977). This study of a large American corporation shows that where promotions to top managerial positions are concerned, not only universalistic criteria of aptitude and ambition, but particularistic criteria of similarities to present incumbents, gender, and personal trust are taken into account as well. And this corporation, most likely, is typical of a host of other corporations of its kind, operating in similar settings.

Also in this context, Danet (1989, p. 45) reports on several studies which tap particularism, for instance in the form of old-boy networks. They show that these norms and practices are well entrenched in Western democracies, including Britain and the United States. In Western countries the application of such criteria would be extremely rare in the allocation of routine goods and services; these can be easily obtained by universalistic criteria alone. But when it comes to goods and services which are more difficult to obtain – such as top-level appointments or access to exceedingly scarce benefits – personal, political and group connections continue to play a role.

Thus particularistic criteria for the distribution of resources have not disappeared. They have merely moved up a notch and have come to be confined to the higher rungs of the hierarchy. Which is another way of saying that they coexist with objective ones precisely at the level at which elites and sub-elites interface with each other or with would-be elites. And it is this coexistence of seemingly incompatible codes which makes it relatively easy for elites and sub-elites to collude with each other. For while such collusions may run counter to universalistic norms, it is easy for those involved to invoke particularistic norms to justify them. And when inconsistent norms coexist rather comfortably in people's action-space, it is unlikely that real sanctions would be attached to them.

## The subjugation of elites and sub-elites: some recent examples

It is for different combinations of these reasons, then, that from Europe, through the United States, to Australia, the history of Western democracies has been replete with instances of both the subjugation and collusion of elites and sub-elites. While this has been the case ever since the inception of democracy, elite autonomy has been under siege particularly in recent years. In support of this argument some recent celebrated examples of such phenomena are now listed. Thereby the intent is not to expose hitherto concealed facts, but to bring out the significance of already well publicized ones, in the light of this argument.

At first sight the phenomena listed below are separate from each other and have little in common. In fact, however, they have a common denominator in that they all entail attempts at the subjugation of elites and sub-elites by encroaching on or threatening their control of resources.

## Restricting freedom of information

One example of this kind concerns recent restrictions on access to an important symbolic resource – information – in the United States and Britain. It is no secret that after 1980 the US government cut down the spread of information. It did so by reducing the volume of material previously available through government agencies (using economy as a justification). It also expanded the range of information protected by government classification in the name of national security. This was supplemented by threats of prosecution against the media for publishing information, frequently arbitrarily labelled secret. A further back-up has been the use of contracts to bind civil servants to lifelong censorship, and the subjecting of their writings and speeches to censorship, to prevent them from publicizing waste and corruption (Demac, 1984; Collins, 1988; Jansen, 1988).

In Britain, much publicity has surrounded the attempts by the government to prevent the media from reporting the views of leaders of the Irish Republican Army (IRA), and to suppress the publication of *Spycatcher*, the memoirs of a retired intelligence operative. This, however, was merely part of a wider pattern. During its eleven years in office, the Thatcher government resorted to the Official Secrets Act of 1911 – which made it illegal for public servants to disclose any information without authorization – more frequently than any previous government. By 1988, that government had used the Act in at least twenty-four prosecutions, compared with thirty-four in the previous sixty-eight years.

At the beginning of 1990, a new Official Secrets Act came into force in Britain. It was hailed by the government as a 'charter of liberty' because, compared to the 1911 Act, it more clearly defined the categories of secret information which were not to be divulged.[1] It also included the provision that the prosecution would have to satisfy specific tests of harm involving unauthorized disclosures by most people who are not intelligence officers, including journalists. It was nonetheless condemned by critics, including the National Council for Civil Liberties, as a further tightening of government control on information. This was so chiefly because of its failure to provide for a public interest or previous publication defence. Therefore it was considered by this body's representatives that it gave the government greater power to conceal information than the previous Act had done before.

The British government's attempts to restrict freedom of information were evident also in its treatment of the national, but ostensibly independent British Broadcasting Corporation. As my own study on this topic has shown (Etzioni-Halevy, 1987), subtle but increasingly formidable pressures were brought to bear on it in order to bring it to heel. Recently these pressures were exacerbated further, a major instrument used being that of appointing to the BBC's board of governors people sympathetic to the government. Another instrument was that of subtle intervention in programming, even in news and public affairs coverage, thus leading to the gradual taming of the one-time unruly national broadcaster. Other broadcasting companies were put under similar pressure. According to the periodical *Labour Research* (May 1989, pp. 9–11), from 1979 to 1989 the government put pressure on television companies to ban, reschedule or withdraw, at least seventeen programmes on Northern Ireland.

## Union bashing

A second, seemingly unrelated, example has been concerted attacks by the British and American governments respectively on the trade unions, popularly known as union bashing. These attacks have taken the form of encroaching on both their material and their administrative/organizational resources, thus limiting their ability to manifest their independence by waging industrial conflict.

In Britain, since the Conservative government came to office at the end of the 1970s a plethora of laws aimed at restricting the organizational power of unions has been passed. These included *inter alia* the law that industrial disputes must be confined to employees and their employers, secondary action being outlawed. Also, unions were legally required to hold secret ballots before industrial action, and failing to do so made them liable for prosecution and claims for damages. Closed shops now had to be affirmed by secret ballots to avoid claims of unfair dismissal from those who refused to join the unions. Unions were also required to hold secret ballots for elections of executive committees, as well as for political funds (*Labour Research*, June 1987, p. 16).

On its own, each of these laws looks reasonable and justifiable, particularly in the face of the previous (some would say excessive) accumulation of trade union power. But together they nonetheless can be seen to have been part of a concerted strategy aimed at weakening unions and removing several of their (by now) traditional immunities. In addition, the police were used more than previously to maintain rights of access to, for instance, coal pits by strike-breakers. These were precisely the rights which union leaders felt they had to restrict in order to succeed in industrial action. For this and other reasons, unions have indeed been weakened, and union membership has slumped considerably in recent years: in 1979 nearly 50 per cent of British employees belonged to unions; in 1988 union membership was down to about 35 per cent of the workforce (Kettler and Meja, 1988).

In America, union power peaked during the Second World War, but in 1947 the Taft-Hartley law restrained such power by requiring the cooling off of strikes through compulsory arbitration, and by reducing closed shops to a minimum. The strongest blow to union power came in 1981, when President Ronald Reagan responded to the general strike of the unionized flight controllers by summarily dismisssing them and replacing them by non-unionized ones. Thereby he instantly destroyed an entire trade union.

Another step in what has also been referred to as the progressive sterilization of trade unions came in 1991. At that time, the administration – with the cooperation of Congress – once more made short shrift of a general strike it considered as damaging to the economy, this time the strike of railway workers. On the request of the transport secretary, legislation to prohibit the strike was speeded through Congress in a matter of hours, and was immediately signed by President George Bush. Thus it took no longer than forty hours to force several hundred thousands of railway workers back to work.

American unions have still had some achievements. In 1989 they succeeded in obtaining a raise in minimum wages, and they have succeeded in convincing Congress to legislate for a compulsory notice of two months before dismissal. But they have been working more as pressure groups lobbying Congress, and they have shown less of a tendency to manifest relative independence through their traditional conflictual means of strikes and other industrial action: barring some exceptions, strikes have been mostly small scale and on the local level. As in Britain, the trends of the weakening of independent union power have been reflected in a decline in membership: in 1968 30 per cent of American workers were union members; by 1988, membership comprised no more than around 17 per cent of the workforce.

## Repoliticizing the bureaucracy

Another example from a seemingly separate area concerns recent changes towards greater politicization in the government bureaucracy in both Britain and the United States. In Britain, as a result of previous struggles and reforms, the bureaucratic elite had gained a large degree of control of the combined material/administrative resource of its own appointments and promotions. It had thus gained the ability to stand relatively aloof from party-politics (though not necessarily from all political controversy). Recently, however, it has no longer been – like Caesar's wife – above suspicion. During her term of office, Prime Minister Margaret Thatcher took a more interventionist role than did her predecessors in the major (previously relatively independent) resource of bureaucratic appointments and promotions. This led to a greater intrusion of political criteria into bureaucratic staffing and decison-making than had previously been the case.

This was so not in the sense that appointments and actions became party political. Rather, it took the form of top appointments and promotions going to people who were enthusiastic about the government's policies, while those who showed no such enthusiasm tended not to flourish. Although prime ministerial intervention concerned chiefly the appointments at the highest level (such as those of permanent secretaries and deputy secretaries), top appointees were then influential in more junior ones – leading to a trickle-down effect of subtle but significant bureaucratic politicization (Ridley, 1983; Wass, 1985; Ponting, 1986; Hennessy, 1989).

In the United States, following previous reforms, the government elite has some, but only limited control of the resource of bureaucratic appointments: only a relatively small top layer of officials in the federal administration can be political appointees. But here, too, there has been a partial regression to a more politicized pattern. Thus, the numbers of political presidential appointees have tripled in the last twenty years.

President Reagan used to make as many patronage appointments as he could to top positions not insulated by public service rules. He did so to a greater extent than his recent predecessors, and there were signs that this trend was being perpetuated by President Bush, for instance in his diplomatic appointments.

Further, closer political control was imposed on civil servants by administrative means: political appointees were given a greater leverage over career officials of various ranks than had been the case before. Such career officials could now be relocated even against their will. While only a small proportion of actual relocations were forced ones, career officials soon realized that such relocations were possible. Not surprisingly, this made most of them more politically compliant. And those who did not take the hint had close political supervision imposed on them (Goldenberg, 1984).

## Teaching higher education a lesson

An additional, ostensibly disparate, instance concerns increasing government pressures on higher education, primarily in Britain. In the postwar era, British universities have been funded chiefly by the government; in the 1970s they depended on the central government for about three-quarters of their revenue, that is, their material resources. They were nonetheless protected from government interference by the University Grants Committee (UGC), designed to allocate funds to universities while keeping the government at arm's length from the institutions it funded. Although the universities were subject to some UGC control, which increased somewhat in the 1970s, outside intervention in their affairs was still marginal.

In the 1980s, however, pressure began to be applied to universities through infringement of their material resources: grant reductions which led to the early retirement of large numbers of senior academics. These reductions also led to a widespread feeling among the remaining academics that their positions were under threat. In addition, the UGC was abolished, and replaced by the new University Finance Commission. This commission, which for all practical purposes was an agent of the government, has exercised a much firmer grip on the universities than the UGC did in the past: through a variety of contractual funding arrangements, it has had the power to control their policies. In this manner, the universities were brought practically under the direct administrative control of the government.

In conjunction with this, academic staff have lost some of their previous control over the combined material/administrative resource of tenure of office: such tenure was all but abolished. The 1988 Education Reform Act provided for an appropriate body capable of dismissing academic staff by reason of 'redundancy' or for other 'good cause'. The redundancy provisions applied only to persons whose contract of employment commenced or was altered after 20 November 1987. This, however, signified that tenure had now been abolished for academics appointed or promoted after that date (Griffith, 1988). Unless the Act is changed, the next generation not only of junior academics, but of senior academics as well, will be untenured. The aim of these reforms in teaching higher education a lesson and in circumscribing its manifestations of independence, as well as the achievements in this respect, are clear: 'with university lecturers feeling insecure in employment an important source of criticism [of the government] has been subdued' (Bealey, 1988, p. 188).

## The collusion of elites and sub-elites: some recent examples

The following recent phenomena ostensibly involve an entirely different facet of politics. It will be seen later on, however, that they are closely related to the previous ones: they, too, involve trespassing on the autonomy of elites. However, they involve the voluntary, illicit collusion (rather than the subjugation) of elites and sub-elites.

### Extraparliamentary interests of parliamentarians

In Britain there has been a longstanding custom, whose dimensions have grown even further in recent years, for members of parliament to maintain extraparliamentary interests: to receive financial benefits through connections with private companies and trade unions. The standards of propriety require that ministers divest themselves of any interest they may hold in a company, but other members of parliament have not been required to do so. Various constitutional provisions, Acts and parliamentary resolutions have prohibited members accepting payment for parliamentary services. But these provisions have been vague. As Pinto-Duschinsky points out, they merely mean that 'there must be no explicit *quid pro quo* though, in practice, an implicit one is all right' (1981, p. 240).

Members of parliament have been required to register their pecuniary interests in registers of members' interests which are available for inspection by the public. These registers have some shortcomings. For instance, members are not required to register the magnitude of their interests: some may be major, others may be trifling. The registers still present the closest available approximation to what is actually going on.

From the 1987 *Register of Members' Interests* it transpires that a significant proportion (26.7 per cent) of (particularly Conservative) MPs have held directorships of companies. Also, a significant proportion (34 per cent) have held consultancies for companies and lobby organizations – the word consultancy being a euphemism for representing the client's interests in parliament. Indeed, the practice of large companies employing MPs as consultants to represent them in parliament is so widespread that most of them have had at least one MP in their employment. A significant proportion (23.6 per cent) of (almost exclusively Labour) members, for their part, have been sponsored by trade unions. Such sponsorship entails payments helping to defray their electoral and constituency expenses, such as those of maintaining an office and a secretary in the electorate.

My own study (Etzioni-Halevy, 1990), based on interviews with members of parliament,[2] has shown that in return members have supplied those that retain them with a variety of resources in the form of services. Companies or unions have tended to retain members who are in sympathy with their general aims and so would be promoting them in any case. Nonetheless, it was reported by respondents that there is much that parliamentarians have been doing specifically in favour of their retaining companies or unions. They have supplied them with symbolic resources: pertinent information and advice, including information on the House of Commons and on the government's way of thinking about matters that are of concern to them. In this manner they have provided them with an 'early warning system', which was 'worth a lot' to them. They have also provided their clients with access to the House, to ministers and to the civil service, for instance by arranging visits, which otherwise might be more difficult to obtain.

Members have also become an organizational outpost, so to speak, for their retainers, by lobbying on their behalf behind the scenes. At times members of parliament have become lobbyists on their own, and at times they have become part of lobbying firms. Either way they have lobbied parliament on behalf of their clients, for instance in the party room, in a committee or in parliament itself. While members generally vote according to the party line (except on matters of conscience), and while they cannot vote on issues in which they have an interest, they can lobby for legislation in its preliminary stage. Or else, lobbying may take place by having 'a quiet word with the minister' on behalf of a retainer. The member would then have to declare his or her interest. Nonetheless, the possibility that a minister might be influenced by members' submissions on behalf of their clients cannot be ruled out.

Most respondents saw these practices as legitimate although, not surprisingly, Conservative members were more likely to legitimize private interests while Labour members were more likely to justify union sponsorship. Legitimation of both practices was generally based on several norms and lines of reasoning. One of these was British tradition. In the past, parliamentarians were not paid, and then were paid only small amounts. Following this tradition, they continued not to be paid 'full' salaries, that is, they were earning less than they would have been had they worked in the private sector or in the civil service. Hence they had to supplement their incomes. Further, if they were required to sever their links with companies they had worked for before, and then lost their seats in parliament, they might be too old to find new jobs.

In addition, members connected with companies, so the reasoning went, were better able to keep in touch with the community. They were not 'cut off' from the 'real world' and this made them better MPs. Similarly, trade union sponsorhip was said to serve as a 'grassroot connection'. Moreover, respondents argued that it was basically a matter of honour. Members of parliament were called 'honourable', and this had to be relied on. Although they were retained by companies or sponsored by unions, they were not 'bribed' or 'bought' by them. This was so especially since interests had to be declared. For corruption could occur only if matters were concealed. Since everything was 'open and above board', it could not be corrupt.

Yet the practice also raised concerns among some participants. The concerns were that it interfered with members' loyalty to their constituencies by creating loyalties to other interests. Some respondents showed ambivalence, as expressed, for instance, in the following statement: 'There could be a conflict of interest, but if interests are declared there is not much danger of that because others would be suspicious. But there is a danger. If too many members have consultancies it would put business interests first.' Finally, there was a concern that the practices gained over-representation for the interests of those who could afford to retain MPs. As a member of the Committee on Members' Interests put it, this was hardly fair on others who 'do not have access to this sort of cash to put forward their point of view'.

## The PACking of legislators' interests

In the United States there has recently been an explosion in the expenditures involved in election campaigns. Yet candidates for Congress (like other candidates) must now fund a large part of their own elections. This has led to a situation where such candidates have gained the financial resources necessary for their campaigns through backing by individuals (particularly, though not only, business and industrial magnates or smaller business people) and interest groups, as represented by Political Action Committees (PACs). Recently there has been a boom in such PACs: from 139 in 1975, their number has mushroomed to several thousands at the turn of the 1990s. While there are PACs to represent most interest groups, the interests of the wealthy, the capitalists, the corporate sector are evidently better PACked than are other interests.

There are some restrictions on the size of election campaign contributions by any single individual or PAC. But, as Etzioni (1984) and others have pointed out, these can be easily circumvented. Contributions have usually gone to candidates or incumbents who are sympathetic to the contributors' interests. Or else candidates who have been supported have been expected to promote those interests once they are elected. Explicitly offering a member of Congress money in exchange for a legislative vote is in transgression of the law. But deals can be struck implicitly. As one member of Congress quoted by Etzioni (1984) put it, 'I cannot be bought.' He then added as an afterthought, 'But I can be rented.' As in Britain, then, the money flow to legislators has opened a path of influence on the political process for those who can pay for it, which is denied to others.

## Huddling at HUD

Another example concerns recent occurrences at the United States Department of Housing and Urban Development (HUD). Here senior position holders and their political allies have been huddling together to their mutual advantage. Such connivance was made possible by the party political character of the higher rungs of the departmental bureaucracy. It was thus the outcome of the previous politicization of the bureaucracy. This, however, resulted in voluntary mutual back-scratching by exchange of resources among position holders.

In April 1989 the department's inspector general issued a report documenting the fact that millions of dollars in departmental contracts and subsidies had been steered to developers who had once held high-level political posts at the agency. Or else monies had been channelled to people who had paid hundreds of thousands of dollars to consultants who had been such former officials, or were well connected in the Republican party. These consultants, earning millions of dollars, engaged in peddling influence in return for money by persuading top officials in the department to approve federal housing subsidies and other support for their clients' projects.

Since senior posts in the department were filled by people selected for their political connections, this was not difficult to achieve. Republican consultants, developers or politicians could secure such favours for their clients, or for those in other ways connected to them, by appealing to the political loyalties of the top departmental managers. Favouritism at HUD was also enjoyed by Democrats, who were using administrative leverage to help secure financial benefits for friends and constituents.

## Politics in the police

Half across the world from Washington, on the other side of the Pacific Ocean, lies the Australian state of Queensland. Because of its warm and sunny climate, it has also been named the Sunshine State. Recently, however, Queensland has not been quite so sunny. It has been beset by an explosive corruption scandal, and consequently has been renamed by some as the Moonlight State. A commission of inquiry (Fitzgerald, 1989) found that the police force had been debilitated by widely institutionalized misconduct. This was manifested in large-scale bribes to certain members of the force from the prostitution, gambling, betting and drug industries, in return for tacit acceptance and police protection of their illegal operations. Some of the proceeds of these transactions were flowing upwards in the direction of high rungs in the police hierarchy.

The commission also found that this protection racket was closely connected to the politicization of the police force, which was contrary to a longstanding Australian convention. The then police commissioner was clearly a political appointee: in 1976 he was appointed by the then state premier to be assistant police commissioner, and this involved his elevation 'without justification or explanation' (Fitzgerald, 1989, p. 205) over and above a hundred more senior officers. It was also done by overruling the wishes of the then commissioner, thereby forcing his resignation. This was definitely the overpowering of the police commissioner by the government. Thereupon, however, the assistant commissioner was appointed as the commissioner's successor, and from then onwards the intimate relationship between the government and the top and other senior officers of the police was entirely voluntary on both sides.

According to the Fitzgerald report, the new police commissioner came to be heavily involved in politics. He provided uncompromising support to the premier and his (National party) state government by supplying them with a variety of symbolic resources. Thus he supplied the premier with information by conducting political opinion polls for him among police, and by having his and his ministers' political opponents investigated by the police. Prior to an election he went as far as to make a public statement in favour of the premier. He also discussed police matters and appointments with politicians (see also Dickie, 1989, p. 268). Other senior officers in the police also cooperated by supplying the premier and his ministers with information they used to the disadvantage of a member of the opposition (the Australian Labor party) (Fitzgerald, 1989, p. 82).

For their part, the premier and some other members of the state government were deeply involved in police matters. Thereby they supplied the police commissioner with a variety of administrative/material resources which strengthened his position. These resources, in turn, had direct ramifications for the development and persistence of police misconduct, which opened a flow of material resources to higher rungs of police officers, that is, a large part of the police elite and sub-elite.

One of the police commissioner's first achievements in office was that – although there was an internal investigation unit that was responsible for the investigation of police misbehaviour – he ordered that no such investigations be conducted (Fitzgerald, 1989, p. 49). Subsequently the commissioner victimized police officers who had been involved in attempts to uncover police misdeeds, while his own friends enjoyed successful careers. In all this, the premier and top state politicians stood staunchly behind him. They not only closed an eye to police corruption, but helped him defeat officers who were involved in attempts to combat it (pp. 5l, 75). Thus, 'while he was commissioner, senior officers, including those whom police officers generally accepted were engaged in misconduct, not only had the authority of their positions but the political support of the Premier ...' (p. 205). Symbolic resources also flowed from the government to the top and senior echelons of the police: when allegations of police misconduct were made, top politicians vilified those who made the allegations.

## Conclusion and discussion

There is nothing novel in the listing of these phenomena. They have all been reported in the press (albeit of different countries) at one time or another. Thus, what I have referred to as recent attempts at the subjugation of elites and sub-elites have been highlighted in the press as violations of democratic principles. They have usually been cited in separation from each other, because they each involve the subversion of a different principle. Restrictions on information have been cited as infringing freedom of information. The weakening of trade unions has been invoked as contravening freedom of association. Bearing down on higher education has been condemned as breaching academic freedom. It may be added that politicization of the bureaucracy detracts from the separation of powers within the state. Each of these democratic principles protects citizens' rights and liberties, and their infraction has also been seen as a threat to these immunities.

All this is correct, of course. But what has not been pointed out is that on top of involving transgressions of different democratic principles, these processes have something in common. They all entail assaults on the autonomy of elites and sub-elites, thereby putting this autonomy under siege. And it is *these assaults on elite autonomy* which also contain the threat these processes pose to civil liberties and the rights of citizens.

Thus, while restrictions on information obviate freedom of information for the public, such freedom can only be protected by a relatively autonomous media elite and sub-elite. And any restrictions on this freedom curtail the symbolic resources that form a necessary basis for the activities of that category of people. 'Union bashing', while contravening freedom of association, simultaneously detracts from the independent organizational resources, and thus from the power of trade unions. Thereby it enfeebles the autonomy of their leaders and activists, which for over a century now has formed one of the main pillars of Western democracy.

Along the same line, greater politicization of the government bureaucracy is simultaneously a weakening of the bureaucratic elite's control over the administrative/material resources of bureaucratic appointments and promotions; and thus a weakening of that elite's independence. It is thereby that it also diminishes the separation of state powers. Imposing greater government control on universities involves the curbing of academic freedom. But this is so because it threatens the autonomy of the academic elite and sub-elite – professorial and lecturing staff who, through their employment of symbolic resources, may be the bearers and guardians of such freedom.

While subjugations such as these generally raise concern as negating civil rights and liberties, the phenomena of voluntary collusion usually raise concern in the press as instances of impropriety or corruption. Once again, it does not get pointed out that these examples, too, involve inroads into the autonomy of elites and sub-elites.

Thus, for example, extraparliamentary pecuniary interests of legislators make them partly (though not totally) reliant on material resources from capitalists and trade unions. Hence they entail a diminution of the autonomy of the political elite, as manifested in the services this elite renders to those other elites. Influence peddling involves an illicitly intimate exchange relationship of material and administrative resources among members of the political, bureaucratic and capitalist elites and sub-elites, which thus become partly (though not entirely) reliant on each other for resources. Police misconduct with government blessing is connected with an illegitimately close relationship between the highest and middle rungs of the police and the political elite of the government, in which symbolic as well as administrative and material resources flow back and forth between the two groups, entailing a partial symbiosis of resources between them. In contrast to the previous examples, however, the present ones involve not the ascendancy of the government elite over other elites, but rather a voluntary accommodation between two (or more) elites and those immediately surrounding them, to their mutual advantage.

Generally the examples reviewed do not spell a coercive or complete suppression or amalgamation of elites. But they entail steps, however small, in this direction, and as such they are of special concern. Thus the phenomenon of other elites and sub-elites being partly overpowered by the government is of special concern because it is inversely related to citizens' rights and liberties. As noted at the beginning of this chapter, it can itself be explained *inter alia* on the basis of the existing balance of power between the government and the other elites: a government which has great power already is more likely than a weaker government to overpower other elites and sub-elites, and if these are already relatively weak, they will find it more difficult than more powerful ones to resist attacks on their autonomy. But what is the lesson to be learned from this?

If we use the Thatcher government in Britain as an example of a relatively powerful government, with special proneness to subjugate elites, can it then be said that the Thatcher decade suggests that no amount of 'elite autonomy' and its tradition – as it has developed in Britain for over a century – can provide a defence against the determined use of state or government power? To my mind this conclusion, though *prima facie* convincing, would be unjustifiably fatalistic. It would imply that once a government shows sufficient strength and determination to subdue other power holders, all that is left for those to do is to accept the situation and submit to it.

However, just as the power of the government to subjugate other elites depends among other things on the personal resources of ambition and determination of its members, so does the ability of those other elites to resist such subjugation depend among other things on the personal resources of ambition and determination among *their* members. To put it differently, the Thatcher decade can also be taken to drive home the lesson that elites and sub-elites must be aware of the crucial role which their relative autonomy from the government fulfils for democracy, and be determined enough to struggle for this autonomy, if democracy is to survive.

Turning now to the voluntary collusion of elites, involving impropriety or corruption – this, too, is of special interest, for it has certain implications for the exacerbation of socioeconomic inequalities. This is so because it generally involves an exchange of resources between members of two or more power groups. This leads to the interests of these people (such as capitalists of various magnitudes, or union activists of various ranks) being over-represented in the policy-making arena. Thereby it *ipso facto* also leads to all other interests being under-represented.

For instance, British MPs have become mediators between the

interests of corporate elites (those of private corporations and trade unions) and the political elite (parliament and government). Each mediating act may not amount to much. But when all such acts are combined, they may be seen to have a formidable impact on how information, views and pressures are fed into parliamentary and government decisions in favour of capitalists and those in charge of trade unions. The same processes also lead to the acqusition by politicians of economic resources which enhance their chances of gaining and perpetuating their power. In a circular way these exchanges thus work to enhance the resources of those involved, who already enjoy significant advantages in the control of resources. Since resources are scarce, these exchanges are at the expense of all those who are not included. That is, they are at the expense of the general public, to the detriment of democracy.

Putting elite autonomy under siege is connected to the inconsistency of democratic principles and of other codes of behaviour. Governments attempting to overpower academic, bureaucratic or trade union elites could justify themselves on the basis of the electoral principle: they were, after all, legitimately elected power holders, exerting authority over non-elected, or not generally elected, ones. The elites and sub-elites whose independence was under threat could justify their self-defence by invoking the principles of freedom of information and of association, or those of the separation of powers. HUD bureaucrats who gave advantages to their political cronies were transgressing norms of objectivity and fairness. But they could justify their actions on the basis of norms of political loyalty. British parliamentarians could justify their transactions with capitalist and trade union elites on the basis of British tradition and codes of parliamentary honour. Yet they raised concern because they contravened the equally prominent norms of the loyalty of the elected to their constituencies, as well as those of fair access for all to the policy-making process, thus creating inequalities.

Needless to say, the inequalities created by the collusion of elites are not the most blatant inequalities that pervade Western societies. But they are especially significant because they entail a weakening of the autonomy of established elites, which in turn forms the basis for the autonomy of the elites and sub-elites of social movements. And it is these which have the potential of providing some of the most egalitarian mechanisms of Western societieties. These are dealt with in the next chapter.

## Notes

1   These categories include: security and intelligence, international relations, confidential information obtained from other governments or international organizations; information useful to criminals and likely to result in crime; official phone tapping and mail interceptions under statutory warrant.
2   Only the House of Commons has been included in the study.

# 10

# Social protest movements and the potential of Western democracy

---

In the course of this discussion I have made the claim that both the demo-elite perspective and the Western democratic regimes to which it pertains have dynamic and progressive potential. It is now time to substantiate this claim. In the framework of this perspective, I argue that some seeds of change which Western democracies carry within them are contained in the democratic meta-principle of the autonomy of elites. And a major linchpin which connects this principle to change consists of social protest movements and their elites and sub-elites.

The initiators and organizers of social movements thus form a uniquely dynamic element in Western regimes. But this is so not because by clamouring for change they can directly bring it about. Rather, it is so because the principle of elite autonomy (however imperfectly implemented) prevents governments from suppressing them. Thereby it forces them to employ alternative, less coercive but more manipulative strategies in order to dissipate their threat. These strategies, here referred to as the absorption of protest, are aimed at stabilizing the system. Yet in the process of stabilization they – paradoxically – lead to change.

This paradoxical process may also be seen as a distinctive 'learning mechanism'[1] of Western democracies, which turns them into more flexible and change-oriented systems than would otherwise be the case. And the change generated in this manner is frequently (though not always) in the direction of more democracy and greater equality. Because of the relative autonomy of elites and sub-elites in Western democracies, the very exertion of government power thus also opens up prospects for social progress.

# Major theories fail to come to terms with social movements

Democratic change through social movements is something with which several other major theories have failed to come to terms. Pluralist and pluralist elite theories, by conceiving of the political arena in Western countries as a balance of power between a multiplicity of pressure groups, convey the picture of an equilibrium, and fail to identify what it is that may lead this equilibrium to change. Because several of them are also satisfied with the democratic system as it exists today, the impetus to search for mechanisms leading to social progress – such as social movements – is largely removed from the scene.

Several elite theories, by emphasizing the concerted power of elites in a democracy, and by seeing the public as a relatively passive receptacle of elite power, also do not provide a handle which could help us come to grips with processes of change. Since established elites have a stake in the existing state of affairs, and if they are concerted in their power, it is not at all clear where the push for sociopolitical change may derive from. Certainly not many elite theorists view social movements in this capacity. Participatory theories of democracy provide us with a vision of how democracy ought to look in the future. But several of them fail to provide an adequate analysis of social movements as the mechanisms which could lead us from here to there.

Strange as it may sound, even Marxist theories – although they are basically theories of conflict and change – have not made an important contribution to the analysis of change in Western democracies. For by setting their sights almost exclusively on revolutionary and other so-called class struggles, they have neglected the analysis of alternative, no less significant, and possibly more dynamic struggles in capitalist regimes. Although some scholars with Marxists affinities have analysed recent social movements (Offe, 1985, 1990), they have not really been able to utilize much of the traditional Marxist framework for their analysis. In the words of Carl Boggs:

> Marxism presents the image of a bipolar world characterized by epochal struggles between . . . wage labor and capital . . . Economic crisis leading to revolutionary transformation is the projected outcome of this dialectical confrontation. Such a polarized conflict . . . was expected to produce a relatively homogeneous working class community, permeated with anti-capitalist consciousness. However appropriate this scenario might have looked in earlier phases of competitive capitalism . . . it now

seems quite outdated in the more complex and fragmented world inhabited by the new movements. . . . To retain a conventional Marxian framework . . . in the face of this fundamentally new historical reality is to reduce theory to a dogmatic, reified enterprise no longer capable of grasping social change. (1986, pp. 57–8)

# The demo-elite perspective and social movements in the West

By contrast, the demo-elite perspective is practically forced by its inner logic to deal with movement generated change. For by defining elites and sub-elites *inter alia* on the basis of personal resources such as those of charisma and energy, it must include in its analysis leaders and activists of social movements as well. As explained before, the organizations of the establishment are repositories of society's main resources. They are also the power bases for the most powerful elites. At the same time, disproportionate personal resources are not dependent on organizations. Hence, by this definition, elites and sub-elites are not only those who sit atop established organizational power structures. They are also those who challenge and wish to change them. In short, the demo-elite perspective is compelled by its own definition of elites and sub-elites to deal with the challenge posed by leaders and activists of social movements. This is the task of the present chapter.

In this context, movements should be distinguished from interest and pressure groups. Both pressure groups and social movements are in some way concerned with the redistribution of resources. But while pressure groups are concerned primarily with the distribution of resources in favour of their own interests, protest movements are concerned with the redistribution of resources – sometimes in their own favour – as part of broader moral/ideological issues.

This difference is related to another one. While pressure groups act within the confines of the extant system, social movements act to promote (and occasionally to prevent) the change of at least some of its aspects. In addition, pressure groups are usually organized and engage in institutionalized modes of action such as petitioning and lobbying. Social movements, on the other hand, are generally less organized and engage in non-institutionalized, less institutionalized or only partly institutionalized modes of action, including demonstrations, rioting, sit-ins, camp-ins and the like. As Offe (1990) shows, how far movements are institutionalized changes through their life histories.

Occasionally interest groups and social movements may shade into each other. Sometimes movements turn into pressure groups or even into political parties. But mostly, at any given point in time, it is not difficult to tell them apart.

Like pressure groups, social movements vary in their size and in the weight they carry in the political arena. The elites of most social movements (like the elites of most pressure groups) may not be very powerful. But occasionally elites of major movements may become quite significant. For this the Greens in West Germany, before they became institutionalized, furnish an apt example. Furthermore, together, the elites (occasionally referred to as counter-elites) and sub-elites of social movements hold strategic importance – and great potential – in democratic regimes.

This is so because in clamouring for change of existing power structures, the leaders of movements pose a potential threat to the established elites. Thereby they become highly visible to them. By being so visible to the establishment on the one hand, while also maintaining close contact with parts of the public on the other hand, they provide a relatively effective channel through which messages may flow from one to the other. By their intensive interaction with the public, they also encourage relatively widespread political participation from below, and thus a more participatory democracy than would otherwise be the case.

## The relative autonomy of elites and the proliferation of social movements

All this would mean very little, however, if governments in democratic regimes could simply crush and eliminate social movements, as their counterparts have done in so many other regimes. And this would be the case were it not for the democratic meta-principle of the relative autonomy of elites. For it is the evolution of this principle, and its – albeit imperfect – implementation, which has made it increasingly difficult for governments to suppress other elites and sub-elites, including those of social movements.

By Western rules the resources of coercion are legitimately mono-polized by the state. But the meta-principle of the autonomy of elites has made it impossible for the elites of the state, in particular the government, to use those means against other elites – for instance the elites of the opposition, the media and intellectual elites – however much they may feel the urge to do so. Hence it is the same meta-principle which these other elites must defend in order to sustain their own positions. And by defending this principle in general, these elites, whether they like it or not, also defend the autonomy of the counter-elites of social protest movements. The ability of government elites to suppress or repress movements has thus been greatly curtailed.

By repression of a protest movement I refer to a combination of two elements: the use of coercion or the threat of coercion; and coercion's effect in making the movement disappear, or preventing it from acting, or altering its nature to such an extent that it no longer remains the same entity.

On the basis of this definition it would be difficult to claim that no coercive repression has ever been applied to social movements in the West. For instance, before the passing of the Wagner Act of 1935 in the United States, the labour movement there was clearly confronted by coercive repression applied by the state and by capitalists. At that time the courts, the police and federal and state troops acted in most localities in alliance with business to put down the labour movement by frequent arrests, jailings, beatings and shootings of its activists (Barbalet, unpublished, and 1989).

But, on the whole, such measures diminished after the last part of the nineteenth century and during the first half of the twentieth century. There has recently been a weakening in trade unionism in several Western countries. But (as explained in the previous chapter with respect to Britain and the United States) this does not amount to actual coercive repression by the state. And while the elites of newer social movements have occasionally been harassed (Bottomore, 1979), as long as they have remained non-violent they have mostly been allowed to express their grievances through a variety of protest activities. Despite their potential threat, their development could not be prevented: the principle of the autonomy of elites has contained within it the seeds of their proliferation.

In the last few decades (particularly from the 1960s onwards) social movements have, in fact, proliferated all over the Western world. They have, of course, included the students' movement in several Western countries, the interrelated civil rights and black power movements, as well as the anti-Vietnam War movement particularly in the United States. They have also included the women's liberation movement, homosexual liberation movements, the environmental, anti-nuclear and peace movements, and a variety of related movements in various

Western countries. Thus in West Germany alone a recent estimate suggested there were 38,000 citizen action groups in existence, backed by 2.3 million members, supporters and sympathizers (Mushaben, 1985). And the situation is not much different in several other countries in the West.

## The relative autonomy of elites and the absorption of protest

The mushrooming of social movements in the West does not imply that they have been allowed to run loose. On the contrary, governments have made continuous efforts to curb them. But, being unable to suppress social movements by force, they have been led to employ other, less repressive but more manipulative, strategies in order to control them. These are here referred to as strategies for the absorption of protest. One of the most important developments in Western democracies has been the governing elites' gradual shift from strategies of repression to such strategies of absorption.

The absorption of a movement's protest differs from its repression in two ways:

- It does not involve coercion directly. While coercion is always there in the background, and available as a last resort, the actual strategy of control is a step removed from coercion;
- The aim and/or result of the mechanism is not to eliminate the movement and its activities, or even to alter it completely, but rather to let it persist while dissipating its threat; the aim is to eliminate not the movement itself, but its destabilizing potential.

The absorption of protest is necessarily based on the utilization of the (non-coercive) state resources of which the government has charge. These form the basis of its own power, and can also be used by it to avert threats to this power, including threats of destabilization posed by social movements. This cannot be done in a straightforward manner. For, sustained by the principle of the relative autonomy of elites, social movements and their elites are not directly dependent on state resources. They have been allowed to accumulate material resources of their own (for instance through membership fees and private contributions) and these are relatively free from state control. Their leaders' own elite positions are accorded to them by these movements, and not by the state. For their administrative resources, they are also not dependent on the state, or the governing elite.

On the other hand, again, the independence of social movements and their elites and sub-elites is never complete. Thus these movements' leaders and their aides may be affected by state resources, of which the government has control, in a variety of ways. For instance, in order to maintain their elite positions they must be able to 'deliver' at least some achievements to their supporters. These achievements must be in the shape of reforms, and for these they frequently are dependent on the government. In addition, while in Western democracies the leaders and activists of social movements may have independent sources of livelihood that have nothing to do with the state, their personal rewards may be greatly enhanced by the government, for instance by means of various appointments. Hence the ability of the government elite to use the state resources at its disposal with the aim of absorbing protest and taming protest movements.

There is a certain similarity between the absorption of protest and the subjugation of elites and sub-elites dealt with in the previous chapter. In both cases the government uses the resources at its disposal in order to make another elite and sub-elite more pliable. There are, however, some important differences. The absorption of protest is not necessarily in contradiction to the rules of democracy, or even on the borderline of what is permissible by these rules. Further, as distinct from the subjugation of elites, the absorption of protest entails a certain price that has to be paid to the leaders and activists of movements in the form of 'achievements' for the movement itself. And it is this convergence between the taming of the movement and the price (however small) which has to be paid in exchange for the willingness to be tamed that opens an important channel of sociopolitical change in Western democracies. This becomes evident when we consider the various strategies that governments commonly engage in for taming movements through the absorption of protest.

## Strategies for the absorption of protest

As noted before, the resources under the control of the government include (apart from coercive resources) a variety of symbolic, administrative/organizational and material (economic) resources. They may be used by the government as either negative sanctions (curbs) or positive sanctions (inducements) or both, following the stick and carrot methods. Thus state resources may be used by the government as negative sanctions to penalize movements and their elites when they get out of hand, that is, for non compliance, deviance or 'radicalism'. Or they may be used as positive sanctions or inducements, to reward and elicit moderation. That is, they may be handed out by the government to the movements' leaders, their potential leaders, their members, or all three, in exchange for acquiescence in its own rule or moderation of their demands.

Such strategies for the absorption of protest include, first, sanctions, drawing on *symbolic resources*. On the negative side, they may take the form of denigration of extremist or otherwise threatening movements. Such negative symbolic sanctions may, of course, misfire. But this does not alter their aim of discrediting the movements, of 'extraditing' them, as it were, beyond the pale of what is acceptable.

An apt example of such an attempt occurred in Israel some years ago. At that time a movement of young Jews from Middle Eastern countries, calling themselves 'Black Panthers', took shape. In protest against alleged discrimination, their leaders instigated demonstrations and some mild acts of violence against property. In response, the then prime minister Golda Meir pronounced them to be 'not nice'. This expression had a boomerang effect, and has since found its way into the folklore of Israeli anti-establishment humour. At the time, however, it was a clear attempt to delegitimize the Black Panthers in the eyes of the public.

Another example of such symbolic extradition is the implicit imputation of criminality or deviance. Thus the Australian prime minister Bob Hawke, in a 1987 television appearance, reacted to demands from the gay movement for the decriminalization of adult homosexuality by saying that his government would not do so (Altman, 1989, p. 51). Thereby he implied that there was in fact something criminal, not in the movement itself, but in the cause for which it stood.

Other examples of symbolic extraditions of movements include questioning their basic loyalty and allegiance. Communist and other radical movements have occasionally met with this response from the establishment. For this, the McCarthy allegations that communism contravened the 'American way of life' may serve as a prominent example. More recently, in Israel, activists of the left-wing movement Peace Now have been labelled by government leaders as supporters of the Palestine Liberation Organization (PLO).

On the positive side, the use of symbolic resources may take the form of reassurances, such as politicians' expressions of support for the movements' causes and demands. A good example would be a statement made by the same Australian prime minister in response to a protest demonstration against alleged discrimination held by Aborigines on the occasion of the bicentenary of white settlement in Australia, in 1988. In this statement the prime minister referred to a previous ministerial statement, saying that

> It acknowledges the descendants of the Aboriginal people of Australia as the . . . original owners of this land. It acknowledges the dispossession of their land by subsequent European occupation . . . It acknowledges the deep disadvantages and deprivations the aboriginals have thereby suffered – and continue to suffer. And it pledges the Australian government . . . to an earnest and continuing effort of rectification and reconciliation. (*The Australian*, 26 January 1988, p. 15).

Apart from soothing statements, symbolic reassurances may take the form of the establishment of commissions of inquiry to investigate the movements' complaints and demands, and the publication of their reports. Prominent cases in point would be the commissions of inquiry into the conditions of blacks and women set up in the wake of the civil rights movement and the women's movement, and the publication of their reports in the United States and some other Western countries.

Similarly, government response to the green movement in Germany included public hearings into nuclear programmes and into environmental policy, and commissions of inquiry constituted on these topics in the government and established opposition parties. On the basis of their recommendations they all either adopted or claimed adherence to many of the movement's aims (Papadakis, 1989, p. 91).

Strategies for the absorption of protest include, secondly, *administrative/organizational* devices. On the negative side they entail utilization of the state's power structures to curb social movements. This may take the form of restrictive (which is less than repressive) legislation. This includes laws, regulations or verdicts in various Western countries, which are designed to regulate and restrict (but not to prevent completely) street marches and demonstrations. A case in point is the recent decision of a West German federal court declaring all sit-down demonstrations (for instance, in front of military installations) a criminal offence (Offe, 1990, p. 238).

On the positive side, organizational devices may take the form of co-optation. This entails letting movements' leaders or potential leaders gain a certain share of power in the establishment by their incorporation into existing organizational structures, in return for acceptance of those structures. Cases in point would include the incorporation of increasing numbers of blacks into administrative/political structures in the United States (Berns, 1984) and the incorporation of environmental and nuclear movements and their leaders into the parliamentary and electoral structures in several Western, especially European, countries, with the Greens in West Germany as the most prominent example.

Strategies of protest absorption include, thirdly, *material* devices. On the negative side, they may take the form of depriving certain movements or their leaders of monetary resources accruing to other movements. For instance, in Israel's pre-state era, the semi-autonomous Jewish National Authorities, established under British Mandatory rule, used to allocate funds derived from the World Zionist Organization only to those parties and movements that accepted their authority, and to deny such funds to the more 'extremist' movements (Horowitz and Lissak, 1971). This practice has been perpetuated into the post-state era as well, despite widespread opposition to it.

On the positive side material devices may take the form of policies entailing acceptance of some of the movements' demands for the reallocation of material resources. In some Western countries, for instance, governing and legislative elites have responded to the women's movement with legislation and policies leading to decreases in the earning differentials between men and women (Costain and Costain, 1985; Jones, 1983; 1984). Also, the response of the established parties in West Germany to the green movement included the funding of large-scale, movement-linked projects and enterprises (Papadakis, 1989, p. 91).

In addition there are, of course, combined or mixed devices for the absorption of protest. Thus, on the negative side, during the McCarthy era in the United States state elites attempted to put drastic curbs on (without coercively eliminating) communist and related organizations and movements, by restricting access by their members and sympathizers to existing organized power structures and employment, at the same time as discrediting them in the eyes of the public.

On the positive side, mixed devices were applied, for instance, to protest activity in Britain in the nineteenth century. According to Tilly (1986), collective protest action, which had been proceeding in a relatively low key, exploded in the years 1830-1 (with over 600 such gatherings in 1830 and approximately 1,000 in 1831). This was then speedily followed by the Reform Act of 1832, which provided for the extension of the franchise and some other reforms which had the effect of increasing and institutionalizing the organizational basis of power for activists and potential activists of protest movements. It was further followed by the Factory Act of 1833, which had to do with material resources, providing for the enforcement of shorter working hours for children. These reforms do not seem much by present standards, but they were a step forward at the time.

I suggest (although I cannot provide quantitative proof for this) that the strategies devised by Western governments for the purpose of coping with the new social protest movements in the last few decades have been most prominently those that employ positive rather than negative sanctions. Thus the shift has been not only from coercive repression to other strategies of control, but also towards positive rather than negative sanctions, inducements rather than curbs. And among the positive devices the most prominent has been that of co-optation, of incorporating elites of social movements into existing power structures in exchange for moderation.

It has been argued, quite plausibly, that this 'generous' approach on the part of the governing elites took shape in the framework of the complacency generated by the growing affluence of Western societies, particularly in the postwar era. Graver economic downturns than those experienced since the early 1970s might well have led to a more restrictive approach on the part of the powers that be, one in which curbs might well have outweighed inducements in the control of social movements.

Be this as it may, it is noteworthy that the inducements that have been offered to movements and their elites have not been such as to allow them to cause fundamental changes in the power structures and patterns of resource allocation in Western societies. There is, of course, no generally accepted yardstick to indicate where a limited change ends and a fundamental one begins. But three criteria have been applied here:

- Nowhere in recent decades have the movements' leaders been allowed to become major power holders within existing establishments.
- Wherever changes in the allocation of resources have occurred, they have not measured up to the movements' demands.
- Where the movements' demands have resulted in some reallocations

of resources in favour of disadvantaged groups, these reallocations have not abolished those disadvantages. They have not gone as far as to put the disadvantaged groups on a par with the more advantaged groups in society.

For instance, leaders of environmental and anti-nuclear movements have not become major components of Western governing elites, and despite a decrease in the differentials between men and women's earnings, average women's pay for fulltime year-round work is still only between two-thirds and three-quarters that of men's pay in the various countries of the Western world (Etzioni-Halevy, 1989a, ch. 7).

## Protest and progress

The absorption of protest, thus, has not been a motor for drastic changes in the distribution of resources. It has nonetheless been an important impetus for social progress, but in a roundabout way. For the strategies of protest absorption, and particularly co-optation, have quite frequently been crowned with success. That is to say, several (though certainly not all) of the leaders, activists or potential leaders of movements have let themselves be co-opted into the existing establishments. This seems to have been the case partly because of the personal rewards involved, and partly because without such co-optation the achievements they could have delivered to their supporters would usually have been even smaller.

Roberto Michels clarified long ago that when the then non-established elites of labour unions and parties came to share power within the existing establishments, the very establishments they had previously undertaken to transform, their revolutionary zeal abated, and they became increasingly willing to accept the status quo. And the same is still true today. Possibly this is one of the major reasons why Western capitalist democracies have not been riddled by major revolts or rebellions.

However, while Michels was correct in his factual analysis, he nevertheless missed an important point which now, with the hindsight of almost a century, has become much clearer. The point being that, in the very process of becoming incorporated into the establishment, the core people of the labour movement have still managed to achieve certain changes in the allocation of resources in favour of their supporters. And the same is true for the leaders of more recent social movements. While these achievements have been limited, this is not to say that they have not been valuable, or that no real and substantial improvements may result from them. For even small achievements may be incremental and add up to more significant achievements in the long run.

The absorption of protest, and most prominently co-optation, thus entails a two-sided process. It is largely responsible for the dissipation of the threat of social movements. It has a prominent share in the 'domestication', so to speak, of potentially radical movements. Because the absorption of protest is successful, the representatives of social movements generally settle for much less than they initially demanded. But it is also a mechanism that prevents ossification of the system. Because of it there have been no major rebellions or revolutions, and hence no far-reaching transformations. But because of it, there is also some (albeit limited) change.

This is significant in particular since in Western democracies counter-elites and sub-elites of social movements have frequently (though not always) championed the interests of some disadavantaged classes or groups in society. Those interests lie in change towards a more egalitarian distribution of power and material resources. And since leaders and activists of social movements can maintain their positions only if they deliver at least some achievements to their supporters, there is always a likelihood that they will push for a more egalitarian distribution of resources. In other words, there is a chance that they will push for social progress.

As noted before, this is what happened in the past. It was precisely the struggles of non-established elites which mediated the manner in which a variety of socioeconomic reforms towards a lessening of inequalities in the distribution of resources were achieved. By the same token, there is no reason why it should not happen again. It is true that recently the distributive achievements of social movements have been less impressive than those of movements in the past, particularly towards the end of the nineteenth and the beginning of the twentieth century.

This is so because several of the most recent movements have been fragmented (Boggs, 1986), and have moved from '"Red" to "Green"' (Fehér and Heller, 1984). And in the process, they have abandoned the clamour for the redistribution of material resources in favour of quality of life issues and postmaterialist values (Inglehart, 1981; Lipset, 1985). Consequently many of them and their elites have not been representing the particular interests of the most disadvantaged classes, and have not been concerned chiefly with a more egalitarian redistribution of resources (Offe, 1985).

But this is not to say that no social movements have been concerned with material inequality and redistribution. Moreover, several of the new movements have been concerned particularly with more autonomy for individuals and a more participatory style of politics (Boggs, 1986, chs 2, 6; Desai, 1985). That is to say, they have been concerned with a more egalitarian distribution of power, or with greater democratization, and it is in this area that they have the greatest potential of affecting Western societies.

If, as has been argued before, the changes brought about by social movements' elites have occurred precisely in the process of their protest being absorbed, and if several of these changes have been towards greater redistribution of material and/or power resources, then it must be concluded that in Western democracies co-optation of relatively autonomous non-established elites is a major process through which redistributive changes, that is social progress, occurs. The elites who have let themselves be co-opted by the establishment have frequently been accused by their supporters of betrayal, and in many cases those accusations were justifiable. Nonetheless it was in the very process of co-optation that non-established elites have been a force of (albeit hesitant) progress in democratic societies.

## Conclusion and discussion

In Western democracies important changes come about through the relative autonomy of elites and sub-elites of social movements. However, they come about not through those elites' activities as such, but rather through the governing elites' strategies for the absorption of their protest. Such strategies, including first and foremost co-optation, form attempts to domesticate social movements. Yet they also entail a certain price that has to be paid in return for their willingness to be domesticated. This price is usually paid first and foremost through personal rewards to the movements' leaders and activists, or to those who have the potential of becoming such leaders and activists. But because the leaders must be able to show some achievements to their supporters, the price must also be paid in the denomination of concessions, even if only minor ones, to the movements' demands for change. The relative autonomy of movements' elites is thus important not because it leads to change in a straightforward manner, but because it leads to strategies of control and stabilization which – unintentionally – also lead to change.

Even in non-Western regimes, where there is no, or much less autonomy of elites than there is in the West, people with the potential of destabilizing the system are frequently bought off through a variety of personal rewards. But in Western democracies, where there is a more pronounced autonomy of elites and sub-elites, including those of social movements, the co-optation of such elites with destabilizing potential exacts an additional price: concessions to the movements on which their power is based. Even in non-Western regimes a social movement, if it arises at all, may leave behind a certain legacy of reforms. But there the occurrence would be exceptional. In Western democracies, on the other hand, concessions to movements in return for their domestication are now made on a routine basis. They have become part of the manner in which the machinations of power work to preserve the system, while also leading to change.

In other words, the recurring cycles of the generation of relatively autonomous movements, the absorption of their protest by co-optation of their elites, according some limited concessions to them, their consequent acceptance of the status quo, and finally the generation of yet other relatively autonomous counter-elites to take their place, may be seen as a major 'learning mechanism', or a major channel through which progress in Western democracies takes place. The reallocation of resources that takes place in this manner at any particular point in time may not be large or impressive; at times it may stop altogether, and at other times it may proceed at a snail's pace. But looked at over longer timespans, the changes that do occur may be seen to be incremental and cumulative.

This pattern has already involved significant reallocations of economic and other resources over the last centuries. The redistribution may have been less impressive in recent years, and great inequalities still remain. But once the present phase of postmaterialism is succeeded by the phase of post-postmaterialism – as it eventually must be – there is no reason why social movements should not once more be concerned with the equalization of economic resources as well. Hence it is not inconceivable that greater redistributions may once again occur in the future.

The elites of whatever movements for greater democracy and equality emerge in the future may well be co-opted, as their predecessors have been in the past. They may betray their rank-and-file members by becoming staunch supporters of the status quo. But as in the past, so in the future, it is precisely through their betrayal – through the price they exact for it – that changes towards greater equality may occur. And the greater the autonomy of the counter-elites at the time of co-optation, the higher the price – in concessions for their movements – which they can exact from established elites in return for their willingness to be co-opted. Hence also the greater the changes towards equality they can achieve. And if, or when, they get co-opted, others may well come to take their place.

Thus the relative autonomy of elites of social movements, although it brings about only limited achievements at any given time, still turns democracy into a more dynamic and progressive system than would otherwise be the case. Not all social movements are necessarily progressive and not all necessarily deserve support. But, in general, the ability of social movements and their elites and sub-elites to express themselves autonomously (as long as they do not turn to violence) certainly needs to be defended and encouraged. And understanding the democratic role of those who instigate, organize and lead autonomous movements helps not only in understanding democracy, but also in understanding how democracy can be encouraged to breed a more democratic, equitable and egalitarian democracy in the future.

## Note

1   As noted above, this concept has been suggested by Boulding, 1990.

# Conclusion

The aim of this book has been to highlight some major aspects of how a system of the type that we call Western-style democracy comes about and how it functions and malfunctions in the world today. The aim has also been to sound a warning bell on some threats to its integrity, and to explore the prospects of countering such threats – while also reforming the system.

The argument has been that a distinctive feature of democracy is the relative autonomy of elites and sub-elites in the control of resources; that this is a major (though implicit) metaprinciple of democracy and an integral part of what the principles of democracy – when stripped of their rhetoric – are really about. It has also been argued that this relative autonomy has been an important precondition for the stabilization and even for the emergence of democracy, and that it protects the principles of democracy, and is in return protected by them.

A modicum of cooperation among elites and sub-elites is necessary for the working of any political system, including a democratic one. Such cooperation does not necessarily contradict elite autonomy in the control of resources. But if it does, if the elites' cooperation is based on the infringement of each others' autonomy beyond what (implicitly) is regarded as acceptable by democratic principles and rules, this endangers the human rights and civil liberties which make democracy preferable to non-democratic regimes.

This argument has given rise to the warning that ever since its inception democracy has not been secure, and that this is even more so today. The most immediate danger to it stems not from external enemies, but from within. It stems from attempts by elites to obviate autonomy, sometimes in subjugation of other elites and sub-elites and sometimes in collusion with them – usually at the expense of the public.

So far the tradition of the freedom of elites and sub-elites from repressive legal and other restraints, and their control of independent resources, is still relatively strong in Western democracies. Where there have been deviations from this tradition, these have still been sedate. Where there have been subjugations and collusions of elites, these have still been circumspect. The limitations still besetting these practices in Western democracies become evident in particular when the situation is compared to that in non-democratic countries. Thus the yearly report of the International Confederation of Free Trade Unions, presented in Geneva on 19 June 1989, documented that in the previous year 650 leaders and representatives of trade unions had been murdered and over 6,500 had been imprisoned, for instance in Latin America, Africa and South Korea.

Comparisons such as these, however, entail the risk of making people in the West overly complacent with their own lot. They entail the hazard of making them disregard the warning bell that is sounded by subversions of elite autonomy, which endanger citizens' rights, in their own backyards. If these assaults are taken in people's stride, there is a distinct possibility that they may become more formidable in the future. Some would counter this by saying that as long as free, competitive elections are not in jeopardy, democracy is secure and there is no occasion for concern. But with weakening elite autonomy, Western regimes would gradually be transformed from liberal democracies into what Lord Hailsham has termed 'elective dictatorships'; and eventually even free elections could not be preserved.

All this is an attempted diagnosis of a problem, not a prescription for a remedy. But it is evident that any step towards rectifying the situation must be preceded by an explicit recognition of what is wrong. This, in turn, requires an explicit acknowledgment of the importance of the autonomy of key elites and sub-elites (as distinct from the broader phenomena of 'pluralism' or of 'civil society') for Western democracy.

So far, elites – and by implication, elite theory – have all too often been regarded as the antithesis of democracy. A first step in the right direction would be the explicit, popular recognition that elites may be either democratic or undemocratic. But when they are kept institutionally separate from each other in the *sources* of their *resources*, when they therefore have interest in limiting each other's power, they have the potential of strengthening democracy – democracy, that is, not as it emerges in slogans or in utopian ideals, but as it can exist in reality. Once elite autonomy is recognized as an explicit principle of democracy, vague conventions now preserving such autonomy can be transformed into explicit ones.

This is not to say that Western democracies ought to be frozen or mummified into their present casts. In this sense the end of history is both impossible and undesirable. Ever since their inception, Western democracies have been changing, and they must continue to change if they are to survive. But if democracies are to adapt to the future they must, as a first step, preserve the achievements that have been the results of past struggles within them. If they are to cope with the challenge of trends towards democratization in Communist countries, they must at the very least refrain from adopting authoritarian patterns of the subversion of elite autonomy which have been the hallmark (and apparently the downfall) of those regimes themselves.

Further, it must be recognized that as elite autonomy has been achieved through elite struggles, so can it only be preserved through elite struggles. Some would counter this by saying that if governments are powerful and determined enough, there is little that other elites and sub-elites can do to stand up to them. But there is no reason why other elites should be less determined than overbearing governments. If, on the other hand, elites and sub-elites will not show determination in struggling for their own self-determination, nobody will perform this task for them. If elites relinquish their control of resources, if they become overly compliant to government dictates, if they embrace other elites with excessive affection, if they do not struggle to free themselves from suffocating bear-hugs of other elites, the battle for democracy is lost already.

Finally, it must be recognized that the autonomy of elites may also play an egalitarian role, and that in this respect the counter-elites and sub-elites of social movements have a strategic place. Enjoying, as they do, the relative autonomy which other elites have struggled for in the past, it is now up to them to help perpetuate such autonomy into the times that lie ahead. It is up to them to do so not as an end in itself, but because in the process of preserving what has been attained so far, they have the potential – and therefore also the responsibility – to open the prospect for change not towards an elite-less, but nonetheless towards a more equitable, egalitarian and democratic democracy in the future.

# References

Abercrombie, Nicholas and Urry, John 1983: *Capital, Labour and the Middle Classes*. London: George Allen & Unwin.

Abraham, David 1986: *The Collapse of the Weimar Republic*, 2nd edn. New York: Holmes & Meyer.

Abramovitch, Raphael 1962: *The Soviet Revolution 1917–1939*. London: George Allen & Unwin.

Almond, Gabriel A. 1988: Return to the state. *American Political Science Review*, 82, 854–74.

Althusser, L. 1971: Ideology and ideological state apparatuses. In his *Lenin and Philosophy and Other Essays*, trans. B. Brewster, London: New Left Books, 123–73.

Altman, Denis 1989: The emergence of gay identity in the USA and Australia. In Christine Jennett and Randal G. Stewart (eds), *Politics of the Future*, Melbourne: Macmillan, 30–53.

Altschull, Herbert J. 1975: Chronicle of a democratic press in Germany before the Hitler takeover. *Journalism Quarterly*, 52, 229–38.

Aron, Raymond 1968: *Progress and Disillusion*. London: Pall Mall.

—— 1978: *Politics and History*, trans. M. Bernheim-Conant. New York: Free Press.

Arrighi, Giovanni, Hopkins, Terence K. and Wallerstein, Immanuel 1987: The liberation of class struggle? *Review*, 10, 403–24.

Barbalet, Jack M. 1989: Social movements and the state. In Christine Jennett and Randal G. Stewart (eds), *Politics of the Future*, Melbourne: Macmillan, 237–61.

—— (unpublished): Social organization and group processes in power relations.

Barber, Benjamin R. 1984: *Strong Democracy*. Berkeley: University of California Press.

Barnett, Clifford R. 1958: *Poland*. New Haven: Hraf.

Bealey, Frank 1988: *Democracy and the Contemporary State*. New York: Oxford University Press.

Bechhofer, Frank, Elliot, Brian and McCrone, David 1978: Structure consciousness and action. *British Journal of Sociology*, 29, 410–36.

Bédarida, François 1991: *A Social History of England 1850–1990*, trans. A.S. Forster and J. Hodgkinson. London: Routledge.

Bell, Daniel 1973: *The Coming of Post-Industrial Socieity*. New York: Basic Books.

Bentham, Jeremy 1960: *Fragment on Government*, ed. W. Harrison. Oxford: Blackwell.

Berelson, Bernard R., Lazarsfeld, Paul F. and McPhee, W.M. 1954: *Voting*. Chicago: Chicago University Press.

Berghahn, V.R. 1987: *Modern Germany*. Cambridge: Cambridge University Press.

Berns, Walter 1984: *In Defense of Liberal Democracy*. Chicago: Gateway.

Bernstein, Paul 1976: *Workplace Democratization*. Kent, Ohio: Kent State University Press.

Birnbaum, Pierre 1988: *States and Collective Action*. Cambridge: Cambridge University Press.

Bismarck, Otto von 1889–1919: *Gedanken und Erinnerungen*, 3 vols. Stuttgart: Gotta'sche Buchandlung.

—— 1943: *Der Kanzler*, 16th edn. Ebenhaufen: Wilhelm Langewiesche-Brandt.

Blackbourn, David 1987: *Populists and Patricians: Essays in Modern German History*. London: Allen & Unwin.

Bleuel, H.P. 1968: *Deutschland's Bekenner: Professoren zwischen Kaiserreich und Diktatur*. Bern: Scherz.

Block, Fred 1987: *Revising State Theory*. Philadelphia: Temple University Press.

Bociurkiw, Bohdan 1966: Religion and Soviet society. *Survey*, 60, 62–71.

Boggs, Carl 1986: *Social Movements and Political Power*. Philadelphia: Temple University Press.

Bottomore, Tom 1979: *Political Sociology*. London: Hutchinson.

Bowles, Samuel and Gintis, Herbert 1986: *Democracy and Capitalism*. London: Routledge & Kegan Paul.

Boulding, Kenneth E. 1990: Book Review on Eva Etzioni-Halevy: Fragile Democracy. *Social Science Quarterly*, 71, 4.

Bourdieu, Pierre 1988-9: Vive la crise! For heterodoxy in social science.

*Theory and Society*, 17, 773–87.

Braverman, H. 1975: *Labor and Monopoly Capital*. New York: Monthly Review Press.

Burton, Michael G. and Higley, John 1987: Elite settlements. *American Sociological Review*, 52, 295–307.

Carchedi, G. 1977: *On the Economic Identification of Social Classes*. London: Routlege & Kegan Paul.

Cawson, Alan 1983: Functional representation and democratic politics. In G. Duncan (ed.), *Democratic Theory and Practice*, New York: Cambridge University Press, 178–98.

— 1986: Hostile brothers: the role of firms in the politics of industry sectors. Paper presented to the XI World Congress of Sociology, New Delhi, August.

Clarke, Oliver 1987: Industrial democracy in Great Britain. *International Studies of Management and Organization*, 17, 38–51.

Cole, George D. H. 1950: *A Short History of the British Working Class Movement: 1789–1947*, trans. J. Azaria. Hakibbutz Hame'uhad (Hebrew).

Coleman, James 1990: *Foundations of Social Theory*. Cambridge: Belknap.

Collins, Thomas 1988: Closing the gate on the fourth estate. *The Guardian*, 20 June, 23.

Connell, Robert W. 1977: *Ruling Class, Ruling Culture*. Cambridge: Cambridge University Press.

Costain, A.N. and Costain, W.D. 1985: Movements and gatekeepers. *Congress and the Presidency*, 12, 21–42.

Crouch, Colin 1979: The state, capital and liberal democracy. In Colin Crouch (ed.), *State and Economy in Contemporary Capitalism*, London: Croom Helm, 13–54.

Dahl, Robert A. 1956: *Preface to Democractic Theory*. Chicago: University of Chicago Press.

— 1961: *Who Governs?* New Haven: Yale University Press.

— 1967: *Pluralist Democracy in the United States*. Chicago: Rand McNally.

— 1971: *Polyarchy*. New Haven: Yale University Press.

— 1982: *Dilemmas of Pluralist Democracy*. New Haven: Yale University Press.

— 1984: Polyarchy, pluralism and scale. *Scandinavian Political Studies*, 7 (New Series), 225–40.

— 1985: *A Preface to Economic Democracy*. Cambridge: Polity.

Dahl, Robert A. and Lindblom, Charles E. 1976: *Politics, Economics and Welfare*. Chicago: University of Chicago Press.

Dahrendorf, Ralf 1959: *Class and Class Conflict in Industrial Society*. Stanford: Stanford University Press.
—— 1961: Demokratie und Sozialstruktur in Deutschland. In his *Gesellschaft und Freiheit*, Munich: Piper, 260–99.
—— 1967: *Society and Democracy in Germany*. New York: Doubleday.
Danet, Brenda 1989: *Pulling Strings*. Albany: State University of New York Press.
Demac, Donna A. 1984: *Keeping America Uninformed: Government Secrecy in the 1980s*. New York: Pilgrim.
Desai, Uday 1985: Citizens' participation and environmental policy implementation. Paper prepared for the XIII World Congress of the International Political Science Association, Paris, July.
Diamond, Larry, Linz, Juan J. and Lipset, Seymour M. 1989–90: *Democracy in Developing Countries*. Boulder: Lynne Rienner.
Dickie, Phil 1989: *The Road to Fitzgerald and Beyond*. St Lucia, Queensland: University of Queensland Press.
Domhoff, G. William 1983: *Who Rules America Now?* Englewood Cliffs, NJ: Prentice Hall.
Dunlop, John B. 1989: Gorbachev and Russian Orthodoxy. *Problems of Communism*, 41, 96–116.
Dye, Thomas R. 1985: *Who's Running America? The Conservative Years*. Englewood Cliffs, NJ: Prentice Hall.
Dye, Thomas R. and Zeigler, Harmon L. 1987: *The Irony of Democracy*, 7th edn. Monterey, Calif.: Brooks Cole.
Edelstein, J. David and Warner, Malcolm 1979: *Comparative Union Democracy*, rev. edn. New Brunswick: Transaction.
Ehrenreich, B. and Ehrenreich, J. 1979: The professional-managerial class. In Walker, P. (ed.), *Between Labour and Capital*, New York: Monthly Review Press, 5–45.
Eisenstadt, Shmuel N. 1966: *Modernization: Protest and Change*. Englewood Cliffs, NJ: Prentice Hall.
Etzioni, Amitai 1961: *A Comparative Analysis of Complex Organizations*. Glencoe, Ill.: Free Press.
—— 1984: *Capital Corruption*. New York: Harcourt, Brace, Jovanovitch.
Etzioni-Halevy, Eva 1985: *Bureaucracy and Democracy*, rev. edn. London: Routledge & Kegan Paul.
—— 1987: *National Broadcasting under Siege*. London: Macmillan.
—— 1989a: *Fragile Democracy*. New Brunswick: Transaction.
—— 1989b: Elite power, manipulation and corruption: a demo-elite perspective. *Government and Opposition*, 24, 215–31.

— 1990: Comparing semi-corruption among parliamentarians in Britain and Australia. In Else Oyen (ed.), *Comparative Methodology*, London: Sage, 113–33.

Evans, Richard J. 1982: *The German Working Class 1888–1933*. London: Croom Helm.

Eyck, Erich 1958: *Bismarck and the German Empire*. London: George Allen & Unwin.

Fainsod, Merle 1953: *How Russia is Ruled*. Cambridge, Mass.: Harvard University Press.

— 1958: The party in the post-Stalin Era. *Problems of Communism*, 7, 7–13.

Fairbrother, Peter 1986: Union democracy in Australia. *Journal of Industrial Relations*, 28, 171–90.

Fehér, Ferenc and Heller, Agnes 1984: From red to green. *Telos*, 59, 35–44.

Feuer, Lewis S. 1970: The intelligentsia in opposition. *Problems of Communism*, 19, 1–16.

Field, G. Lowell and Higley, John 1980: *Elitism*. London: Routledge & Kegan Paul.

Fitzgerald, G.E. 1989: *Report of the Commission of Inquiry into Possible Illegal Activities and Associated Police Misconduct*. Brisbane: Queensland.

Fraenkel, Ernst 1964: *Deutschland und die Westlichen Demokratien*. Stuttgart: Kolhammer.

French, D. and French, E. 1975: *Working Communally*. New York: Russell Sage Foundation.

Frentzel-Zagorska, J. 1989: Semi-free elections in Poland. Research School of Social Sciences, Australian National University (unpublished).

— 1990: Civil society in Poland and Hungary. *Soviet Studies*, 42, 759–77.

Galbraith, J.K. 1952: *American Capitalism*. Boston: Houghton Mifflin.

— 1967: *The New Industrial State*. Boston: Houghton Mifflin.

Gamarnikov, Michael 1967: Poland: political pluralism in a one-party state. *Problems of Communism*, 16, 1–14.

Gamson, Zelda F. and Levin, Henry M. 1984: Obstacles to the survival of democratic workplaces. In Robert Jackall and Henry M. Levin (eds), *Worker Cooperatives in America*, Berkeley: University of California Press, 219–44.

Gerth, H.H. and Mills, C.W. 1958: *From Max Weber: Essays in Sociology*. New York: Oxford University Press.

Giddens, Anthony 1973: *The Class Structure of Advanced Societies*. London: Hutchinson.

— 1982a: Power, the dialectic of control, and class structuration. In Anthony Giddens and Gavin McKenzie (eds), *Social Class and the Division of Labour*, Cambridge: Cambridge University Press, 29–45.

—— 1982b: *Profiles and Critiques in Social Theory*. London: Macmillan.

Giddens, Anthony and McKenzie, Gavin (eds) 1982: *Social Class and the Division of Labour*. Cambridge: Cambridge University Press.

Goldenberg, E.N. 1984: The permanent government in an era of retrenchment and redirection. In L.S. Salmon and M.S. Lund (eds), *The Reagan Presidency and the Government of America*, Washington, DC: Urban Institute Press.

Goldthorpe, J.H. 1978: The current inflation: towards a sociological account. In F. Hirsch and J.H. Goldthorpe (eds), *The Political Economy of Inflation*, Oxford: Martin Robertson, 186–214.

—— 1980: *Social Mobility and Class Structure in Modern Britain*. Oxford: Clarendon.

—— 1982: On the service class, its formation and future. In Anthony Giddens and Gavin McKenzie (eds), *Social Class and the Division of Labour*, Cambridge: Cambridge University Press, 162–85.

Grant, Wyn (ed.) 1985: *The Political Economy of Corporatism*. New York: St Martin's.

Grebing, Helga 1985: *The History of the German Labour Movement*, 2nd edn, trans. E. Korner. Leamington, Warwickshire: Berg.

Greenberg, Edward S. 1984: Producer democracy and democratic theory. In Robert Jackall and Henry M. Levin (eds), *Worker Cooperatives in America*, Berkeley: University of California Press.

—— 1986: *Workplace Democracy*. Ithaca: Cornell University Press.

Griffith, John 1989: The threat to higher education. *Political Quarterly*, 60, 50–62.

Gulowsen, Jon 1985: Hearocracy. *Organization Studies*, 6, 349–65.

Habermas, Jürgen 1989: What does a crisis mean today? In Steven Seidman (ed.), *Jürgen Habermas on Society and Politics: A Reader*, Boston: Beacon, 267–83.

Hans, Nicholas 1964: *History of Russian Educational Policy*. New York: Russell.

Held, David 1987: *Models of Democracy*. Cambridge: Polity.

Hemingway, John 1978: *Conflict and Democracy*. Oxford: Clarendon.

Hennessy, Peter 1989: *Whitehall*. London: Martin Secker & Warburg.

Herman, Edward S. and Chomsky, Noam 1988: *Manufacturing Consent*. New York: Pantheon.

Herz, John H. (ed.) 1982: *From Dictatorship to Democracy*. Westport: Greenwood.

Hibbing, John R. and Patterson, Samuel C. 1991: The emergence of democratic parliaments in Central and Eastern Europe. Paper prepared for the XVth World Congress of the International Political Science Association, Buenos Aires, July.

Higley, John and Burton, Michael J. 1989: The elite variable in democratic transitions and breakdowns. *American Sociological Review*, 54, 17–32.

Hindess, Barry 1989: *Political Choice and Social Structure*. Aldershot, Hants: Edward Elgar.

Hirszowicz, Maria 1978: Intelligentsia versus bureaucracy? The revival of a myth in Poland. *Soviet Studies*, 30, 336–61.

Hobsbawm, E.J. 1962: *The Age of Revolution 1789–1848*. New York: Mentor Books.

— 1968: *Labouring Men*, 2nd edn. London: Weidenfeld & Nicolson.

— 1975: *The Age of Capital 1848–1875*. London: Weidenfeld & Nicolson.

Hobson, John A. 1917: *The Evolution of Modern Capitalism*, new edn. London: Walter Scott.

Horowitz, Dan and Lissak, Moshe 1971: Authority without sovereignty. In Moshe Lissak and E. Gutman (eds), *Political Institutions in Israel*, Jerusalem: Akademon.

Ingelhart, R. 1981: Post materialism in an environment of insecurity. *American Political Science Review*, 75, 880–900.

Jackall, Robert and Levin, Henry M. (eds) 1984: *Worker Cooperatives in America*. Berkeley: University of California Press.

Jäger, Oskar 1910: *Deutsche Geschichte*, vol. 2. Munich: Beck'sche Verlagsbuchhandlung.

Jansen, Sue Curry 1988: *Censorship*. New York: Oxford University Press.

Jarausch, Konrad H. 1982: *Students, Society and Politics in Imperial Germany*. Princeton: Princeton University Press.

Jessop, Bob 1978: Capitalism and democracy. In G. Littlejohn, G. Smart, B. Wakeford, and N. Yuval-Davis (eds), *Power and the State*, London: Croom Helm, 10–15.

— 1979: Corporatism, parliamentarism and social democracy. In P.C. Schmitter and G. Lehmbruch (eds), *Trends toward Corporatist Intermediation*, Beverly Hills: Sage, 185–212.

Jones, Frank L. 1983: Sources of gender inequality. *Social Forces*, 12, 134–52.

— 1984: Income inequality. In D.H. Broom (ed.), *Unfinished Business: Social Justice for Women*. Sydney: George Allen & Unwin.

Joravsky, David 1977–8: Political authorities and the learned estate. *Survey*, 23, 37–41.

Kaiser, Robert G. 1976: *Russia*. New York: Atheneum.

Kanter, Rosabeth Moss 1977: *Men and Women of the Corporation*. New York: Basic Books.

Karpinski, Jakub 1987: Polish intellectuals in opposition. *Problems of Communism*, 36, 444–57.

Keane, John (ed.) 1988: *Civil Society and the State: New European Perspectives*. London: Verso.

Keep, J.L.H. 1963: *The Rise of Social Democracy in Russia*. Oxford: Clarendon.

Kehr, Eckhart 1965: *Der Primat der Innenpolitik*. Berlin: Walter de Gruyter.

Kennedy, Michael D. 1991: *Professionals, Power and Solidarity in Poland*. Cambridge: Cambridge University Press.

Kesselman, Mark 1983: From state theory to class struggle and compromise. *Social Science Quarterly*, 64, 826–45.

Kettler, David and Meja, Volker 1988: The end of trade unionism in the West? Paper presented to the International Conference on Social Progress and Sociological Theory, Krakow, 28 June–1 July.

Knowles, L.C.A. 1932: *Economic Development in the Nineteenth Century*. London: Routledge & Kegan Paul.

Kornhauser, A.W. 1959: *Problems of Power in American Democracy*. Detroit: Wayne State University Press.

Korpi, Walter 1983: *The Democratic Class Struggle*. London: Routledge & Kegan Paul.

Lamprecht, Karl 1904: *Zur Jüngsten Deutschen Vergangenheit*. Freiburg: Heyfelder.

Landecker, Werner S. 1981: *Class Crystallization*. New Brunswick: Rutgers University Press.

Lansbury, R.D. (ed.) 1980: *Democracy in the Workplace*. Melbourne: Longman Cheshire.

Lasswell, Harold D. and Kaplan, Abraham 1950: *Power and Society*. New Haven: Yale University Press.

Lehmbruch, Gerhard 1985: Neocorporatism in Western Europe. Paper presented to the XIII World Congress of the International Political Science Association, Paris, July.

Lenski, G. 1954: Status crystallization. *American Sociological Review*, 19, 405–13.

Lepsius, M. R. 1978: From fragmented party democracy to government by emergency decree and national socialist takeover: Germany. In J. Linz and A. Stepan (eds), *The Breakdown of Democratic Regimes: Europe*, Baltimore: Johns Hopkins University Press, 34–79.

Leslie, R.F. (ed.) 1980: *The History of Poland since 1863*. Cambridge: Cambridge University Press.

Levi, Margaret 1988: *Of Rule and Revenue*. Berkeley: University of California Press.

Liedman, Sven-Eric 1986: Institutions and ideas: mandarins and non-mandarins in the German academic intelligentsia. *Comparative Studies in Society and History*, 28, 119–44.

Lindblom, Charles E. 1965: *The Intelligence of Democracy*. New York: Free Press.

—— 1977: *Politics and Markets*. New York: Basic Books.

Linz, Juan J. 1978: *The Breakdown of Democratic Regimes: Crisis, Breakdown and Reequilibration*. Baltimore: Johns Hopkins University Press.

Lipset, Seymour Martin 1967: Political sociology. In Neil J. Smelser (ed.), *Sociology: An Introduction*. New York: John Wiley.

—— 1968: History and sociology. In Seymour Martin Lipset and Richard Hofstadter (eds), *Sociology and History: Methods*. New York: Basic Books.

—— 1981: *Political Man: The Social Bases of Politics*, expanded edn. Baltimore: Johns Hopkins University Press.

—— 1985: *Consensus and Conflict: Essays in Political Sociology*. New Brunswick: Transaction.

Lipset, Seymour Martin, Trow, M.A. and Coleman, J.S. 1956: *Union Democracy*. Glencoe: Free Press.

Lockwood, D. 1958: *The Blackcoated Worker*. London: Allen & Unwin.

Lovell, David 1984: *From Marx to Lenin*. Cambridge: Cambridge University Press.

McLennan, Gregor 1989: *Marxism, Pluralism and Beyond*. Cambridge: Polity.

Mandel, Ernest 1975: *Late Capitalism*. London: New Left Books.

—— 1989: *Beyond Perestroika*, trans. G. Fagan. London: Verso.

Manley, John F. 1983: Neo-pluralism. *American Political Science Review*, 77, 368–83.

Mann, Michael 1984: The autonomous power of the state. *European Journal of Sociology*, 25, 185–213.

—— 1986: *The Sources of Social Power*, vol. 1: *A History of Power in Agrarian Societies*. New York: Cambridge University Press.

March, James G. and Olsen, Johan P. 1989: *Rediscovering Institutions: The Organizational Basis of Politics*. New York: Free Press.

Marx, Karl 1969a: *The Civil War in France* (1871). In vol. 2 of Karl Marx and Friedrich Engels, *Selected Works*, 3 vols, Moscow: Progress.

—— 1969b: *The Class Struggles in France* (1850). In vol. 1 of Karl Marx and Friedrich Engels, *Selected Works*, 3 vols, Moscow: Progress.

—— 1976: *Capital*, vol. 1 (1867), trans. B. Fowkes. Harmondsworth: Penguin.

Marx, Karl and Engels, Friedrich 1969a: *The German Ideology* (1845–6). In vol. 1 of their *Selected Works*, 3 vols, Moscow: Progress.

—— 1969b: *Manifesto of the Communist Party* (1848). In vol. 1 of their *Selected Works*, 3 vols, Moscow: Progress.

Mathias, Peter and Pollard, Sidney 1989: *The Cambridge Economic History of Europe*, vol. 8. Cambridge: Cambridge University Press.

Merrill, John C. 1968: *The Elite Press*. New York: Pittman.

Michels, Robert 1915: *Political Parties*, trans. E. Paul and C. Paul. London: Jarold.

Middlemas, Keith 1979: *Politics in Industrial Society: The Experience of the British System since 1911*. London: André Deutsch.

Milbrath, Lester W. and Goel, M.L. 1965: *Political Participation*, 2nd edn. Chicago: Rand McNally.

Miliband, Ralph 1973: *The State in Capitalist Society*. London: Quartet.

—— 1977: *Marxism and Politics*. Oxford: Oxford University Press.

—— 1989a: *Divided Societies*. Oxford: Clarendon.

—— 1989b: Reflections on the crisis of Communist regimes. *New Left Review*, 177, 27–36.

Mill, James 1937: *An Essay on Government*. Cambridge: Cambridge University Press.

Mill, John S. 1982: *On Liberty*. Harmondsworth: Penguin.

Miller, Robert F. 1990a: Civil society in communist regimes: some introductory remarks. Paper presented at the Conference on the Development of Civil Society in Communist Systems, Canberra, Australian National University, March.

—— 1990b: The development of civil society in Yugoslavia. Paper presented at the Conference on the Development of Civil Society in Communist Systems, Canberra, Australian National University, March.

Mills, C. Wright 1959: *The Power Elite*. London: Oxford University Press.

Mommsen, Wolfgang J. 1974: *The Age of Bureaucracy*. Oxford: Blackwell.

Montesquieu, Charles 1952: *The Spirit of Laws*. Chicago: William Benton.

Moore Jr, Barrington 1969: *Social Origins of Dictatorship and Democracy*. Harmondsworth: Penguin.

Morlino, Leonardo 1987: Democratic establishments. In Enrique A. Baloyra (ed.), *Comparing New Democracies*, Boulder: Westview.

Mosca, Gaetano 1939: *The Ruling Class*, trans. H. D. Kahn. New York: McGraw Hill.

Moyser, G. and Wagstaffe, M. 1987: Studying elites. In G. Moyser and M. Wagstaffe (eds), *Research Methods for Elite Studies*, London: Allen & Unwin.

Mushaben, J.M. 1985: Cycles of peace protest in West Germany. *West European Politics*, 8, 24–40.

Nordlinger, Eric E. 1981: *On the Autonomy of the Democractic State*.

Cambridge, Mass.: Harvard University Press.

Nowak, Jan 1982: The church in Poland. *Problems of Communism*, 31, 1–16.

O'Connor, James 1987: *The Meaning of Crisis*. Oxford: Blackwell.

O'Donnell, Guillermo and Schmitter, Philippe C. 1986: Tentative conclusions about uncertain democracies. In Guillermo O'Donnell, Philippe C. Schmitter and Laurence Whitehead (eds), *Transitions from Authoritarian Rule: Prospects for Democracy*, Baltimore: Johns Hopkins University Press.

Offe, Claus 1984: *Contradictions of the Welfare State*. Cambridge, Mass.: MIT Press.

— 1985: New social movements. *Social Research*, 52, 817–68.

— 1990: Reflections on the institutional self-transformation of movement politics. In R. Dalton and M. Vuchler (eds), *Challenging the Political Order*, Cambridge: Polity.

Ogden, S.G. 1982: Trade unions, industrial democracy and collective bargaining. *Sociology*, 16, 544–63.

Pachter, Henry M. 1978: *Modern Germany: A Social, Cultural and Political History*. Boulder: Westview.

Pakulski, Jan 1991: *Social Movements*. Melbourne: Longman Cheshire.

Palmer, Alan 1976: *Bismarck*. New York: Scribner.

Panitch, L. 1981: Trade unions and the capitalist state. *New Left Review*, 125, 21–43.

Papadakis, Elim 1989: Struggles for social change. In Christine Jennett and Randal G. Stewart, (eds), *Politics of the Future*, Melbourne: Macmillan, 76–97.

Parenti, Michael 1986: *Inventing Reality*. New York: St Martin's.

Pares, Bernard 1962: *Russia between Reform and Revolution*. New York: Schocken.

Pareto, Vilfredo 1935: *The Mind and Society*, trans. and ed. A. Livingston, 4 vols. New York: Harcourt Brace Jovanovitch.

Parkin, F. 1979: *Marxism and Class Theory: A Bourgeois Critique*. London: Tavistock.

Pateman, Carole 1970: *Participation and Democratic Theory*. Cambridge: Cambridge University Press.

Pennar, Jaan 1960: The party and the universities. *Problems of Communism*, 9, 59–61.

Perkin, Harold 1969: *The Origins of Modern British Society 1780–1880*. London: Routledge & Kegan Paul.

— 1989: *The Rise of Professional Society*. London: Routledge.

Peterson, A.D.C. 1952: *A Hundred Years of Education*. London: Duckworth.

Pinto-Duschinsky, Michael 1981: *British Political Finance*. Washington: American Enterprise Institute for Public Policy.

Pipes, Richard 1989: *Russia Observed: Collected Essays on Russian and Soviet History*. Boulder: Westview.

Pittman, Rita H. 1990: Perestroika and Soviet cultural politics. *Soviet Studies*, 42, 111–32.

Poggi, Gianfranco 1978: *The Development of the Modern State*. London: Hutchinson.

Polonsky, Antony 1972: *Politics in Independent Poland 1921–1939*. Oxford: Clarendon.

Polsby, Nelson W. 1985: Prospects for pluralism. *Society*, 22, 30–4.

Ponting, Clive 1986: *Whitehall: Tragedy and Farce*. London: Hamish Hamilton.

Poulantzas, Nicos 1975: *Political Power and Social Classes*. London: New Left Books.

—— 1977: The new petty bourgeoisie. In A. Hunt (ed.), *Class and Class Structure*, London: Lawrence & Wisehart, 113–24.

—— 1978: *Classes in Contemporary Capitalism*, trans. David Fernbach. London: Verso.

Przeworski, Adam 1977: Proletariat into a class. *Politics and Society*, 7, 343–402.

Pushkarev, Sergei 1966: *The Emergence of Modern Russia 1801–1917*. New York: Holt, Rinehart & Winston.

Putnam, Robert 1976: *The Comparative Study of Political Elites*. Englewood Cliffs, NJ: Prentice Hall.

Ramet, Pedro 1984: Religious ferment in Eastern Europe. *Survey*, 28, 87–116.

*Register of Members' Interests on the 8th December 1987*, 1987. London: Her Majesty's Stationery Office.

Rey, Lucienne 1957: Intellectual and literary revival in Poland. *Problems of Communism*, 6, 26–33.

Ridley, F.F. 1983: The British civil service and politics. *Parliamentary Affairs*, 36, 28–48.

Riesman, David 1961: *The Lonely Crowd*. New Haven: Yale University Press.

Rigby, T.H. 1990a: The development of civil society in communist systems. Australian National University (unpublished).

—— 1990b: Changes in the Soviet Union. Paper prepared for presentation at the Annual Conference of the Academy of the Social Sciences in Australia, Canberra, November.

Ringer, Fritz K. 1986: Differences and cross-national similarities among mandarins. *Comparative Studies in Society and History*, 28, 145–64.

Ritter, Franz 1981: *Theorie und Praxis des Demokratischen Sozialismus in der Weimarer Republik*. Frankfurt: Campus.

Roemer, J. 1986: New directions in the Marxist theory of exploitation and class. In J. Roemer (ed.), *Analytical Marxism*, Cambridge: Cambridge University Press.

Rokkan, Stein 1966: Norway: numerical democracy and corporate pluralism. In Robert A. Dahl (ed.), *Political Opposition in Western Europe*, New Haven: Yale University Press, 70–115.

Rosenberg, Arthur 1928: *Die Entstehung der Deutschen Republik 1871–1918*. Berlin: Ernst Rwohlt.

—— 1943: Harepublika Hagermanit: Lejdatah Ush'kiatah (The German Republic: Its Birth and Decline), trans. Y. Shimoni. Tel-Aviv: Am Oved (Hebrew).

Rosner, Menachem and Cohen, Nissim 1983: Is direct democracy feasible in modern society? The lesson of the kibbutz experience. In Ernest Krausz (ed.), *The Sociology of the Kibbutz*, New Brunswick: Transaction.

Roth, Günther 1963: *The Social Democrats in Imperial Germany*. Totowa: Bedminster.

Rothschild, Joyce and Whitt, J. Allen 1986: *The Cooperative Workplace*. ASA Rose Monograph Series. Cambridge: Cambridge University Press.

Rothschild-Whitt, Joyce 1979: The collectivist organization. *American Sociological Review*, 44, 509–27.

Roy, E.P. 1976: *Co-operatives*, 3rd edn. Danville, Ill.: Interstate.

Sartori, Giovanni 1987: *The Theory of Democracy Revisited*. Chatham (USA): Chatham Publishers.

Schmitter, Philippe 1985: Neo-corporatism and the state. In Wyn Grant (ed.), *The Political Economy of Corporatism*, New York: St Martin's, 32–62.

—— 1988: The consolidation of democracy in Southern Europe (unpublished).

Schmitter, Philippe C. and Lehmbruch, Gerhard (eds) 1979: *Trends toward Corporatist Intermediation*. Beverly Hills: Sage.

Schneiderman, S.L. 1963: Eclipse of the Polish October. *Problems of Communism*, 12, 64–8.

Schumpeter, Joseph A. 1962: *Capitalism, Socialism and Democracy*, 3rd edn. New York: Harper.

Schwartz, Harry 1961: *The Red Phoenix*. New York: Praeger.

Seifert, Wolfgang 1988: Some thoughts on the problem of internal union democracy in Japan. *Economic and Industrial Democracy* (UK), 9, 373–95.

Seton-Watson, Hugh 1952: *The Decline of Imperial Russia 1855–1914*. New York: Praeger.

— 1967: *The Russian Empire 1801–1917*. Oxford: Clarendon.

Skocpol, Theda 1979: *States and Social Revolutions*. Cambridge: Cambridge University Press.

Smith, Hedrick 1973: *The Russians*. London: Sphere.

Staniszkis, J. 1990: History and chance (unpublished).

Stephens, John, D. 1989: Democratic transitions and breakdowns in Western Europe, 1879–1939: a test of the Moore thesis. *American Journal of Sociology*, 94, 1019–77.

Stern, Fritz 1972: *The Failure of Illiberalism*. London: George Allen & Unwin.

Stewart, A., Prandy, K. and Blackburn, R. M. 1980: *Social Stratification and Occupations*. London: Macmillan.

Stirling, John, Mallor, Mary and Hannah, Janet 1987: Managing Co-operatively. *Employee Relations* (UK), 9, 22–6.

Stone, Clarence 1987: Elite distemper versus the promise of democracy. In William G. Domhoff and Thomas Dye (eds), *Power Elites and Organizations*, Newbury Park: Sage, 239–65.

Therborn, Goran 1977: The rule of capital and the rise of democracy. *New Left Review*, 103, 3–41.

— 1978: *What Does the Ruling Class Do when it Rules?* London: New Left Books.

Thompson, E.P. 1980: *The Making of the English Working Class*. London: Gollancz.

Thompson, John M. 1990: *Russia and the Soviet Union*. Boulder: Westview.

Tilly, Charles 1981: *As Sociology Meets History*. New York: Academic Press.

— 1986: Structural change and contention in Great Britain in 1758–1834. New School of Social Research, New York (unpublished).

Tilly, Louise and Tilly, Charles 1981: *Class Conflict and Collective Action*. Beverly Hills: Sage.

Truman, David 1971: *The Governmental Process*, 2nd edn. New York: Knopf.

Turner, Jr, Henry Ashby 1985: *German Big Business and the Rise of Hitler*. New York: Oxford University Press.

Useem, Michael 1984: *The Inner Circle*. New York: Oxford University Press.

Vaughan, Michalina and Archer, Margaret Scottford 1971: *Social Conflict and Education Change in England and in France 1789–1848*. Cambridge: Cambridge University Press.

Wallace, Donald Mackenzie 1961: *Russia on the Eve of War and Revolution*. New York: Vintage.

Wardell, Mark and Johnston, Robert L. 1987: Class struggle and industrial transformation. *Theory and Society*, 16, 781–808.

Wass, D. 1985: The civil service at the crossroads. *Political Quarterly*, 227–41.

Weber, Max 1947: *The Theory of Social and Economic Organization*, trans. A.M. Henderson. New York: Free Press.

—— 1958: *The Protestant Ethic and the Spirit of Capitalism*, trans. T. Parsons. New York: Charles Scribner's Sons.

—— 1968: *Economy and Society*, 3 vols. New York: Bedminster.

Weinreich, Max 1946: *Hitler's Professors*. New York: Yivo.

Wetherly, Paul 1988: Class struggle and the welfare state. *Critical Social Policy*, 8, 24–40.

Wildman, Allan K. 1967: *The Making of a Workers' Revolution*. Chicago: University of Chicago Press.

Willey, Richard 1971: *Democracy in the West German Trade Unions*. London: Sage.

Wilson, H.T. 1984: *Political Management*. Berlin: Walter de Gruyter.

Wippler, Reinhard 1986: Oligarchic tendencies in democratic organizations. *Netherlands Journal of Sociology*, 22, 1–17.

Wright, Erik O. 1980: Varieties of Marxist conceptions of class struggle. *Politics and Society*, 7, 343–402.

—— 1985: *Classes*. London: New Left Books.

# Index